BOUNCE BACK!

UPPER PRIMARY TO JUNIOR SECONDARY

Teacher's Resource Book

Helen McGrath and Toni Noble

Sydney, Melbourne, Brisbane, Perth, Adelaide
and associated companies around the world

Copyright © Helen McGrath and Toni Noble 2003

Pearson Rigby
An imprint of Pearson Australia
A division of Pearson Australia Group Pty Ltd
20 Thackray Road, Port Melbourne, Victoria 3207
PO Box 460, Port Melbourne, Victoria 3207
www.pearsoned.com.au/schools/

All rights reserved. Except under the conditions described in the Copyright Act 1968 of Australia and subsequent amendments, no part of this publication may be reproduced, stored in a retrieval system or transmitted in any form or by any means, electronic, mechanical, photocopying, recording or otherwise, without the prior written permission of the copyright owner.

Senior Acquisitions Editor: Diane Gee-Clough
Senior Project Editor: Natasha Dupont
Copy Editor: Felicity Shea
Proofreader: Janice Keynton
Cover and internal design by R.T.J. Klinkhamer
Illustrations by Techa Noble
Typeset by Midland Typesetters, Maryborough, Vic.

Printed in Malaysia, LSP

8 9 10   11 10 09

National Library of Australia
Cataloguing-in-Publication Data

> McGrath, Helen.
> Bounce back!: teacher's resource book: level three: upper primary and junior secondary.
>
> Bibliography.
> ISBN 978 0 7339 9956 7.
>
> 1. Resilience (Personality trait) in children.
> 2. Resilience (Personality trait) in adolescence. I. Noble, Toni. II. Title.
>
> 370.153

Bounce Back Resiliency® is a registered Trade Mark under the Trade Marks Act, 1995, Commonwealth of Australia.

Every effort has been made to trace and acknowledge copyright. However, should any infringement have occurred, the publishers tender their apologies and invite copyright owners to contact them.

CONTENTS

1 Core values *1*

2 Elasticity *33*

3 People bouncing back *49*

4 Courage *79*

5 The bright side *100*

6 Emotions *119*

7 Relationships *150*

8 Humour *183*

9 Bullying *200*

10 Winners *230*

INTRODUCTION

Welcome to the BOUNCE BACK! Classroom Resiliency Program. This program contains resource materials and strategies to teach young people the personal skills that underpin resiliency, that is, the capacity to 'bounce back' after encountering problems, difficulties and down times. Young people have *always* needed effective coping skills, but there is evidence that today's world is more challenging and that young people may have fewer resources to deal with those challenges than previous generations had. Although most young people still live healthy, satisfying and productive lives, an increasing number report being depressed and suicidal, and an increasing number engage in maladaptive coping strategies such as substance abuse and antisocial behaviour.

The BOUNCE BACK! Classroom Resiliency Program contains four books:

1. The Teacher's Handbook

The *Handbook* provides an overview of the research into the concept of resilience and the personal skills and environmental resources that help to protect young people from the negative effects of difficult times in their lives. It discusses ways in which schools can foster resilience through whole-school and classroom practices. It also contains a number of assessment instruments that can assist in identifying the capacity for resilient behaviour in individual students as well as the degree to which specific classrooms and teachers foster resilience. A detailed chapter on managing school bullying is included and some suggestions for working collaboratively with parents. The last two chapters contain step-by-step details of the cooperative learning strategies, games and resources that are featured in the curriculum activities throughout the three Teacher's Resource Books.

2. Teacher's Resource Book: Level One—Lower Primary

One of the principles underpinning the BOUNCE BACK! Classroom Resiliency Program is that it is essential that the skills of resilience be taught as early as possible in a child's life. This book contains curriculum materials and strategies that are suitable for students in their first three years of primary schooling (i.e. aged approximately five to seven years).

3. Teacher's Resource Book: Level Two—Middle Primary

This book contains curriculum materials and strategies that are suitable for students in Years 3 and 4 of primary schooling (i.e. aged approximately eight to ten years). Many of the activities and ideas can be easily adapted for younger or older students.

4. Teacher's Resource Book: Level Three—Upper Primary/Junior Secondary

This book contains curriculum materials and strategies that are suitable for students in the final two years of primary schooling and the first two years of secondary schooling (i.e. aged approximately eleven to fourteen years). Some of the activities and ideas can be adapted for younger or older students.

There are ten units of work in each of the three Teacher's Resource Books. Each unit contains a summary of the key points to communicate to students, introductory tasks followed by suggested discussion questions, activities based around picture books and novels, games, music and art ideas, opportunities for drama, and many activities and worksheets that can be used in a variety of key learning areas. There is also a strong focus on cooperative learning and opportunities for self-reflection through self-assessment tasks and quizzes. The ten units are summarised below.

Unit 1: Core values

- Integrity: being honest, fair, responsible and loyal
- Support: supporting and caring for other people and showing compassion
- Cooperation: cooperating with others
- Acceptance: Understanding and accepting the differences between oneself and others, and including others socially
- Respect: respecting the rights of others
- Friendliness: being friendly and socially responsible, and including others.

Unit 2: Elasticity

- Investigating and experimenting with elastic forces
- Elastic animals (e.g. kangaroos and springboks)
- Springs: how they work and their uses
- Inflatables (e.g. tyres and balloons).

Unit 3: People bouncing back

- The ways in which 'nature' bounces back (e.g. bush regeneration and skin repair)
- High-profile people who have 'bounced back' after hard times or hardship
- The BOUNCE BACK! acronym and ways to teach it (the acronym poster is featured in the *Teacher's Handbook*)
- Using helpful thinking and reality checks
- Using balanced causation to work out personal responsibility in difficult times.

Unit 4: Courage

- Understanding the differences between everyday courage, courage in response to misfortune, heroism, thrill seeking, professional risk-taking and foolhardiness
- Understanding that fear and courage are relative
- Developing the skills and perceptions that lead to being more courageous.

Unit 5: The bright side

- Positive tracking, that is, focusing on the positive aspects of situations
- Positive conversion of negative events and mistakes into opportunities to learn
- Accepting that bad times are temporary and don't have to spoil other parts of your life
- Finding hope in difficult times.

Unit 6: Emotions

- Understanding that how you think about something can either exaggerate your feelings or help you cope
- Recognising and managing one's own negative emotions and enjoying positive emotions
- Recognising the feelings and intentions of others and responding empathically.

Unit 7: Relationships

- Skills for getting along well with others and being accepted
- Understanding and managing shyness
- Skills for making and keeping friends
- Conflict management skills
- Leadership skills (upper unit only).

Unit 8: Humour

- Understanding the processes and styles of humour and how humour can help with coping
- Using humour to help, not harm
- Five-minute humorous activities that can be used as a stress-break in class.

Unit 9: Bullying

- Making bullying uncool
- Investigating the legal and workplace issues related to bullying
- Understanding the similarities between bullying and historical/global situations of oppression and persecution
- Strategies for understanding and managing peer pressure to take part in harassment
- Skills for dealing with being bullied
- Teaching the skills and attitudes that enable bystanders to support those being bullied.

Unit 10: Success

- Identifying relative strengths and weaknesses on the basis of evidence
- Skills of self-discipline and self-management
- Skills of goal achievement, initiative and resourcefulness.

UNIT 1
CORE VALUES

KEY POINTS

Having a set of personal values increases self-esteem and self-respect.
Values give you direction about how to behave towards other people. Doing the right thing by others as well as yourself helps you develop self-respect.

Personal values are easy to talk about but harder to act on.
The real test is whether you still follow your own personal rules when it is inconvenient for you or when there might be unpleasant outcomes for you. Nobody is perfect, but you can try to do what you believe is the 'right thing', even though you may not always succeed.

It is important to develop a sense of integrity.
If you have integrity, then you try to act according to your values, even when there is a personal cost to doing so. Acting with integrity also means:
- Being honest, by telling the truth, not stealing or cheating, and 'owning up'
- Being fair, by trying to make things as equal as possible, following rules, returning favours and kindnesses, and helping others to get a fair deal (i.e. gain justice, food, shelter, medical treatment and schooling)
- Being responsible, by not letting people down, honouring commitments, letting people know what is happening, and helping people in trouble or those who are less able to look after themselves.

Not everyone tries to achieve a sense of integrity.
Some people say that they believe in certain values but they do not act in accordance with those values. A few other people have no positive personal values to guide them and are prepared to do anything to get what they want, no matter how harmful or wrong their actions are. They usually don't have much self-respect.

It is important to care about and support others and to act with compassion.
Supporting and caring about other people and being compassionate means helping, being kind and thoughtful, giving encouragement, and listening. It also means being patient and trying to understand.

It is important to cooperate.
Cooperating means working together to achieve something by sharing, communicating, encouraging others, doing your share of the work, making sure everyone's ideas are heard and negotiating solutions so that everyone gets *some* of what they want.

It is important to accept that it is okay for people to be different.
Acceptance means acknowledging the right of others to be different to you and learning to live comfortably with and find the positives in the ways in which they are different from you.

It is important to show respect to other people.
Respect is about showing consideration for the rights and feelings of others. It means treating others as you want them to treat you. One aspect of respect is good manners.

It is important to be friendly.
Being friendly means being kind and welcoming to others by being interested in them, making eye contact, smiling, taking the time to say hello and talk to them, finding something funny to laugh about together and offering help if they need it. Being friendly also means including others in activities and conversations even if they are not close friends.

UNIT 1—CORE VALUES

Class discussion—Integrity: acting fairly, honestly and responsibly *3*
- BOOKS
- *The Great White Man-Eating Shark* *3*
- *The Gizmo* *4*
- VIDEO
- *Big Fat Liar* *4*
- ACTIVITY
- Think-Pair-Share *4*
- MEDIA ACTIVITY
- Truth in advertising *4*
- SCIENCE/ENGLISH ACTIVITY
- Lie detecting *4*

Class discussion—Fairness and responsibility *5*
- BOOK
- *The Pain and the Great One* *6*
- ACTIVITY
- Information scavenger hunt: Justice *6*

Class discussion—Support, kindness and compassion *6*
- BOOK
- *Stargirl* *7*
- ACTIVITY
- Collective classroom research *7*

Class discussion—Cooperation *8*
- BOOK
- *Piggybook* *8*
- ACTIVITIES
- Cooperative technology bug game *9*
- All together now *9*
- Cooperative hoops *9*
- Cooperative group walk *9*
- All touch the ball *9*

Cooperative activities and games *10*
- MATHS/ENGLISH ACTIVITY
- What makes teams work well together? *11*
- MEDIA ACTIVITY
- Cooperation *11*
- ACTIVITY
- Musical groups and cooperation *11*

Class discussion—Cooperating to protect our environment *11*
- SOCIAL STUDIES INVESTIGATION
- 'If everyone just . . .' *12*

Class discussion—Acceptance of diversity and not judging others *13*
- BOOKS
- *Little White Dogs Can't Jump* *13*
- *Luke's Way of Looking* *14*
- BOOK AND PLAY
- *Boss of the Pool* *14*
- VIDEO
- *Remember the Titans* *14*
- ACTIVITIES
- People pie (or class survey) about differences *14*
- Personal poll *14*

Class discussion—Respect *15*
- INVESTIGATION
- Which bad manners drive you mad? *16*

Class discussion—Friendliness *16*
- CLASSROOM ORGANISATION
- Cooperative committee *17*

Consolidation *17*
- Core values cartoons *17*
- Balloon burst quotes *17*
- Antonyms and synonyms *17*
- Designing a board game *17*
- Class recommendations *17*
- Newspaper analysis *17*
- Cross-offs *18*

Resources *18*

BLM 1.1—Postbox *19*

BLM 1.2—The Pinocchio effect *20*

BLM 1.3—The ten thinking tracks *21*

BLM 1.4—Amnesty International *23*

BLM 1.5—The Smith Family *24*

BLM 1.6—Fred Hollows *25*

BLM 1.7—Caroline Chisholm *26*

BLM 1.8—Clean Up Australia *27*

BLM 1.9—People scavenger hunt on differences *28*

BLM 1.10—Social biodiversity *29*

BLM 1.11—Core values cartoons *30*

BLM 1.12—Cross-offs *32*

UNIT 1—CORE VALUES

CLASS DISCUSSION INTEGRITY: ACTING FAIRLY, HONESTLY AND RESPONSIBLY

Introduce 'integrity' by having students complete the postbox questions on BLM 1.1. Discuss the findings. Alternatively, you could:
- Read to the class and discuss the picture book *The Great Man-Eating Shark* (see below).
- Read the simple chapter book *The Gizmo* (see below).
- Show the video *The Big Fat Liar* (see below).

Discussion questions

Use the postbox strategy (see Chapter 10 of the *Teacher's Handbook*) with BLM 1.1. The results can be the basis of the discussion. Discuss one question at a time.
- Why is it good to have values? (They help you to decide how to behave when things are unclear; they give you self-respect; the community works better if people have shared positive values.)
- What are some examples of honesty and dishonesty?
- When is it hardest to tell the truth and why?
- How would you feel if someone gave you a compliment and later you found out that they had lied to you?
- Most police officers are honest, so how do you feel when you read about the few who are dishonest?
- Tell about a time when someone lied to you. How did it make you feel? ('no names' rule)
- What is the most common kind of cheating you have witnessed?
- Why do you think people cheat in games?
- Why do some people find it hard to be honest?
- In what situations might you tell a white lie? (e.g. to be tactful, such as if a friend got a new haircut or outfit you didn't like)
- What happens when people consistently act dishonestly? How does their dishonesty affect them? (They may have low self-esteem.) How does it affect others? (Others feel that the person can't be trusted.)
- What are some of the ways in which shop owners attempt to deter dishonest people? What happens to those who are caught shoplifting? How does shoplifting affect the whole community?

Follow-up activities

- In pairs, students interview two local shopkeepers about shoplifting and write a report.
- Students research the cost of shoplifting to the community.
- Students complete BLM 1.2, 'The Pinocchio effect', and follow-up activities.
- Students use BLM 1.3, 'The ten thinking tracks', on the ideas of:
  - Local shopkeepers keeping a shared 'shoplifters' register' with photographs
  - Red-eye cameras
  - The honesty phone (see BLM 1.2 for descriptions).

BOOKS
The Great White Man-Eating Shark (Picture book)

This is a modern version of the fable of the boy who cried 'wolf', relocated to a beachside setting with Norvin, a selfish young boy, as the protagonist.

The Gizmo (Simple chapter book)

Stephen's supposed mate Floggit cons Stephen into stealing something from a market stall. It turns out to be a gizmo that makes you swap clothes with whoever you stand next to. Stephen learns a lot about honesty and about the shallowness of some so-called mates.

VIDEO
Big Fat Liar

In this comedy a young high school student continually lies to everyone about why his homework hasn't been done and why he is late. He writes a story which is stolen by a film producer and made into a movie and no one believes him. The boy and his friend pursue the producer to make him admit the truth.

ACTIVITY
Think–Pair–Share

✗ See Chapter 10 of the Teacher's Handbook.

Is it ever okay to break a promise? What do you think about these situations?
- You saw your uncle bash up your aunt, but she makes you promise not to tell anyone else in your family.
- Your older sister starts to talk about killing herself, but she makes you promise not to tell anyone else.
- Your older brother is being given a really hard time by three kids at school, but he makes you promise not to tell a teacher because he is frightened of their revenge.
- Two kids at school tell you that they shoplift in the local department store, but they make you promise not to let anyone know that they do it.

MEDIA ACTIVITY
Truth in advertising

- Discuss: How important is truth in advertising and why?
- Research: What safeguards are in place to try to make sure that people advertising goods and services do not deceive or con others?
- In groups of three students, analyse a television or magazine advertisement aimed at the youth market. What information is missing in the advertisement? What would you ask the advertiser if you could? Is the advertisement 'truthful'?

SCIENCE/ENGLISH ACTIVITY
Lie detecting

In pairs students investigate whether their pulse rate increases when they tell a small lie. Each thinks of three 'facts', two that are true and one that is a small fib. Each pair makes a small ball of playdough and sticks a toothpick in it (pointy end in the playdough). They take turns to lie their arm flat on a table and place the ball on their pulse (they may need to move it around to find the strongest beat). Does the toothpick waver when they fib? Can they detect when their partner fibs?

UNIT 1—CORE VALUES

CLASS DISCUSSION **FAIRNESS AND RESPONSIBILITY**

Prepare for this topic by asking students to each survey three people about what they think 'being unfair' means and to give examples of fair and unfair behaviour. Another way to start is to use the 'partner retell' strategy (see Chapter 10 of the *Teacher's Handbook*) and ask students to talk about a time when they felt they were unfairly treated or they saw someone else being unfairly treated.

Discussion questions

Use the results of the survey or the 'partner retell' where appropriate.
- What does fairness mean? (see below)
- Is it fair that some convicted criminals make money from books written about their crimes or similar crimes (such as Chopper Read or Ronald Biggs)?
- Why is fairness sometimes a subjective thing? (there are many different perceptions in any situation)
- What might cause a student to think a teacher is being unfair when the teacher is actually being fair?
- What do we mean by being responsible? (see key points)
- What are the advantages of behaving responsibly? (being trusted, self respect) What are the disadvantages? (inconvenience)

Follow-up activities

Students work in groups to:
- Develop a set of criteria for 'fair' and 'unfair'. For example, 'fair' involves:
    - consistency (e.g. in applying rules)
    - equal or reasonable division of resources
    - an unbiased reaction or response, in proportion to what happened, and a controlled rather than an emotional response (e.g. in punishments)
    - responses based on respect, understanding and open-mindedness (rather than being judgmental)
    - no misuse of power
    - advertised and predictable consequences.
  Students can use the criteria for judging the fairness of different school rules and their consequences.
- Give students newspapers and ask them to work in pairs to find examples of fairness and unfairness and apply the criteria above.
- In pairs, students brainstorm some of the things kids their age sometimes see as 'unfair'. Then in a second column they write down the other person's perspective on that situation. For example:
    - Kids not allowed to eat in the classroom. The cleaners' perspective is that they have to clean up the mess.
    - Students not allowed to stand for the Student Representative Council (SRC), because they have been disrespectful to a teacher.
- Use the 'Think–Pair–Share' strategy (see Chapter 10 of the *Teacher's Handbook*) to discuss and list individuals or groups in our community who don't get a fair deal. Brainstorm how the class could make a difference to these people, even in a small way.
- Use the 'ten thinking tracks' strategy (see BLM 1.3) on the idea of parents having a microchip surgically implanted in their child's arm (and not removed till the child is 18 years of age) so that the child can be tracked to make sure he or she is safe, *or* on the

idea of students being allowed to have only see-through backpacks in order to avoid weapon carrying etc.
- Read to the class the picture book *The Pain and the Great One* (see below) in relation to 'fairness'. Students can make a similar picture book for younger children.
- In pairs students research the following topics in terms of fairness and justice:
  - Aboriginal land rights issues and reconciliation
  - child poverty
  - globalisation and the exploitation of child labour or poorly paid Asian labour
  - legal aid.

BOOK
The Pain and the Great One (Picture book)

A girl and her younger brother each believe that they are unfairly treated compared with the other and that they are not as loved by the parents as the other. The first half of the story outlines the sister's perceptions about her brother ('the pain'), and the second half gives the brother's perceptions about his sister ('the great one').

ACTIVITY
Information scavenger hunt: Justice

X See Chapter 10 of the Teacher's Handbook.

- What is the symbol for justice and why is that symbol used?
- What does an ombudsman do and what are two examples of ombudsmen?
- How does the Small Claims Tribunal help people get a fair deal? Give its phone number and address.
- Give one reason why an individual would go to the Industrial Relations Commission.
- How is a magistrate different from a judge?
- What do the different courts do?

CLASS DISCUSSION — SUPPORT, KINDNESS AND COMPASSION

Introduce the class discussion by reading to the class the chapter book *Stargirl* (see below). You could also read to the class and discuss *Wilfred Gordon McDonald Partridge*, a picture book about a small boy's kindness towards an elderly resident in the neighbouring nursing home.

Discussion questions

- How do humans support each other and show compassion for each other? (encouragement; food and resources; help and assistance; being understanding and showing empathy; being patient with someone; listening to someone who has a problem to talk over; wishing someone well in a difficult venture; protecting someone; standing up for somebody; including someone)
- Do we show support and compassion only for people close to us? (we support loved ones and friends more, but we can also show compassion and support to people we don't know or who we're not close to)

- Why is compassion a positive aspect of the human species? (We survive better together; trust develops; it is often reciprocal.)
- What does the word 'altruism' mean? (helping another with no return to oneself) When have you or someone you know behaved altruistically?

Follow-up activities

- Use the 'jigsaw' strategy (see Chapter 10 of the *Teacher's Handbook*) with BLM 1.4, 'Amnesty International', BLM 1.5, 'The Smith Family', BLM 1.6, 'Fred Hollows' and BLM 1.7, 'Caroline Chisholm'. Remove the comprehension questions if using as a jigsaw. Leave them in if using as worksheets.
- Provide newspapers and ask students working in pairs to find examples of people offering support or compassion or needing it.
- Students search for songs and movies on the theme of human compassion and support for each other.
- Each student chooses one member of their family and performs various kind acts for them for one week. They record who, what, where and the results of each act of kindness. Follow up with a 'partner retell' (see Chapter 10 of the *Teacher's Handbook*) and with the students writing a report.
- Discuss ways in which the class could offer support to people in their community or the larger society who may be struggling or in need of care, concern or support (e.g. those struggling with poverty here or overseas, the elderly).

BOOK
Stargirl (Chapter book)

'Stargirl' arrives at her new high school, a complete non-conformist in the nicest possible way. She is a bit of a fey spirit who dresses in her own style and performs acts of kindness towards others. She becomes socially ostracised and bullied for not bowing to peer pressure. The book is also used in the Bullying Unit (Unit 9).

ACTIVITY
Collective classroom research

X See Chapter 10 of the Teacher's Handbook.

Students research some of the following organisations that support people who need help:
- World Vision
- Lifeline
- Kids Helpline
- RSPCA
- The Red Cross
- The Salvation Army
- The Brotherhood of St Lawrence.

The following websites should prove helpful:
- *Australian charities:* www.auscharity.org
  This website details hundreds of charities nationwide. It links to volunteer and philanthropic organisations as well as providing information on the 'history of charity'.
- *St Vincent de Paul:* www.vinnies.org.au
  This site outlines services ranging from drug and alcohol centres to family support and visits to hospital, prison or the streets to care for the mentally ill and homeless. There is also information about the founder, Frederic Ozanam.

- *The Hunger Site:* www.hungersite.com
  This site gives details about world hunger, and it blacks out a country on the world map every time someone dies of starvation (i.e. every few seconds). Visitors to the site can help the hungry by clicking on a 'give free food' icon and sponsors then give money.
- *Plan International:* www.plan.org.au
  Plan International supports struggling communities overseas. It provides bulletins on community development, news on 'hot zones' where disasters and social unrest are making life hard, and an area that children can access to gain details about the food, cultural differences, languages and stories of other countries.

CLASS DISCUSSION COOPERATION

Read to the class and discuss the picture book *Piggybook* (see below).

Discussion questions

- What do we mean by cooperation? (working together for a shared goal; team-work and collaboration)
- What are some other words that mean 'cooperation'?
- What skills do you need to be able to cooperate well? (sharing and taking turns; listening to all ideas; negotiation—finding a way for everyone to get some of what they wanted; doing your share of a task in a friendly way; conflict management skills)
- Can you cooperate only with people you like? (no, you can cooperate with anyone with whom you have a goal in common)

Follow-up activities

- Students make a fridge magnet (see Chapter 11 of the *Teacher's Handbook*) with the saying 'TEAM = Together Everyone Achieves More'.
- Students use collective classroom research on famous 'teams', such as explorers, bands, researchers, sports teams etc.
- Use some of these whole-class cooperative projects:
  - a class book of cooperation (i.e. a record of things accomplished that would not be possible without cooperation, including photos)
  - a class newsletter or newspaper
  - a class bulletin board
  - class committees (see Chapter 5 of the *Teacher's Handbook* for ideas).

BOOK
Piggybook (Picture book)

None of Mrs Piggott's family cooperate. Eventually she gets so tired of doing all the work that she leaves home. After Mrs Piggott leaves, her husband and sons get messier and messier until eventually all three turn into pigs!

UNIT 1—CORE VALUES

ACTIVITIES

Cooperative technology bug game

Provide a variety of craft and junk for students to select from. Each group negotiates in advance to decide on their way to make a large bug with detachable pieces and a rope to pull it with. They will need parts to make:
- A body (e.g. small plastic bucket, a large yoghurt container etc.)
- A head (must have a way of attaching a rope to it)
- Two antennae
- Two eyes
- One tail
- Six legs

Each group throws a dice in turn and attaches the body part they throw.
- a 6 must be thrown first to start with the body.
- a 5 is needed next for the head
- a 4 is needed for each one of the six legs
- a 3 is needed for the tail
- a 2 is needed for each one of the two antennae
- a 1 is needed for each one of the two eyes

When a group has completed their bug they have to quickly tie a rope around its neck and drag it across a pre-designated finishing line some distance away.

All together now

Draw a large chalk circle. Ask the whole class to stand completely within it. Then draw a smaller one and ask them to do the same. Keep reducing the circle's size so that they have to cooperate to fit within it.

Cooperative hoops

Students stand in a circle and hold hands. Start one hoop hanging over one pair of joined hands. Each person in the circle must pass the hoop over him/herself and on to the next person without letting go of hands. They cannot use their fingers at all! It takes cooperation. Have two hoops going in opposite directions so that at some point they have to pass through each other.

Cooperative group walk

Students cooperate in a group of five or six for this activity. They line up shoulder to shoulder, each student's right foot next to the left foot of the student to their right. The challenge to the group is to 'walk forward' as a group—with each group step every student steps forward with one (and only one) foot (keeping their feet touching the feet of the students on either side of them). This is more difficult than it sounds.

All touch the ball

Use a variety of objects in a variety of sizes e.g. a soccer ball, a softball, a tennis ball, a golf ball, a large clip, and a dollar coin. Start with the biggest item and work down to the smallest. A group of ten or so stands in a circle. They must find a way to cooperate so that everyone is touching the object for ten seconds at the same time but without touching each other.

Cooperative activities and games

- Each team makes a *pop-up book* (e.g. about Egypt).
- Plan, cost, advertise, design and road-test recipes and publish a class *cookbook*. Each team contributes one recipe.
- Organise and shop for a *class lunch* with another class.
- Play *'Cooperative ball pass'* in groups of six with six small balls. The students chant 1, 2, 3 and on '3' they all pass their ball to the person on their left and receive the ball being passed to them on their right. Try to go faster and faster.
- Plan and carry out the *perfect class picnic* by pooling every group's ideas and then implementing the best.
- Play *'Time bomb'*. Hide a picture of a time bomb and use a kitchen timer set for 4 minutes. Each group takes turns to try to find it by asking no more than 20 questions to which only a 'Yes' or 'No' answer can be given. They need time beforehand to negotiate about tactics.
- Play *'Sting'* in two teams of about 10–15 students. You also need two referees per team with a notepad for recording. Each team has a specific colour. Each member of the team has a ball in that colour. Everyone's ball is in play at once and everyone gently moves their team's balls with their foot. The aim is to never have a 'dead' ball (i.e. one that is not moving). Everyone must play and the whole designated area must be used. Both teams play at once in a designated area.
  - A dead ball is called a SPLAT.
  - A ball that has left the ground or has been moved too aggressively is called a SWILL.
  - A STING is the penalty your team is given if one of the four referees sees a SPLAT or a SWILL for your team.
  - Ten stings and your team loses the round.
- Play *'Word Mastermind'* with a partner. Each pair selects a four-letter or five-letter word (with no repeated letters) for another pair to guess. Each pair takes turns to guess the other pair's word in less than ten guesses. They give the following feedback to the guessing pair:
  - A tick is given under each letter that is correct and in the right place.
  - A dot is given under each letter that is in the word but in a different place.
  - A cross is given if that letter is not in the word.
  Each pair can play against five other pairs to see if they can lower or maintain their average score (i.e. number of questions used).
- In groups of three, students undertake *Marble challenges* using old boxes, marbles, cups, and material for making ramps.
  - Make a marble run in which the marble must start approximately 40 cm from the ground. It must change direction three times and land in a cup at least three times.
  - As above, but the marble must take 4 seconds to get from the top to the bottom of the marble run.
  - As for the first challenge, but there must be a starting mechanism so that no one has to directly touch the marble to start the marble down the marble run.
- Play *'Mystery square'* in pairs against another pair. The aim is to guess the other pair's 'mystery square' using no more than ten questions. Each pair draws up a 5 × 5 grid and writes a word in each of the 25 squares, making one the mystery word. They team up with another pair and swap grids. Give each group 5 minutes to plan eliminating questions that can only be answered by 'yes' or 'no'. One pair then questions the other pair until they identify the mystery word, noting how many questions they used. Then the other group has its turn. Banning location questions (e.g. which row or section) or not using a grid makes the game harder. Each pair can play against five other pairs to see if they can lower or maintain their average score (i.e. number of questions used).

- Play *'Cooperative Newspaper Walk'*. Form teams of four. Each team has two sheets of an average-sized newspaper. The aim is for the team to reach the finishing line by walking only on 2 sheets of newspaper. No one's feet must touch the ground between the starting and finishing lines. Teams compete against each other or against a specified time.
- Use the *'Mergers'* activity in *The Creative Kaleidoscope* (see 'Resources' section on page 18) in which groups of students are companies and have to cooperatively merge with other companies.
- Students make a *Peace garden* or *Peace wall mural*.

MATHS/ENGLISH ACTIVITY
What makes teams work well together?

Students each ask two people who play on a sporting team, 'In your opinion, what makes a team work well together?' They collate and interpret the common themes, and then write a report or make a visual display.

MEDIA ACTIVITY
Cooperation

In groups students tape 3-minute video segments of shows that demonstrate cooperation (e.g. sports teams, police shows, family shows). The class devises a checklist of cooperative skills and analyses each videotaped segment using the checklist.

ACTIVITY
Musical groups and cooperation

Students select a music group and identify the different contributions each person in the group makes to the group's performances and products. Who does what? Is anyone less important than another? Would the group be the same if any one person were replaced?

CLASS DISCUSSION COOPERATING TO PROTECT OUR ENVIRONMENT

Read to the class and discuss the picture book *The Lorax*. This book highlights the importance of working together to protect our environment. Then tell the story of the starfish. This is one of those stories that many people tell but its original authorship is unknown.

> One day a man is walking along the beach. The tide had gone out and has left lots of starfish stranded on the sand. The man knows that the starfish will die if left on the sand, so he starts to throw some back into the water. Another man walks past and says, 'You're wasting your time. All along the coast for hundreds of kilometres there are stranded starfish just like these. What difference will it make if you throw a few starfish back into the water?' The first man replies, 'Well, that may be true, but it will definitely make a difference to *these* starfish.'

Discussion questions

- Can a single person make a difference in protecting our environment and the animals in it? (yes, and if there are many participants, they will make a large cumulative difference)

- What sorts of things have you or your family done that have made a small difference to the environment?
- What are some of the things we could all start to do that we aren't doing at the moment?
- What do you know about how cooperation is involved in:
  - Saving beached whales?
  - Saving injured bush animals?
  - The Antarctic Treaty? (It was signed in 1959 by 12 countries. By 1997, 43 countries including Australia and New Zealand were parties to the treaty, which is an agreement to maintain Antarctica strictly for scientific and peaceful purposes. The protocol on Environmental Protection bans mining and mineral explosion for 50 years.)

Follow-up activities

- Students read BLM 1.8, 'Clean Up Australia', and follow up on the website at www.cleanup.com.au. Another relevant website can be found at www.conservationvolunteer.com.au. Consider a similar local project.
- Students write their own version of the starfish story.
- Students compose a rap on the importance of not littering.
- To rid China of a fly plague each Chinese citizen was asked to kill ten flies a day. Use 'ten thinking tracks' (BLM 1.3) to discuss whether Australians could get rid of their fly problem if everyone cooperated and took responsibility for getting rid of just three flies per day without using sprays of any kind.

SOCIAL STUDIES INVESTIGATION
'If everyone just . . .'

The cooperation of many people together can achieve great outcomes even if each person makes only one small effort.

Mark an area of the playground with chalk. Then ask everyone in the class to drop just one piece of rubbish within that area sometime over one day. Take 'before' and 'after' photos of the area. At the end of the day students can look at how much rubbish there is in the area because everybody dropped just one piece. This, of course, is how we get rubbish problems. Everyone thinks that their one piece makes no difference, but together 'things happen'. Then, on another day, everyone can pick up just one piece of rubbish in a specified (and usually messy) area to show the difference that can be made if people cooperated and 'everyone just . . .' Once again take 'before' and 'after' photos.

Follow up with students in groups designing an advertising campaign based on the notion of 'if everyone just . . .' on an issue such as:
- Used hankies instead of tissues
- Took cuttings and seeds from plants twice a year
- Smiled four extra times per day
- Performed one act of random kindness a week.

UNIT 1—CORE VALUES   13

CLASS DISCUSSION ACCEPTANCE OF DIVERSITY AND NOT JUDGING OTHERS

Introduce this value by using one of these alternatives:
- Read to the class and discuss the picture book *Little White Dogs Can't Jump* (see below).
- Read to the class and discuss the picture book *Luke's Way of Looking* (see below).
- Use the 'People scavenger hunt' activity (BLM 1.9).
- Show and discuss the video *Remember the Titans* (see below).
- Read to the class and discuss the simple chapter book *Boss of the Pool* (see below).

Discussion questions

- Ask several students to share one thing they learned about a classmate in relation to each question from the people scavenger hunt (BLM 1.9).
- How are we different from each other? (Different experiences, cultural backgrounds, strengths and weaknesses, abilities, family structures, values, opinions, preferences, personalities, goals)
- What are some examples of discrimination based on 'difference'?
- How might it feel to be discriminated against? What are the long-term effects?
- What does acceptance of difference mean? How can we demonstrate this? (acknowledge diversity as a good thing; tolerate those differences we may not like in others; find the good ways in which people are different; welcome others and include them in fun, work or conversation; notice when someone is left out and invite them in; avoid stereotyping, using putdowns and 'excluding')
- Students can write a children's story for younger students about an animal who is 'different' e.g. a ladybird with only one spot, a tiger with spots instead of stripes etc.

Follow-up activities

- Students read BLM 1.10, 'Social biodiversity', and then write/draw about ways in which their own life has improved because of social biodiversity.
- Students talk or write about a time when they felt 'different'.
- Students research different artists' impressions of similar subject matter (beach/sea, the country, still life) through different painting styles, such as impressionism, expressionism, surrealism, cubism or modernism.
- Use the song 'Walk a Mile in my Shoes' as a poetry activity. It was written and performed by Joe South in the 1970s and there are also versions by Elvis Presley and Bryan Ferry. Try 1970s compilation CDs or CD collections by Elvis Presley or Bryan Ferry. Lyrics are at: www.superseventies.com and also at www.absolutelyric.com.

BOOKS
Little White Dogs Can't Jump (Picture book)

This is the story of Smudge, a chubby little white dog who can't get into the 'tall' car his family have because his legs are too short and stumpy. His family try to find a way to help him to get into the car as they want to take him with them. Eventually they solve the problem by buying a low-slung sports car instead. The message is that everyone is different and sometimes we have to accommodate those differences rather than judge and expect change.

BOUNCE BACK!

Luke's Way of Looking (Picture book)

Luke is very artistic and doesn't see things the way his teacher says he should. He discovers that it's okay to be different.

BOOK AND PLAY
Boss of the Pool (Simple chapter book) and Boss of the Pool: The Play

Shelley is initially horrified at the indignity of having to spend several days at the hostel for people with disabilities where her mother works. She slowly learns that there are many things that are not fair, apart from her having to be there when she would rather be with her friends. She realises that it's not fair that Ben, one of the intellectually disabled boys at the hostel, has so few opportunities. Shelley slowly warms to Ben and realises that, by teaching him to swim, she can make a difference to Ben's life. In doing so, she makes a big difference to her own. This book has 68 small pages.

VIDEO
Remember the Titans

This video is the story of how initial racial discrimination in a high school football team is overcome by ongoing contact, cooperation and friendliness.

ACTIVITIES
People pie (or class survey) about differences

X See Chapter 10 of the Teacher's Handbook.

Are you or are you not:
- Left-handed?
- Blue-eyed?

   Do you:
- Suffer from allergies?
- Have a step-parent?
- Like to watch tennis on TV?

   Were you:
- Born in Australia?

Personal poll

Would you rather:
- Eat chocolate or strawberry ice-cream?
- Read a book or play on the computer?
- Be rich or famous?
- Be artistic or athletic?
- Be good at school work or musical?
- Have lots of money or lots of friends?
- Be a good reader or a good drawer?
- Be honest or be confident?
- Be creative or be a good organiser?
- Be the captain of the team or the team's best player?
- Go to the beach or go to the ski slopes?

- Watch a video or play a computer game?
- Have a teacher who taught you a lot or was kind to you?

CLASS DISCUSSION RESPECT

Start with students putting together an impromptu story or skit about 'the guest from hell' who comes to stay for a weekend and shows incredibly bad manners at every turn. Debrief and each time the students refer to a bad manner ask, 'What are they not respecting?'

Discussion questions

- What does 'showing respect' for others mean? (treating others with consideration; making sure that others are allowed to have dignity; avoiding insulting, injuring or interfering with others; appreciating what others can do well; showing courtesy and good manners to others; protecting and caring for shared or others' property)
- How do we show disrespect? (using put-downs; talking about people behind their back; misusing their things; not considering them or their rights; speaking rudely)
- Why is it important to use good manners? (people feel respected so hostility is reduced; people respond to you more positively; it acknowledges their right to be treated with respect; they are more likely to behave courteously to you too)
- With rights come responsibilities. What responsibilities do you have at home and at school and how do they relate to some of the rights you have?
- One aspect of responsibility and respect for others is good manners. What are good manners? (respect for and consideration of others; ritualised social skills that have been over-learnt) What are bad manners? (lack of respect for others)
- How do you disagree with someone in a respectful manner? (first find something you agree with that the other person said and then express your own opinion)
- Is spitting a bad manner? (yes, and it spreads germs such as hepatitis) What about kissing in public?

Follow-up activities

- Use the 'partner retell' strategy (see Chapter 10 of the *Teacher's Handbook*) to ask what each person's family considers to be *especially* bad manners.
- Tell the students that RESPECT! stands for 'The Royal Educational Society for the Prevention of Embarrassment and Cruelty to Teachers'. In pairs students can design a tongue-in-cheek booklet of advice to students about how to treat teachers in a humane and thoughtful fashion (e.g. when a teacher makes a mistake, pretend not to notice it; make sure you give your teacher a quality present at the end of the year, and so on).
- Unit 1, 'Core values', in the Level 2 *Teacher's Resource Book* (Middle Primary) contains a collection of 'good manners' which can be used for drama.
- Students search for websites on manners and etiquette.
- Students conduct a 'Manners' survey. They choose four of the following situations and interview five people about what they consider to be good and bad manners in those situations. They then make a brochure or book entitled '(Your name)'s Really Excellent Book of Manners when/relating to . . .'
  - Eating in a food hall or restaurant
  - In a shop
  - In a plane or train

- Using the telephone/mobile phone
- Visiting someone's house
- Entertaining a guest
- Sharing a 4-bed cabin at school camp
- At the movies or any kind of show
- Bodily fluids.
• Students work in groups to make up a good manners quiz for the class.

INVESTIGATION
Which bad manners in public places drive you mad?

Students devise a checklist of bad manners in public places. They then interview two adults to judge each bad manner on a 3-point scale: really annoying, somewhat annoying, doesn't bother me. Collate the class results. Some ideas are: spitting, forcing your car into the traffic, one person taking up two seats on public transport, constant sniffing, smokers blowing smoke in your face, or talking for a long time on the telephone while someone else waits.

CLASS DISCUSSION FRIENDLINESS

In advance, ask students to make a note of any examples they observe of people being friendly to each other. Pool everyone's ideas to come up with a class list of behaviours and attitudes that demonstrate friendliness.

Discussion questions

• Why is friendliness a good thing? (creates a positive environment; people feel like they belong and are accepted; people are kinder to each other and like themselves more; you have more fun and look forward to school; it becomes reciprocal; war is less likely)
• What sorts of attitudes lead to friendliness? (acceptance of difference; the need to be active in reaching out to others; the view that people and relationships are important)
• What do people do to be friendly to people they know well? (look at them and smile; greet and acknowledge them; take the time to talk to them; have a brief conversation; share a laugh; offer help if needed; share information about themselves)
• What do people do to be friendly to people they don't know really well? (as above plus ask them about themselves)
• What could someone do to be more friendly to someone who seems lonely and is not included in a group?
• Why were the Melbourne 1956 Olympics and the Sydney 2002 Olympics both described as the Friendly Olympics? (the 47 000 volunteers in 2002 acted as described above; the people in 1956 also helped by billeting athletes in their own homes when official accommodation ran out)

Follow-up activities

• Read to the class and discuss the picture book *Hooray for Diffendoofer Day*, which is about a school where friendliness, kindness, belonging and caring are the highest priorities. This book is also used in 'The bright side' (Unit 5, p. 102).
• Students devise a brochure that advertises their school as a friendly school.

- Use 'ten thinking tracks' (see BLM 1.3) to discuss the idea of having a rule in the first two years of schooling that 'no one can say that you can't play'.

CLASSROOM ORGANISATION
Cooperative committee

Establish a rotating 'roving' cooperative committee that looks for and reports on core values in practice. Give 'Values in practice' awards. Photograph students throughout the school putting the different values into practice.

CONSOLIDATION
Core values cartoons

Students read and analyse the cartoons in BLM 1.11, 'Core values cartoons', and write in detail what each means and how it relates to one or more of the core values.

Balloon burst

✗ See Chapter 11 of the Teacher's Handbook.

- Those who bring sunshine into the life of others can not keep it from themselves. (J M Barrie)
- Alone we can do so little. Together we can do so much. (Helen Keller)
- Kindness is in our power even if fondness is not. (Samuel Johnson)
- Sometimes kindness means caring for people more than they appear to deserve.
- No act of kindness no matter how small is ever wasted. (Aesop)
- Take care of each other. Share your energies with the group. No one must feel alone or cut off, for that is when you do not make it. (Willie Unsoeld, famous mountaineer)

Antonyms and synonyms

Students find antonyms and synonyms for vocabulary related to the core values e.g. polite, courteous, compassionate, faithful, judgmental, rude etc.

Designing a board game

Students can make a Snakes and Ladders game for younger students using the values of honesty, good manners, care and concern for others, cooperation, fairness and acceptance of difference.

Class recommendations

Students write their recommendations (in a class book) for:
- Books/movies/songs with themes that demonstrate any of the core values
- Websites on any of the values

Newspaper analysis

Bring newspapers to class. In groups, students find and report on stories reflecting one or more of the core values.

 ### Cross-offs

Have students complete BLM 1.12. The message is: Having positive values helps you respect yourself more.

RESOURCES

Books

Judy Blume, 1985, *The Pain and The Great One*, Heinemann, London.
Anthony Browne, 1986, *Piggybook*, Julia MacCrae Books, London.
Mem Fox & Julie Vivas, 1984, *Wilfred Gordon McDonald Partridge*, Ashton Scholastic, Gosford, NSW.
Paul Jennings, 1994, *The Gizmo*, Puffin, Ringwood, Victoria.
Robin Klein, 1986, *Boss of the Pool*, Penguin, Melbourne.
Margaret Mahy & Jonathan Allen, 1989, *The Great White Man-Eating Shark*, Puffin Books, London.
H McGrath & H Edwards, 2002, *The Creative Kaleidoscope*, Hawker Brownlow, Melbourne.
Mary Morris, 1993, *Boss of the Pool: The Play*, Currency Press, Sydney.
Dr Seuss, 1972, *The Lorax*, Collins, London.
Dr Seuss, 1998, *Hooray for Diffendoofer Day*, Collins, London.
Jerry Spinelli, 2001, *Stargirl*, Orchard Books, London.
Bruce Whatley & Rosie Smith, 2001, *Little White Dogs Can't Jump*, Angus & Robertson, Pymble, NSW.
Nadia Wheatley, 1999, *Luke's Way of Looking*, Hodder Children's Books, Australia.

Videos

Remember the Titans (PG, 2000, Buena Vista Home Video)
Big Fat Liar (G rating, 2002, Universal)

POSTBOX

BLM 1.1

Tick the box that best describes what you think you would do.

If I was selling my bike and it had something dangerously wrong with it, I would tell the potential buyers about the problem.
Yes ☐   No ☐   Unsure ☐

....

If I was given too much change in a shop, I would keep it rather than tell the shopkeeper they had made a mistake.
Yes ☐   No ☐   Unsure ☐

....

I would let my older brother drive me home even though he had been drinking a lot.
Yes ☐   No ☐   Unsure ☐

....

I would find it hard to say no to my friends if they wanted to do something that was dangerous or unsafe, such as taking drugs.
Yes ☐   No ☐   Unsure ☐

....

I would steal a small thing from a department store if it wasn't worth much and I thought I could get away with it.
Yes ☐   No ☐   Unsure ☐

....

I know someone who stole something, got caught and was punished.
Yes ☐   No ☐   Unsure ☐

....

What is the main reason you would hate it if someone you knew told you a lie? _____

_____

Why do people feel angry and upset when someone who has made a promise to them doesn't keep it? _____

_____

© Helen McGrath and Toni Noble, 2003. This page from Bounce Back!® may be photocopied for classroom use.

THE PINOCCHIO EFFECT

BLM 1.2

Telling lies really does make your nose grow! When you tell lies, the heart pumps blood a little faster so the nasal tissues swell slightly and itch, so people are more likely to rub or scratch their nose. Other telltale signs of fibbing are:

- Slower answers given to questions
- More 'ums' and 'ers' and throat-clearing (as they delay to try to come up with a convincing response)
- Being unnaturally calm
- Making fewer gestures than normal
- Blinking more than normal (due to increased blood flow around the eyes)
- Too little or too much eye contact
- More scratching and touching (especially mouth and nose)
- Excessive swallowing
- Less smiling than normal
- More shoulder shrugging
- Leaning forward more than normal.

Warning: Some of the indicators that someone may be lying are similar to the signs of nervousness.

Lie detectors/polygraphs
Lie detectors are machines that can often, but not always, tell when a person is lying, by measuring their heart beat and the electricity in their skin. When you tell a lie, your heart usually beats faster than when you are telling the truth. However, some dishonest people are so good at lying that they are not detected as liars using a polygraph machine.

Red-eye photos to detect lies
A thermal-imaging camera (hand-held or fixed) can tell if a person is lying with an 83 per cent accuracy rate, which is about the same accuracy rate as a lie detector (a polygraph). When people tell lies, the blood flow around their eyes increases and hence there are 'hot spots' around the eyes that can be detected by the camera. Unlike the lie detector, the camera can be used without a person's knowledge, it does not require an expert to study the results, and it can be used for mass screening (e.g. at airports when passengers show their passports).

The honesty phone
Lie-detecting phones are now available and have an accuracy rate of 75–80 per cent. When most people lie, their brain sends a signal of either anxiety or excitement to their vocal cords and barely detectible voice tremors are produced. If the phone detects these tremors, it flashes a warning light. The software was originally developed to detect bomb hoaxers who rang in. However, some very low-anxiety people can control these tremors and some anxious people have these tremors even when they are telling the truth.

© Helen McGrath and Toni Noble, 2003. This page from Bounce Back!® may be photocopied for classroom use.

THE TEN THINKING TRACKS

BLM 1.3

Track 1	What is it?	Clearly describe the issue, product or problem we want to think about
Track 2	Knowledge	What do we already know about this? What do we need to know more about? How can we find out what we still need to know? Is this similar to anything else we already know about?
Track 3	Bright side	What are the good features of this? What positive outcomes might there be? What good opportunities might this provide?
Track 4	Down side	What are the not-so-good features of this? What problems might happen?
Track 5	Feelings	How does this make us feel? (use proper *feeling* words e.g. excited, worried, shocked, nervous, pleased) How might this affect the feelings of any of the people involved?
Track 6	Improvements	What changes could make this work better? What could be added, removed, reduced or altered to improve it?
Track 7	Thought police	Have we made any assumptions that could be challenged? Do we have enough evidence for what we have been saying? Are we using a trustworthy source of evidence? What unanswered questions are still bothering us?
Track 8	Is it fair?	Are there any safety or legal issues involved? Are there any moral dilemmas? Have we considered the impact of this on smaller groups of people e.g. with disabilities, elderly, other cultural groups etc.? Are there any parts which might not be fair to one gender? Are there any 'big-picture' or global issues to consider?
Track 9	I-think	What opinion does each one of us have about this and why? (All say 'I think . . . because . . .')
Track 10	We-think	What is our group decision when we put our ideas together and negotiate? What are our three main reasons for this decision? Can we sum up the *opposite* point of view?

© Helen McGrath and Toni Noble, 2003. This page from Bounce Back!® may be photocopied for classroom use.

THE TEN THINKING TRACKS (CONTINUED)

BLM 1.3

In your group, divide up the ten 'tracks' (e.g. by drawing out numbers) so that each person leads two or more of the discussion tracks. Colour in your track when that part of the discussion is complete.

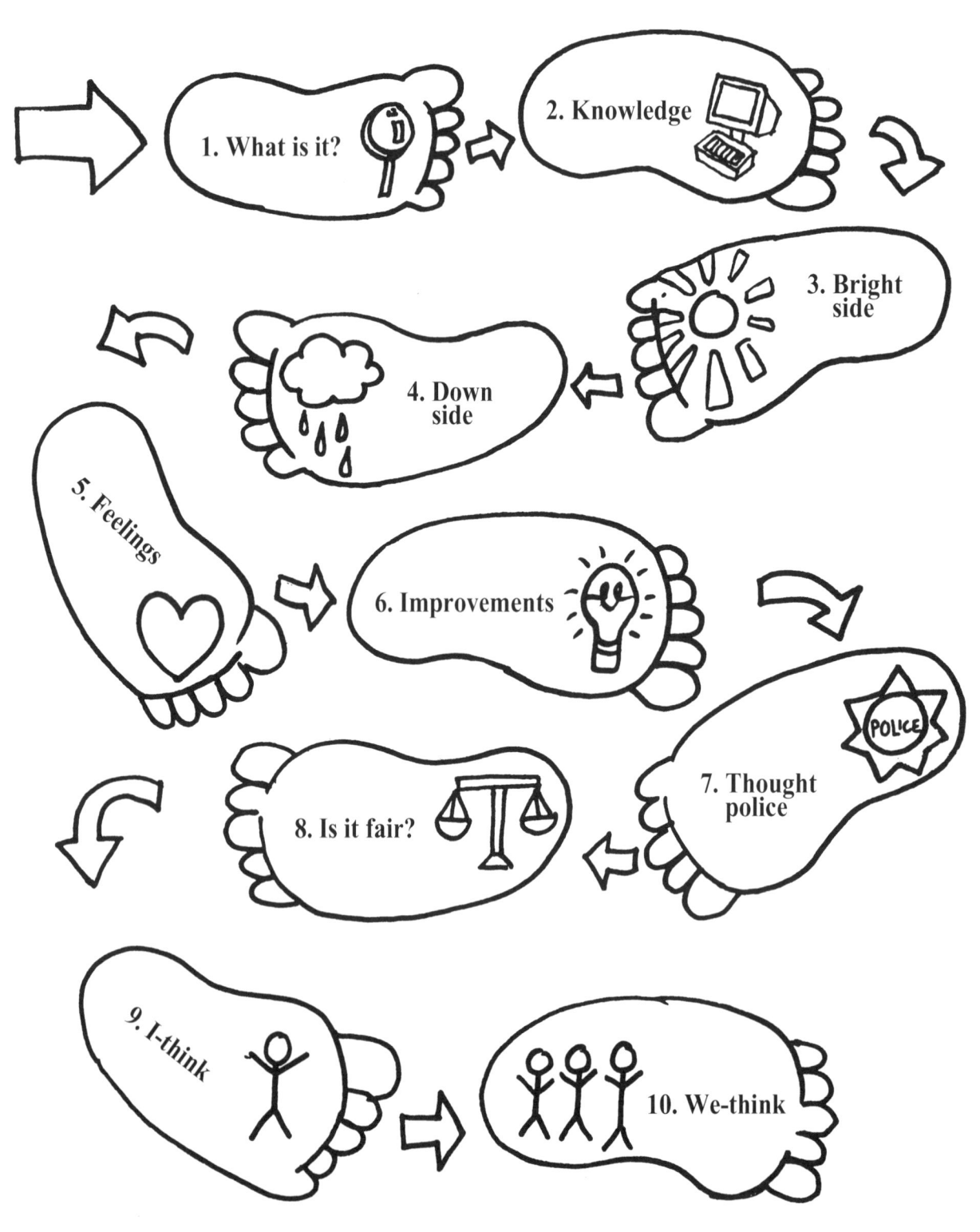

© Helen McGrath and Toni Noble, 2003. This page from Bounce Back!® may be photocopied for classroom use.

AMNESTY INTERNATIONAL

BLM 1.4

Amnesty International (www.amnesty.org.au) is a worldwide organisation that provides a network of help and support. The aim of members of this organisation is to remind countries who do not respect the rights of humans that the world is watching them.

Peter Benenson started Amnesty International in 1961. Benenson had been a defence lawyer for political prisoners in Hungary, South Africa and Spain. He decided to start the organisation after hearing of two Portuguese students who were sent to prison for seven years just for raising their glasses to freedom. He was appalled at the injustice.

Amnesty International focuses on helping three groups of people and offering them hope. The first group are called prisoners of conscience. These are people who have not used violence to express their ideas, but have been persecuted, jailed or tortured for their different religious or political beliefs. The second group consists of political prisoners who have been denied a trial. The third group consists of prisoners who have been mistreated, tortured or who are awaiting execution.

Amnesty International supports people who have been treated unfairly in several ways. It sends lawyers to attend unfair trials. It sends observers to countries where human rights are abused. It writes reports on countries where human rights have been violated. It lobbies governments to stop the abuse of human rights in their countries. It writes letters of hope and encouragement to people who have been unjustly jailed or mistreated in jail.

Amnesty International has offices in more than 40 countries and has over 200 000 members living in more than 100 countries.

1. What is the main aim of Amnesty?

2. What three groups does Amnesty help?

3. What core values are reflected in the way Amnesty helps others?

4. How does offering hope to people in need help them to survive?

5. Research one person or group of people that Amnesty has helped.

6. Think about a situation where a family member or a school friend may lose hope. How could you help them to be hopeful?

© Helen McGrath and Toni Noble, 2003. This page from Bounce Back!® may be photocopied for classroom use.

THE SMITH FAMILY

BLM 1.5

Shortly before Christmas in 1922, five Australian businessmen reflected on their good fortune in being able to afford Christmas presents for their children. They decided that in addition to buying presents for their own children they would share their good fortune by buying presents for children at a local orphanage. When the orphanage asked the men for their names, they answered 'Smith'. And so 'The Smith Family' was founded.

Eighty years later, The Smith Family is one of Australia's biggest charity organisations. Members devote most of their time to assisting Australia's less fortunate families and children.

Over the years The Smith Family has helped poor Australians through a variety of situations. When poor nutrition became a problem during the Depression in the 1930s, the organisation provided food for families who were unable to afford healthy meals. When floods affected Brisbane in 1974, they flew 200 children to Sydney where they were fed and clothed.

The Smith Family also helps children go to school. Through its *Learning for Life* program, 13 000 Australian children are provided with the financial support they need so that they are able to stay at school and make the most of their ability. The Smith Family has also made Christmas a happy time for less fortunate families. Each year they distribute more than 60 000 toys and 20 000 hampers.

Although The Smith Family receives a small amount of money from the government, most of its activities are funded by donations from the public and the support of its sponsors. It also relies on the help of over 1500 volunteers.

1. What are two ways that The Smith Family has helped others?

2. What message can we learn from the way The Smith Family began?

3. What values are reflected in the way The Smith Family helps others?

4. What is one way you have demonstrated one of these values?

© Helen McGrath and Toni Noble, 2003. This page from Bounce Back!® may be photocopied for classroom use.

FRED HOLLOWS

BLM 1.6

Fred Hollows was born into a religious family in New Zealand in 1929. He originally wanted to become a missionary but later decided on a career in medicine. Before long, he decided to specialise in ophthalmology—surgery of the eye.

Fred had always felt a lot of sympathy for those in unfortunate situations. When he heard about the need for doctors to care for Aboriginal people in Sydney, he decided to lend a hand. He played a major role in starting Australia's first Aboriginal Medical Service.

Still interested in the health of Aborigines, Fred found out that large numbers of people living in the outback suffered from eye diseases. He discovered that many of these problems could be prevented with the proper medical treatment and he decided to do something about it.

He launched a program to provide proper eye care for outback Aboriginal people. He was able to organise a team of doctors to volunteer their services to treat those suffering from eye diseases. Over a three-year period, the team treated nearly 30 000 people and provided over 10 000 pairs of glasses.

A few years later, Fred travelled to Eritrea in Africa. He had heard about the millions of people who needed lenses to improve their vision. He decided to ask Australians for donations and was able to raise $6 million for a lens factory. He also trained local doctors to care for the eyes of the Eritreans.

Even when Fred found out in 1989 that he had cancer, he continued his work with the Eritreans. He finally passed away in 1993, but his work in Eritrea and other poor countries is still carried out by his wife, Gabi Hollows.

1. How did Fred Hollows make a significant difference to many people's lives?

2. What values are reflected in the way Fred Hollows helped others?

3. What is one important message we can all learn from Fred Hollows' example?

4. What is one small way you could offer help to someone in your class or your family or your community?

© Helen McGrath and Toni Noble, 2003. This page from Bounce Back!® may be photocopied for classroom use.

CAROLINE CHISHOLM

BLM 1.7

Caroline Chisholm was born in England in 1808. As a young girl, she watched how her parents were always willing to help others. Their home was open to everyone, whether they were rich or poor. As a result, Caroline also became interested in helping others.

Soon after Caroline was married, at the age of 22, she and her husband moved from England to Sydney. When she arrived, Caroline was distressed by the poverty in Sydney. People had come to Australia in search of a better life, but they arrived to find that there were very few jobs or places to live.

Caroline decided to start a home for unemployed women. However, when she asked the Governor of New South Wales for financial help, she was turned down. Caroline was determined and after many more meetings with the Governor her wish was granted. Within two years, the Female Immigrants Home had found jobs and provided shelter for over a thousand women.

Although she had made life a little easier for Australian immigrants, she knew more could be done. Caroline was able to convince the authorities to improve conditions on the ships that brought people to Australia. She also set up Australia's first employment office.

She then turned her attention to the Victorian goldfields. Here she was able to organise land for miners and their families, as well as reasonable shelter for miners making their way to the goldfields.

Caroline Chisholm died in 1877 back in England. By the end of her life she had helped to find jobs and homes for nearly 11 000 migrants. Despite her efforts, she accepted no money for her work and died very poor. Australian history recognises Caroline as 'the immigrant's friend' and she appeared on Australia's five-dollar note for over 20 years.

1. How did Caroline Chisolm help people in need?

2. What values are reflected in the way Caroline helped others?

3. What is one important message we can all learn from Caroline's example?

© Helen McGrath and Toni Noble, 2003. This page from Bounce Back!® may be photocopied for classroom use.

CLEAN UP AUSTRALIA

BLM 1.8

Ian Kiernan was a yachtsman who had sailed all over the world. In his travels he had seen first-hand the damage that rubbish and pollution can do to the environment. So, when he returned to Australia, he decided to do something about cleaning up parts of Australia.

In 1989, with the help of friends, Ian set about cleaning up Sydney Harbour. In only a short time, Ian received an overwhelming response to the idea. Over 40 000 volunteers gave up their time and energy to the Clean Up Sydney Harbour Day.

The following year, Ian turned his attention to all of Australia. The first Clean Up Australia Day in 1990 attracted more than 300 000 volunteers around the country. This proved that a great many Australians were concerned about the state of their environment.

Ever since, Clean Up Australia Day has become an annual event. Its popularity has continued to grow in that time. In 1997, 530 000 volunteers took part in the Clean Up Australia Day in more than 7500 locations. They collected about 17 000 tonnes of rubbish from Australia's parks and waterways.

Keeping Australia clean is too great a job for just a small number of people. But when thousands of people cooperated, the results were spectacular. This proves the old saying that 'many hands make light work'.

In 1994 Ian was recognised for his contribution to keeping Australia clean by being named Australian of the Year.

1. What core values does Ian Kiernan demonstrate in his work for 'Clean up Australia Day'?

2. How does the event illustrate that 'many hands make light work'?

3. How does the principle of 'many hands make light work' operate in a sports team and/or sports club?

© Helen McGrath and Toni Noble, 2003. This page from Bounce Back!® may be photocopied for classroom use.

PEOPLE SCAVENGER HUNT ON DIFFERENCES

BLM 1.9

Find someone who:

Has visited another country. Their name: _____

What is one thing they experienced in this country that was different from Australia?

_____

Was born in another country. Their name: _____

What is one memory they have of their country of origin?

_____

Has eaten food from another country. Their name: _____

What did they like or dislike about the food?

_____

Lives in a different kind of house to you. Their name: _____

Ask them to tell you about one good thing about living in that kind of house.

_____

Has a different family size to yours. Their name: _____

What is one activity their family does together?

_____

Likes to play a different sport to you. Their name: _____

What is it and why do they like it?

_____

Wants to have a different job to you when they leave school. Their

name: _____ What job do they want

and what skill do they now have that will help them in this job?

_____

© Helen McGrath and Toni Noble, 2003. This page from Bounce Back!® may be photocopied for classroom use.

SOCIAL BIODIVERSITY

BLM 1.10

'Diversity' is a term that means 'variety'. Diversity is a very important element in terms of both the environment and society.

Biodiversity

Biodiversity stresses the importance of every living organism in the overall make-up of our planet. It means that every creature makes a unique contribution to the world. The absence of any one organism would upset the careful balance of the environment.

For instance, have you ever wondered why the world needs ants? They seem to be more of a pest than anything else. But ants are very important to our environment. They are a source of food to other species such as birds and lizards. They also distribute the seeds of numerous plants to safe areas where they can grow. If ants became extinct, plant life would be affected and birds and lizards would need to find another source of food. As a result, the environment would become unbalanced.

Cultural diversity

Similarly, think about Australian society as you know it. Now imagine if you removed all the people who weren't born in this country. Then, take away all the aspects of our society that come from other countries. Gone are all the art and music from other cultures. No more Chinese takeaway or pizza (Italy) for dinner. No more Harry Potter books (England) or Pokemon movies (Japan), and you can forget about McDonald's (United States). Pretty boring, isn't it?

Australia's culture is based on the combination of cultures from all over the world. Statistics collected in 2002 suggest that nearly 25 per cent of Australia's population were born overseas. Our country has a reputation for being one of the most culturally diverse nations in the world.

So, the success of our society isn't based on one particular culture. Rather, it is based on the combination of many cultures: Greek, Lebanese, Italian, Turkish, Vietnamese and so on. If we lose just one of these cultures, Australia's culture becomes less diverse and less sophisticated.

1. In what ways is your school 'culturally diverse'?

2. List two ways in which cultural diversity has positive effects in your school.

© Helen McGrath and Toni Noble, 2003. This page from Bounce Back!® may be photocopied for classroom use.

CORE VALUES CARTOONS

BLM 1.11

Write an explanation on a separate sheet about the core values (or lack of them) suggested in each cartoon. What could be improved?

1.

"DID YOU KNOW IT TAKES 26 MUSCLES TO SMILE AND 62 MUSCLES TO FROWN?"

"WELL IT'S WORTH THE EXTRA EFFORT."

2.

TOGETHER
EVERYONE
ARGUES
MORE

"I DON'T THINK THAT'S RIGHT!"

© Helen McGrath and Toni Noble, 2003. This page from Bounce Back!® may be photocopied for classroom use.

CORE VALUES CARTOONS (CONTINUED)

BLM 1.11

3.

- "THANKS A LOT, MRS BASS. I REALLY APPRECIATE YOUR EXTRA HELP."
- "PLEASURE"
- "GUS DOES THIS AMAZING MIND CONTROL THING OVER TEACHERS. SOMETIMES I THINK HE'S AN ALIEN."

4.

- "HA HA... GOTCHA CD!"
- "WHAT WILL YOUR BROTHER BE LIKE WHEN HE FINALLY MATURES?"
- "VERY VERY OLD!"

© Helen McGrath and Toni Noble, 2003. This page from Bounce Back!® may be photocopied for classroom use.

CROSS-OFFS

BLM 1.12

tap	blender	Having	twelve	California	measure	positive
lemon	squash	catamaran	bath	slowly	albatross	yacht
Texas	two	hers	values	nervousness	microwave	sandals
terror	pelican	pillow	helps	Washington	basin	thongs
eight	golf	shower	dreaming	mine	you	treasure
pineapple	soccer	respect	canoe	apple	kayak	slippers
pleasure	snoring	his	boots	fright	penguin	four
tennis	grape	honestly	swan	yourself	stupidly	Florida
toaster	ours	more	banana	eighteen	anxiety	carefully

To find the message, cross off these words:
5 words that are fruits
5 words that are even numbers
4 words that are water birds
4 words that are things in the bathroom
4 words that are games played with a ball
3 words that are electrical appliances in the home
4 words that are adverbs
4 words that mean a kind of fear
4 words that are types of boats
4 words that are possessive pronouns
4 words that are American states
3 words that rhyme with leisure
4 words that are kinds of footwear
3 words that are about sleeping

The secret message is _____

© Helen McGrath and Toni Noble, 2003. This page from Bounce Back!® may be photocopied for classroom use.

UNIT 2
ELASTICITY

KEY POINTS

Energy makes things work.
Energy is the ability of things to do work. The energy of movement is called 'kinetic energy'. 'Potential energy' is energy that is stored within something, such as a machine, a toy or a ball. It is usually stored either in the material that the object is made of or in a part of the object. A jack-in-a-box is a toy that has potential energy in its compressed spring. A ball has potential energy when it is a certain distance from the ground before it is dropped.

Elastic energy is a form of stored energy.
Elasticity can be defined as the capacity of an object or material to return to its original shape after being compressed or squashed, or stretched or forced out of shape. Flexible (elastic) materials can bend and stretch (up to a point) without breaking and tearing. The words 'elasticity' or 'resilience' are used to describe the strength of such forces. Some balls are highly elastic and bounce back close to their original shape. Other balls with less elasticity take longer to return to their shape. This is also true of springs and elastic bands. Rubber, many metals, springs, balloons, spider webs and the air are elastic. Wrinkle-resistant materials (e.g. microfibre or lycra) have elastic properties, whereas fabrics that stay wrinkled (e.g. linen) are not. Some animals use elasticity as a source of energy, such as the kangaroo, the springbok, the grasshopper and the frog.

'Elastic' is different from 'plastic'.
Some materials are plastic rather than elastic. Plastic materials (e.g. clay and putty) are capable of having their shape changed, but they do not return to their original shape and condition. They stay changed. However, some things that are made from a plastic material also have a small 'elastic range'.

The process of bouncing transforms stored energy into kinetic energy.
The degree of stored elasticity in a ball is referred to as its 'bounciness'. When you drop a ball, gravity pulls it towards the floor. The closer the ball gets to the ground the less potential energy it has and the more kinetic energy it has. When the ball hits the floor and stops momentarily, that energy has to go somewhere. It goes into squashing the ball into a new shape. Much of the energy of the ball's downward motion then becomes upward motion as the ball returns to its original shape and bounces into the air.

People can bounce back like a ball does.
When something in their life knocks them down, people can be resilient and bounce back and be (mostly) themselves again, just as balls and springs do. Elasticity is a physical characteristic and resilience is the equivalent psychological characteristic.

UNIT 2—ELASTICITY

ACTIVITY
Circuit brainstorm *35*
MATHS/SCIENCE ACTIVITY
Comparing the elasticity in different balls and surfaces *35*
ACTIVITY
Information scavenger hunt *36*
MATHS ACTIVITY
The angles of bounce *37*
COLLECTIVE CLASSROOM RESEARCH
Elasticised clothing *38*
TECHNOLOGY ACTIVITIES
Elasticised clothing *38*
SCIENCE/TECHNOLOGY ACTIVITIES
Making balls that bounce *38*
Elastic-powered devices *38*
Catapults, maroons and mangonels *39*
Spring challenges *39*

Designing a bungy jump *39*
Designing and making the best jack-in-a-box *40*
Wrinkle tests *40*
Sporting equipment *40*
CATEGORISATION ACTIVITY
Types of springs *41*
MATHS ACTIVITIES
Stretching lolly snakes *41*
Calibrating rubber bands *41*
ACTIVITY
Multiply and merge *42*
DEMONSTRATION
Charging or winding springs *42*
CLASS PRESENTATIONS
How a device with a spring works *42*
MUSIC ACTIVITY
Elastic raps and chants *42*
CREATIVE ARTS ACTIVITIES
Elastic art and design *42*

PE ACTIVITY
Balloon volleyball *43*
ACTIVITIES
Jigsaw strategy *43*

Consolidation *43*
TEAM coaching *43*
A smorgasbord of activities *43*
Before or after? *44*
Cross-offs *44*

BLM 2.1—Springs *45*

BLM 2.2—Animals that Bounce *46*

BLM 2.3—The Elastic Anaconda *47*

BLM 2.4—Cross-offs *48*

UNIT 2—ELASTICITY

ACTIVITY
Circuit brainstorm

X See Chapter 10 of the Teacher's Handbook.

- Name one thing in a home that has a spring in it.
- Name one item of clothing that features elastic in some way.
- Name one living creature that bounces.
- Name one type of sport played with a piece of equipment that has elastic properties.
- Name one form of transport that uses a spring or another kind of elasticity and say where that elasticity is.

MATHS/SCIENCE ACTIVITY
Comparing the elasticity in different balls and surfaces

Use the 'predictor cards' strategy with students in groups of three (see Chapter 10 of the *Teacher's Handbook*). Students make predictions about:
- The relative elasticity of four different balls and then the same ball dropped from four different heights (i.e. how high will they bounce?)
- How high a ball will bounce after being dropped on four different surfaces.

Discuss why it is important to use multiple observations. Students can then plan and carry out an investigation to test out their predictions, using a tennis ball, a golf ball, a cricket ball and a table-tennis ball. Science shops also sell sets of black balls that could be used. They look the same but have different elastic properties. Students create their own data charts and record their results, then write a report on the results and their conclusions. Here is one way to do it if you would rather help them to set it up:

For a comparison of balls

- Tape a tape measure to the top edge of a table. It should hang down so that the zero mark rests on the floor.
- Record the height of the tabletop from the floor.
- Drop a tennis ball several times to practise dropping the balls from the same height each time (i.e. from the top of the table). Balls cannot be pushed or thrown.
- Practise measuring the height of the bounce after the ball hits the floor.
- Drop the tennis ball ten times and each time measure the height of the first bounce.
- Because this measuring technique is not precise, calculate the average height of the ten bounces.
- Repeat the steps with the other three types of balls.

For a comparison of heights from which the ball is dropped

Use the same procedure, but this time use the same ball with three different dropping heights (e.g. 1 metre, ¾ metre and ½ metre).

For a comparison of surfaces

Use the same procedure, but this time use the same ball and dropping height with four different surfaces (e.g. asphalt, concrete, grass, carpet, wood).

There are many aspects of this activity that students can discuss or follow up:
- There are several useful websites on bouncing balls. Try www.physicscentral and search for 'bouncing balls'.
- Some surfaces are very 'bounce absorbing'. If the surface is hard, it allows the ball to recover its shape faster. However, the bounciness of a surface can also interact with the bounciness of the ball.

- The amount of potential energy depends partly on the height from which the ball is dropped. The higher the lift, the more potential energy the ball has.
- When you drop the ball, the potential energy is changed into kinetic energy. As the falling ball rubs against the air, some of the energy is changed into heat. Some energy changes into sound when the ball hits the floor. Because some energy becomes unusable when it changes from one form into another, the ball will never have enough energy to bounce back up to its starting height. You can't ever get as much energy out of a transformation as you put into it.
- A putty or plasticine ball does not bounce at all, so where does the energy go? It is transformed into thermal energy in the form of heat (compare this with the kinetic energy of an elasticised ball).
- A formula for working out the speed of the ball (its velocity in metres per second) just before it hits the ground is v = √(2gh). V (the velocity in metres per second) = square root of (2 × gravity × height of the ball in metres). Gravity is $9.8 m/s^2$ (i.e. 9.8 metres per second). You can multiply by 3.6 to obtain the result in kilometres per hour.
- Why don't we have square balls? (round balls enable us to control the direction of the 'bounce back')
- Why are some footballs not round? What extra skills would be needed to handle these balls?
- What would happen if you put an elastic band around each ball?
- What are many household tennis court surfaces made from? (sand that is regularly sprayed with water and rolled to make it hard and smooth)
- What are tennis racquet strings made from? (try www.pacificstrings and search for 'The Story of Gut')

ACTIVITY
Information scavenger hunt

This activity could also be a collective classroom research activity (see Chapter 10 of the *Teacher's Handbook*).
- What materials are different sporting balls made from?
- Why do tennis players like to play with new balls?
- What kind of surface is used at Wimbeldon? (grass)
- What kind of surface is used at the French Open? (clay)
- What kind of surface is used at the US Open? (asphalt or concrete)
- What kind of surface is used for the Australian Open? (a synthetic surface called 'the synthetic rebound ace court', which is made of nylon mesh with sand rolled into it; it has a rubber mat underneath, coats of acrylic paint and then coats of paint containing both acrylic and fibreglass on top)
- What surfaces does (name a specific world tennis player) prefer?
- How is a plane launched from the deck of an aircraft carrier, given that there is no room for it to take off as planes normally do?
- What was Cathy Freeman's Olympic outfit made of and why?
- Are there any laws relating to bungy jumping?
- Where is the nearest bungy jump to the school? How does it work?
- In what ways are bridges and buildings elastic and why?
- In what way is a tree elastic and why?
- Are muscles elastic? Give your reasons. (yes, so we can to extend and contract them)
- What is rubber and where does it come from?
- Where is elasticity a factor in ageing, urine retention, sexual behaviour and reproduction?

UNIT 2—ELASTICITY

MATHS ACTIVITY
The angles of bounce

For each group of four students you will need:
- A tennis ball or firm rubber ball
- A protractor
- Paper to write on
- A tape measure
- Three pieces of chalk.

In groups of four, students measure the angle of hit and return of balls after they have been kicked along the ground so that they bounce against the bottom edge of a wall. The balls could be rolled instead of kicked. Each student takes on one of these roles:
- Kicker/roller
- Ground-marker (marks on the ground where the ball is kicked from)
- Wall-marker (marks where the ball hits the wall)
- Ball-stopper (stops the ball and marks where it was stopped).

1. The kicker (or roller) kicks the ball straight at the wall. The ball should come straight back and be stopped by the ball stopper. All students do their marking.
2. Then the kicker kicks the ball towards the wall a second time but this time along the ground at an angle. The students do their marking.
3. The ball-stopper draws a line between the point where the ball was kicked, the point of impact, and where it was stopped.
4. Students convert their observations into a diagram and measure with a protractor the angle of incidence (hit) and the angle of reflection (return). They then write up a report on their results and conclusions.

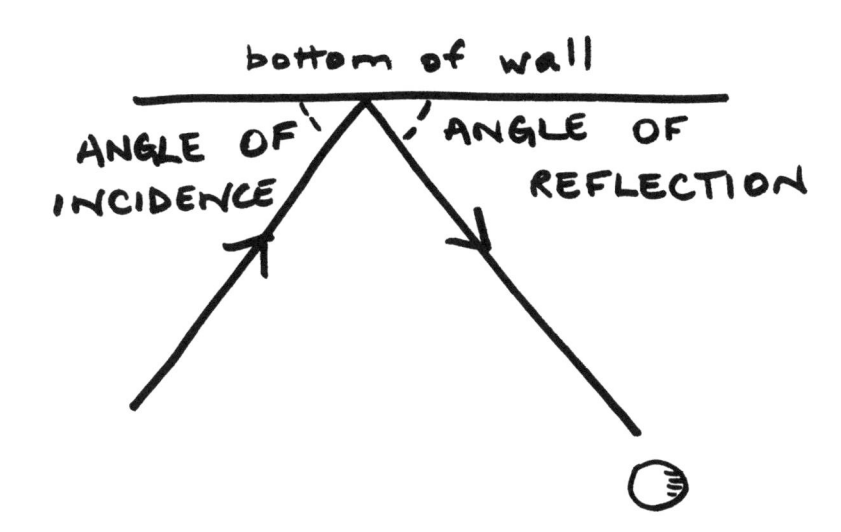

The follow-up discussion could include the following questions:
- Is there a pattern to the angles of bounce? (If the surfaces are perfectly flat, the angle of incidence equals the angle of reflection.)
- If the wall is rough, what will happen to the angles of bounce? (Some error will be introduced. The ball will bounce back more randomly.)
- Does the force of the kick make a difference?
- What does this experiment teach you about playing billiards or pool?

COLLECTIVE CLASSROOM RESEARCH
Elasticised clothing

Have three columns: 'Category of clothing', 'Examples' and 'Advantages'. Use these categories:
- Clothing for water sports and activities
- Clothing for very cold situations
- Sports clothing
- Fashion clothing
- Undergarments.

TECHNOLOGY ACTIVITIES
Elasticised clothing

- Students design an item of sports or fashion clothing that uses stretch fabric.
- Students create a collage based on their own drawings or drawings from magazines, brochures and so on of clothing based on stretch fabric.
- Students work in groups of three to design and make a fashion outfit using stretchy clothing bought from a second-hand shop (which they cut up and re-make). Their budget is $5. Have a fashion parade and a clothesline for displaying the garments.
- Students investigate the history of the use of elastic in a specific item of clothing, such as swimwear. What innovations in fabric production in the twentieth century enhanced the use of elasticised fabric?

SCIENCE/TECHNOLOGY ACTIVITIES
Making balls that bounce

Students can make their own bouncing balls and then test out the bounciness of their productions. Details can be found in Chapter 11 of the *Teacher's Handbook*.

Elastic-powered devices

Start by asking students to place an elastic band against their forehead and stretch it. They can feel the elastic band heat up as it stretches, demonstrating how the student's energy (their stretching) converts to heat energy. You could also ask students to make a simple piece of card with an elastic band threaded through a hole on either side. They can twist the bands and let it go to see the release of stored energy. Then use some of the science and technology activities in David Rowland's book *Problem-Solving in Science and Technology* (1987, Hutchinson Education, London). There are ideas for designing, making and evaluating:
- An elastic-powered device that can slide a large coin 1 metre along a table so that it lands in a 10-centimetre circle.
- An elastic-powered device that can fire a ping-pong ball over a barrier and into a bucket or similar container that is placed 1 metre from the barrier.
- A toy racing car that uses a wound-up rubber band or a mousetrap spring as its source of energy and that can travel a straight, 5-metre path as quickly as possible.

There are also many websites with similar ideas (including rubber band-powered planes and paddle boats). For example:
- www.scienceteacherstuff.com/mousetrapcars.html
- www.publish.csiro.au/helix.

UNIT 2—ELASTICITY

Catapults, maroons and mangonels

This activity may need repeated safety warnings and checks because of the possible misuse of the final product. You will need to provide safety goggles. Long before gunpowder and cannons were invented, large catapults, maroons and mangonels were used to hurl rocks and arrows at the enemy. Often armies had to travel large distances over very rugged and often snow-covered terrain to attack a city. Instead of dragging the huge catapults with them, they would carry only the ropes and other essential gear and then make the catapults at the scene of the battle.

Students research, design, make, test and evaluate their own simple catapult or mangonel.

Spring challenges

Challenge students to work in groups of three to design, make, test and evaluate:
- A mini-trampoline
- A springboard game where things are propelled into a container by a mini-springboard based on paddle-pop sticks joined together and an attached spring.

Designing a bungy jump

Students make a model of a bungy jump to demonstrate the principle of mass versus elasticity in relation to bungy jumping. For each pair of students you will need:
- A number of strong rubber bands
- Different weights
- A tape measure or a metre ruler
- Graph paper.

Instructions

- Use the edge of your desk as the bridge. Decide how low you want your bungy jumper to reach (e.g. 60 cm from the edge of the desk to just above the floor).
- Use a weight and tie some rubber bands together to use as your bungy cord.

- Experiment with different lengths of rubber bands to make the bungy cord, until the cord stops short just above the ground when the weight is released from the table.
- Record the length of the rubber band with the weight attached and the length of the rubber band without the weight attached.
- Repeat the last two steps with different weights, recording both lengths of the bungy cord (with and without the weight).
- Draw a graph with one line showing the length of the bungy cord with the weight attached and the other line showing the length of the cord without the weight attached. What relationship can you observe?
- Bungy instructors use a chart of weight versus length of elasticised jumping cord. Can students make a similar chart using what they have learned?
- Investigate the history of bungy jumping. Who was the first bungy jumper? Plot on a world map where well-known bungy jumps can be found. Find out whether different countries have different laws for bungy-jump operators. How do they calculate weights with tandem bungy jumping? Where would you feel safest if you wanted to make a bungy jump? Have bungy cords ever snapped? Why do they use hundreds of small elastic cables rather than just one large one?

Designing and making the best jack-in-a-box

Students work with a partner to make a jack-in-a-box. The class can draw up a list of the main criteria and another class can rank each of the jack-in-a-boxes on those criteria.

The two guiding principles are that the spring needs to be tightly compressed to work well and the container/box needs to be strong enough to compress the spring and contain the force. Provide students with access to:
- Velcro (to hold down and release the lid)
- Balsa wood
- Nails and hammer
- Empty screw-lid jars ranging from very small to small
- Buttons
- Thick embroidery cotton (for loops to go around buttons as lid-holding devices)
- Double-sided tape
- Plaster of Paris
- Blu-tac or plasticine
- Different-sized springs from unused devices, such as old pumps of the kind found in household cleaners and liquid soap (these are quite small, so consider purchasing some larger compression springs from a hardware store and reuse them each year)
- Polystyrene balls of various sizes.

Wrinkle tests

Resilience/elasticity is the ability of a fibre or fabric to return to its original shape after being stretched and wrinkled. Students work in groups of three to plan and implement a study to compare several types of fabrics in terms of their elasticity (or capacity to overcome wrinkling). They then draw up a grid, form conclusions, and write a report that includes making recommendations for fabrics for travelling.

Sporting equipment

Students can:
- Compare the flexibility of different types of sports shoes.
- Describe how elastic resistance bands can be used for workouts.

- Visit a local gymnasium, sporting venue and/or playground and make a photo study of equipment that is elastic or uses springs. In a labelled drawing of each piece of equipment, students explain how the equipment works and what it is designed to do to improve fitness and health.
- Experiment with a chest expander. In a labelled drawing, students outline how a chest expander improves chest muscle tone.

CATEGORISATION ACTIVITY
Types of springs

Start by asking students to complete BLM 2.1, 'Springs'. Write on cards the names of different objects that have springs. In groups of four, students can classify different objects that use springs according to whether they are compression springs, extension springs or leaf springs.

MATHS ACTIVITIES
Stretching lolly snakes

Bring lolly snakes to school. Students work with a partner to investigate how far the snakes can stretch before they move out of their 'elastic range' and break. Data charts can be made and class averages can be worked out. Have some spare lollies for them to eat later so that they don't try to eat the 'mauled' ones!

Calibrating rubber bands

For each student you will need one large, wide and thick rubber band and a ruler. You will also need a 6-metre tape measure.
- Place the tape measure on the floor and extend it to its full length.
- Each student uses a ruler to shoot a rubber band four times.
- The rubber band should be pulled back a little further each time (e.g. 15 cm, 20 cm, 25 cm, 30 cm).
- The rulers should be held waist-high each time.
- The results of the shooting are recorded on a graph. A curve is produced by plotting the distance of flight on the Y-axis and the distance the rubber band was pulled back from the ruler on the X-axis.
- Then find the parallel white lines on the basketball or four-square court. Measure the distance from one line to another, ensuring that it is within the calibration range of the students' rubber bands.
- Line the students up on one line, tell them the measured distance, and instruct them to use their calibration curves to determine the amount of stretch they need to use to make their rubber bands go exactly the measured distance.
- Students shoot and see how accurate they were.

Variation One
The variables being investigated in this activity are the length and thickness of the rubber band.
- Students can compare three different thicknesses of rubber band and shoot with the same degree of stretch each time.
- They then compare three different lengths.
- The shortest and thinnest rubber bands should travel the furthest because they can be deformed more and hence be stretched more tightly.

Variation Two

The variable being investigated in this activity is the temperature of the rubber band.
- Place the rubber band in ice water for two minutes and then shoot.
- Place the rubber band in hot water for two minutes and then shoot with the same degree of stretch.
- Students then write a statement about the relationship between temperature and elasticity.

ACTIVITY
Multiply and merge

X See Chapter 10 of the Teacher's Handbook.

Students make a negotiated list of the five elastic things (including things with springs in them) which they would hate to have to live without.

DEMONSTRATION
Charging or winding springs

Bring an old wind-up toy or wind-up clock to class. Take off the cover so that students can see the spring as it is wound up. Energy is now stored in the wound-up spring. They can then watch the spring unwind as it slowly gives out energy again.

CLASS PRESENTATIONS
How a device with a spring works

(See the list of 'Things with springs' on pp. 175–76 of the *Teacher's Handbook*.) Students work with a partner to deconstruct a spring-based device. They then present a talk to the class and show the deconstructed object to explain how it works. Items students could use include an old pop-up toaster no longer in working order, a four-colour click ballpoint pen, a mousetrap, a wind-up toy or a chest expander.

MUSIC ACTIVITY
Elasticity raps and chants

Students compose raps and songs that they can sing as they bounce a ball. The song is chanted in time to the bounce of the ball. The bounce of the ball creates a rhythm for their song.

CREATIVE ARTS AND TECHNOLOGY ACTIVITIES
Elastic art and design

- Show students pictures of large-scale interactive mobiles such as those of Alexander Calder. In teams of three, students can design their own mobile and incorporate elasticised parts so that it can bounce. The mobile should first be drawn to scale and then a three-dimensional model can be made. A large-scale mobile could be hung from a tree in the playground or between two buildings. Smaller-scale mobiles can be hung in the classroom. The class can devise criteria to judge each design.
- Students can make a bouncing ball screen-saver or a screen-saver using images of animals that bounce.

- Students work collaboratively to create a class collage, photographic display or paintings of:
  - different objects with springs
  - different objects that bounce
  - elasticised clothing.
- Students design and make a small sculpture with a part that bounces or springs (such as a bouncing head) using wire to construct a spring.
- Students research current ideas for elasticised sportswear on the market and then complete a photographic essay of current designs. They could also design:
  - A new racing suit for a downhill ski racer or a cyclist
  - A wetsuit for a surfboard rider (male, female)
  - An outfit for aerobic exercise or swimming
  - Earrings or other jewellery with spring or bounce.

PE ACTIVITY
Balloon volleyball

Play balloon volleyball, with students standing, sitting on the floor or sitting in desks. You will need two balloons and a rope. A small marble inside the blown-up balloon causes it to be more erratic and can add interest to the game. Stretch a rope between the two teams so that it is just above their reach. Students try to bat a balloon back and forth across the rope. Two balloons provide more action. The opposing team gains one point when a team allows the balloon to touch their floor or a wall.

ACTIVITIES
Jigsaw strategy

X See Chapter 10 of the Teacher's Handbook.

Use BLMs 2.2 and 2.3 on elastic animals.

CONSOLIDATION
TEAM coaching

X See Chapter 10 of the Teacher's Handbook.

Students can be given ten questions on facts about the science of elasticity, based on the work that they have done.

A smorgasbord of activities

- Students research one or more of the following unusual 'bouncers' and explain how they use elastic forces:
  - The quokka
  - The weta
  - Archey's frog
  - The Australian hopping mouse.
- Students use 'flappers' of their choice (see Chapter 10 of the *Teacher's Handbook*) to create questions and answers based on information from any of BLMs 2.1, 2.2 or 2.3.
- Have a bubble-gum-blowing competition and let students draw conclusions about the elasticity of the bubbles blown, and the 'elastic range' of the average bubble-gum.
- Activities based around balloons and elasticity can be found at www.publish.csiro.au/helix. Search for 'Balloons' and 'Elasticity'.

BOUNCE BACK!

Before or after?

X See Chapter 10 of the Teacher's Handbook.

air	flea	rubber
anaconda	frog	spring
ball	grasshopper	springbok
balloon	gravity	squash
bounce	inflatable	stored
bounciness	jump	stretch
catapult	kangaroo	surface
coil	kinetic	trampoline
compression	leaf	transformation
elastic	lycra	tyre
elasticity	plastic	underwear
energy	rebound	velocity
extension	resilient	wrinkle

Cross-offs

Have students complete BLM 2.4. The message is: People are like springs because they can bounce back after being squashed.

SPRINGS

BLM 2.1

What are springs?
Springs are an example of elastic forces in action. Springs are usually made from a special type of steel called 'spring steel'. There are two main types of springs. One is called a 'coil spring' and the other is called a 'leaf spring'.

Coil springs
You will recognise a coil spring by the fact that it looks tightly coiled up in a spiral shape. There are two kinds of coil springs. The first are called 'compression springs'. They provide a force when you push on them. This force is called 'compression'. An example would be the kind of spring you find in the battery compartment of a torch, or in the pump of a liquid-soap dispenser. The second are called 'extension springs', and they provide a force when you pull on them or stretch them. A chest expander is a good example of an extension spring.

Leaf springs
Leaf springs are also known as 'tension springs'. They are made from flat curved strips of metal. An example is the spring in a pop-up toaster. Another example is a tight sliding hair-clip made from two leaf springs (like a bobby pin, which is also a leaf spring).

Car springs
The suspension of a car helps you to drive smoothly over a bumpy road. Springs between the wheel axles and the body of the car cushions the car body from road bumps. There are also springs from the car seats to the body of the car to stop the people in the car from bouncing up and down uncomfortably.

Weighing devices
Springs can also be used to weigh things. When a weight stretches an extension spring downwards, it stretches in proportion to the weight.

Return-springs
Springs can return something to its previous position. A return-spring in a screen door stretches to allow the door to open when pushed. Then, as the person stops pushing the door, the spring contracts and the door is returned to the closed position by itself.

'Charging' springs
Some toys, clocks and music boxes work because their springs are wound up and 'charged'. These things usually have a key or winding mechanism. When the spring is wound up, energy is stored in the spring. This is what 'charging' the spring means. Then the spring unwinds and the energy stored in it is released.

- How is a coil spring different from a leaf spring?
- Name five things not mentioned in the sheet that have springs in them.
- Draw a simple flow chart to show how a screen door closes itself or how a chest expander develops muscles.
- Explain in your own words how a music box works.

© Helen McGrath and Toni Noble, 2003. This page from Bounce Back!® may be photocopied for classroom use.

ANIMALS THAT BOUNCE

BLM 2.2

Kangaroos: Living pogo sticks!
Kangaroos are marsupials that bounce when they move from place to place. They are known as 'macropods' or 'animals with large legs'. The kangaroo bounces on its two large hind legs, which combine with its feet to work like springs. The kangaroo is like a pogo stick. The energy of each bound is recaptured and stored in the kangaroo's legs when it lands, so it can leap again. In this way, the kangaroo can travel fast without using up all its energy. It can hop over large rocks and shrubs and avoid them. It folds its small front legs under its chest and uses them only for balance. Its tail acts like a balancing pole. The longest kangaroo jumps have been measured at over 11 metres, which is much further than an Olympic athlete can jump. It has been calculated that when it travels very fast a kangaroo is airborne about 70 per cent of the time. The kangaroo's hop helps in an environment where there might not be much high-energy food available. The bouncing jump allows kangaroos to move more quickly and use less energy than running on four legs would.

Grasshoppers go!
A grasshopper is an insect that feeds on grass and other plants. It has six legs. The two back legs are for jumping. The four front legs are used only for walking. Its two huge jumping legs fold up and compress like springs. Then the pressure is suddenly released, allowing the grasshopper to make gigantic leaps. Once in the air, the grasshopper uses its wings to fly. Grasshoppers also use their long powerful back legs to jump away from danger. Locusts are one species of grasshopper. Although small, the leg muscles of locusts are about 1,000 times more powerful than an equal weight of human muscle. The longest jump by a locust is about 50 cm, which is equal to ten times its body length. The locust makes its body streamlined when it jumps so it can go as high as possible. The wings remain closed and the legs straighten and tuck under the body.

Bloodsuckers!
Fleas, one of nature's most efficient bloodsuckers, are the champion jumpers for their body size. The cat flea can leap 34 cm. This is at least 100 times its own body length. Fleas go on jumping until they find an animal whose blood they can suck. Fleas can jump hundreds of times each hour for several days. The key to this great feat is two pads of rubbery elastic material called 'resilin'. These pads are on the base of the flea's back legs. Resilin stores and releases energy. If the flea does not land on an animal with the first jump, it will fall back to the ground. It will jump even higher on the rebound.

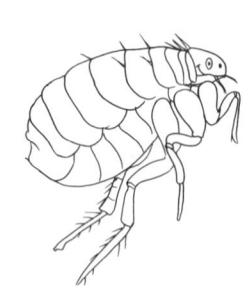

Springboks can pronk!
Springboks live in the deserts of Africa. Their predators are humans, cheetahs, leopards, hyenas and pythons. They travel in herds of 15 to 20 animals looking for food as the seasons change. They are one of the few animals in the world who can 'pronk'. This means that they 'bounce' by jumping in the air with all four legs stretched out and leaving the ground at the same time. They do this to warn the others that a predator is near and to signal to the predator that they can run very fast and therefore discourage it.

© Helen McGrath and Toni Noble, 2003. This page from Bounce Back!® may be photocopied for classroom use.

THE ELASTIC ANACONDA

BLM 2.3

Perhaps you know about the dreaded anaconda from books or movies. The anaconda is considered to be the largest snake in the world. Its average length is 8 metres and its average girth is about 110 centimetres. Anacondas live mainly in the waterways of the tropical rainforests and swamps in Northern Argentina, Paraguay and south-east Bolivia. There is a green variety and a yellow variety of anaconda. Anacondas have very large heads and thick necks. Their eyes are high on the top of their heads, so they can be almost totally submerged in water watching and waiting for prey and not easily seen. They can stay underwater for ten minutes. Anacondas live in shallow caves in the slimy banks of the rivers and other waterways. Anacondas are constrictor snakes, which means that they squeeze their prey tightly until it dies or drowns. They have very sharp teeth and powerful jaws. They can swallow large prey whole because their jaws can unhinge, and their skin and digestive organs are elastic enough to accommodate animals larger than themselves. Their usual prey is large rodents, deer, tapirs, turtles and fish and sometimes alligators. They have been known to eat people but this is rare. Their digestive system is very slow-acting and it can take many days for them to digest what they have swallowed.

- What is 'girth'?

  _____

- What other constrictor snakes have you heard about?

  _____

- Describe three ways in which an anaconda is adapted to the task of surviving.

  _____

- Draw an anaconda just after it has eaten!

© Helen McGrath and Toni Noble, 2003. This page from Bounce Back!® may be photocopied for classroom use.

CROSS-OFFS

BLM 2.4

quartet	grey	apple	index	alsatian	People	are
yoghurt	large	quadrangle	like	Egypt	mauve	terrier
pencil	kangaroo	Mississippi	joy	springs	because	poodle
Danube	milk	koala	swan	anger	storm	they
eraser	mango	quadruplets	magpie	rain	rose	Norway
snow	Amazon	can	envelope	orchid	kookaburra	Nile
cover	page	crimson	hibiscus	petunia	quadruped	sorrow
bounce	sharpener	banana	back	barge	after	garage
Germany	being	fog	cheese	squashed	Iceland	lilac

To find the message, cross off these words:

3 words that are birds
3 words that rhyme with charge
3 words that are dairy products
3 words that are fruits
4 words that are colours
3 words that are feelings
4 words that relate to the number 4
3 words that are breeds of dog
2 words that are types of marsupials
4 words that are countries
3 words that are about books
4 words that are about weather
4 words that are items of office stationery
4 words that are flowers
4 words that are rivers

The secret message is _____

© Helen McGrath and Toni Noble, 2003. This page from Bounce Back!® may be photocopied for classroom use.

UNIT 3
PEOPLE BOUNCING BACK

KEY POINTS

These key points explain each coping statement in the BOUNCE BACK acronym. A copy of the acronym can be found on BLM 4.2 in the *Teacher's Handbook* (p. 185), and there are further details for each statement in Chapter 4 of the *Handbook* on pp. 53–55.

People can bounce back psychologically after being knocked out of shape just like nature does and balls do.
When a ball hits the ground it is temporarily pushed out of shape, but it bounces back and returns almost to the same shape. When the bush is burnt, it can regenerate and bounce back. When you encounter difficulties or hard times in your life that make you feel unhappy, you too can try to bounce back to what you were like before. Sometimes, after bouncing back, you are even stronger than you were before.

Bad times don't last. Things always get better. Stay optimistic.
Bad times and bad feelings are nearly always temporary. Things get better. Sometimes it takes a while for a difficult situation to improve, but it *will* get better. When you are having an unhappy time in some part of your life, just try to get through one day at a time. Don't think about the future until things have got better. (Note: classroom activities based on this point are in Unit 5, 'The bright side'.)

Other people can help if you talk to them. Get a reality check.
Being able to talk to other people when you have bad times and feel unhappy or worried will help you to bounce back. Choose someone you feel that you can trust. When you talk to someone else about a problem, you get a reality check, because they will tell you their view on your problem and may give you other ideas or information. They will also help you and care about you. Talking to someone about your troubles sometimes takes courage, and it is a sign of strength.

Unhelpful thinking makes you feel more upset.
Helpful thinking is based on facts and thinking in this way can make you feel calmer and more hopeful about things. Getting a reality check makes your thinking more helpful. On the other hand, unhelpful thinking makes you feel more upset and reduces hope. Unhelpful thinking is based on jumping to conclusions, trying to read other people's minds, exaggerating, generalising, panicking and thinking that things are simpler than they really are. Helpful thinking is based on reality checking (e.g. getting another opinion, checking facts, sticking to the facts and testing things out). Changing unhelpful thinking to helpful thinking makes you feel better and helps you to make better decisions in your life. (Note: more classroom activities based on this point are in Unit 6, 'Emotions'.)

Nobody is perfect—not you and not others.
Every one makes mistakes, forgets things, fails at some things and is thoughtless at times. It is normal. We are all people just doing our best, and we all have our weaknesses. There is no such thing as a perfect person. If you expect yourself to be perfect, you will be too self-critical. If you expect others to be perfect and never make a mistake, you will be too critical of them and you run the risk of alienating people. Although perfection is not an option, improvement and high standards are.

49

Concentrate on the good bits, no matter how small, and use laughter.
Concentrate on whatever positive aspects you can find in an unhappy or worrying situation, even though they may be small. Concentrate also on any small funny side to a situation. The positives and laughter are things to hang on to when a situation is not good. They won't magically make your problems go away, but they will help you feel a little better and more hopeful about finding solutions and handling things. (Note: classroom activities based on this point are in Unit 8, 'Humour', and Unit 5, 'The bright side'.)

Everybody experiences sadness, hurt, failure, rejection and setbacks sometimes, not just you. It's a normal part of life. Try not to personalise them.
Life is mostly pretty good, but it is normal to sometimes have painful, worrying and distressing times in your life. Unhappy things happen to everyone at times, even though at the time you may feel like they happen only to you. If you incorrectly think that you are especially unlucky, hard-done-by or jinxed, you will be less able to bounce back. Try to see what happens as a normal part of the rich tapestry of anyone's life.

Blame fairly. How much of what happened was due to you, how much was due to others, and how much was due to bad luck or circumstances?
When something bad happens, be fair to yourself and other people when you are trying to explain *how* it happened. Things usually happen as a result of a combination of three things—what you did, what other people did, and bad luck or circumstances beyond your control. Try to work out how much of what happened was because of YOU, how much was because of ANOTHER, and how much was because of BAD LUCK or CIRCUMSTANCES.

Accept the things you can't change, but try to change what you can first.
Do your best to try and change things you don't like in your life. Keep trying to solve the problem but know when it is time to accept that you can't change things. Sometimes you can't change a situation (e.g. when a friend moves or parents separate) because it is not under your control. There is no point in getting upset over what you can't change, because getting upset won't make any difference to the situation. Just say to yourself, 'That's the way things are and I will just have to put up with it. There's nothing else I can do to change things.' If something has already happened and can't be changed, say to yourself, 'What's done is done and can't be undone. I will have to live with it.'

Catastrophising exaggerates worries. Don't believe the worst possible picture.
'Catastrophising' means thinking about the worst thing that could happen in a situation and then assuming that it will happen. Don't panic and make yourself miserable over something that may never happen. Get a reality check. (Note: more classroom activities based on this point are in Unit 6, 'Emotions'.)

Keep things in perspective. A distressing situation is usually only part of your life.
Bad times usually happen in one part of your life. They do not have to spoil other things in your life. You may have a problem with a friend, but your family life is still fine, your pets are still terrific, your school work is still good, and your netball team is still playing well. Bad times are like a few threads in a jumper that have come loose. But the whole jumper hasn't fallen apart. (Note: more classroom activities based on this point are in Unit 5, 'The bright side'.)

UNIT 3—PEOPLE BOUNCING BACK

CLASSROOM ORGANISATION
Bounce Back journal *52*

Class discussion—Life has some ups and downs but you can bounce back *52*

BOOKS
Oh, The Places You'll Go 53
Farewell to Old England Forever 53
Holes 53
Chinese Cinderella 53
Hatchet 53
The True Story of Lilli Stubeck 53
Dougy 54
Slake's Limbo 54
Tomorrow Is a Great Word 54
Goodnight Mr Tom 54

VIDEOS
My Dog Skip 54
Castaway 54

SCIENCE/TECHNOLOGY ACTIVITY
The metaphor of the bounce-backer *54*

Class discussion—Bouncing back from physical damage *55*

Class discussion—Other people can help if you talk to them. Get a reality check *55*

Class discussion—Unhelpful thinking makes you feel more upset *56*

Class discussion—Nobody is perfect—not you and not others *56*

BOOK
Super Dooper Jezebel 57

Class discussion—Everybody experiences sadness, hurt, failure, rejection and setbacks *57*

Class discussion—Blame fairly *58*

Class discussion—Accept the things you can't change, but try to change what you can first *59*

Class discussion—Catastrophising exaggerates your worries. Don't believe the worst possible picture *59*

Class discussion—Keeping things in perspective *60*

BOOKS
It's Not the End of the World 61
Jenna and the Troublemaker 61

Consolidation *61*

Practising the acronym *61*
Wallet card *62*
BOUNCE BACK advertisement *62*
Class recommendations *62*
Media activity *62*
Rewriting BOUNCE BACK statements *62*
The BOUNCE BACK card game *62*
BOUNCE BACK golf ball quiz *62*
Making a life maze *63*
Bouncing and not bouncing *63*
Balloon bursts quotes and proverbs *63*
Cross-offs *64*

Resources *64*

BLM 3.1—AFL star bounces back! *65*

BLM 3.2—If I can't walk, I'll fly instead *66*

BLM 3.3—Bounceback 2000: an environmental recovery project *67*

BLM 3.4—The ship was crushed but not their spirit *68*

BLM 3.5—Reality checks *69*

BLM 3.6—Kids Help Line *70*

BLM 3.7—Helpful and unhelpful thinking *71*

BLM 3.8—Helpful and unhelpful thinking cartoons *72*

BLM 3.9—I'm perfect *73*

BLM 3.10—Absolutely everybody *74*

BLM 3.11—Fair go! *75*

BLM 3.12—How serious is this worry? *76*

BLM 3.13—How can they bounce back? *77*

BLM 3.14—Cross-offs *78*

BOUNCE BACK!

CLASSROOM ORGANISATION
Bounce Back journal

Students can keep a Bounce Back journal to record their reflections and responses to unit activities.

CLASS DISCUSSION — **LIFE HAS SOME UPS AND DOWNS BUT YOU CAN BOUNCE BACK**

Read to the class and discuss the book *Oh, the Places You'll Go* (see below). Select questions for discussion. (Consider using 'partner retell', 'Think–Pair–Share' or 'inside–outside circle'—see Chapter 10 of the *Teacher's Handbook*). You could also play the classic Frank Sinatra song 'That's Life' or use it as a poem (lyrics and music are at www.geocities.com/Broadway/Alley/8212/index-a.htm). Judith Viorst's poem 'Mending' (in *If I Were in Charge of the World and Other Worries*) is a simple statement about the pain of a broken heart. The song 'I Will Survive', sung by Gloria Gaynor, is a triumphant song (or poem) about coping with a romantic break up. Lyrics are at www.absolutelyric.com (search by Gloria Gaynor) and performances are on a variety of CDs such as the soundtrack of *Priscilla: Queen of the Desert*.

Discussion questions

- In *Oh, the Places You'll Go*, what is the writer trying to tell us about life?
- What does the writer mean when he says these things:
  - 'You can steer yourself any direction you choose' (you have choices)
  - 'When things start to happen, don't worry. Don't stew. Just go right along. *You'll* start happening too!' (you'll grow and become stronger)
  - 'You'll play lonely games too. Games you can't win 'cause you'll play against you.' (sometimes you'll be your own worst enemy)
- What are some of the streets about which you might say 'I don't choose to go there!' (e.g. antisocial behaviours, drug taking, bullying, unkindness, greed)?
- What are some of the great places that you might choose to go to? (stress that the 'places' are not just geographical locations, but successes, achievements, friendships, love etc.)
- What is the secret to 'un-slumping' yourself?
- What page best reflects how you are currently feeling?

Follow-up activities

- Students draw their own 'waiting places'.
- Students write a story or create a painting entitled 'Life's a great balancing act!' or make a person balancing on a tightrope as a technology challenge.
- Read and discuss these books using the acronym as a guide: *Holes, Farewell to Old England Forever, Chinese Cinderella, Hatchet, The True Story of Lilli Stubeck, Slake's Limbo, Dougy, Tomorrow Is a Great Word,* or *Goodnight Mr. Tom.*
- Show the video *My Dog Skip.*
- Show the video *Castaway,* starring Tom Hanks.

UNIT 3—PEOPLE BOUNCING BACK

BOOKS

Oh, The Places You'll Go (Picture book)

This is a terrific book about the journey of life and it is an essential book to use in the program. Although it is a picture book for children, it is also very profound. It makes the point, in a humorous way and using Dr Seuss' typical slightly nonsensical rhyming language, that although life contains great joy, success and fun, sometimes you will also be lonely, scared, sad, lost and unsure. It also conveys a timeless message that each person has choices and is responsible for the decisions they make as they travel through life.

Farewell to Old England Forever (Picture book)

The text of this picture book consists of the lines from the verses of 'Botany Bay'. The drawings are evocative and harrowing but make the point that life was very harsh for the convicts who arrived on the boat. There is also a theme of hope of a new beginning after release.

Holes (Chapter book)

Stanley Yelnats, overweight, bullied by a smaller classmate, and short on friends, comes from a family with a history of what he sees as 'bad luck'. He finds himself wrongly accused of stealing a pair of sneakers (formerly owned by a famous baseball player) and is sent to Camp Green Lake for eighteen months where he learns survival skills, the importance of friendship, cooperation, persistence and hope. In the end his resilience and his capacity to not give up pay off. (This book has 50 chapters and is more suitable for Years 7 and 8.)

Chinese Cinderella (Chapter book)

This is a young reader's version of the author's full autobiography entitled *Fallen Leaves*. Adeline's mother died giving birth to her and Adeline was always seen by her family as an omen of bad luck. Her new stepmother was cruel, self-serving and abusive, her siblings tormented her and her father had little affection to give. She was sent to boarding school and 'forgotten' for much of the time, but her strong intellect and feisty nature, plus a warm and positive relationship with her grandfather and aunt, helped her to survive the isolation and mistreatment and eventually become a physician and author.

Hatchet (Chapter book)

Brian, aged thirteen, has had some difficult times as a result of the divorce of his parents. He is on a charter flight to visit his father when the pilot suffers a fatal heart attack and the plane crashes. Brian has to survive for 59 days alone in the Canadian wilderness, using only the small hatchet given to him by his mother before he left. He becomes very resourceful. The book has 18 chapters.

The True Story of Lilli Stubeck (Chapter book)

Lilli comes from an impoverished family who all scavenge to survive. Wealthy Miss Daglish 'buys' Lilli when her family move on and Lilli lives with her for some years. Fiercely independent, Lilli leaves Miss Daglish when her mother and youngest brother return and need her help, but she returns to help Miss Daglish when she becomes ill.

Dougy (Chapter book)

This story is told by Dougy, a young Aboriginal boy in a remote country town. He spends hours watching his sister practise running and she is eventually picked for the state athletics championship. This event triggers dramatic events in the town and black and white relations reach explosion point. In the end it is up to Dougy to persevere, overcome significant obstacles, not give up and save his family.

Slake's Limbo (Simple chapter book)

Artemis Slake is an orphan with no one who really cares about him. He is tormented and bullied at school and lives in a state of constant fear. After being pursued by his tormentors on one occasion, he escapes by finding a kind of excavated cave, 8 feet by 4 feet, in a wall in the New York subway system. He decides that he can't face the fearful life he has any more, so he lives in his subway refuge for many months, showing great resourcefulness in terms of finding food, work and warmth. The book is available in sets.

Tomorrow Is a Great Word (Simple chapter book)

Louisa, a young teenager, writes in her diary all her feelings and problems in relation to her family, friends, school and 'boyfriends'. When an earthquake occurs while she is alone in the family's Adelaide apartment, she finds herself trapped underneath the rubble for six days. Over the six days she demonstrates optimism and effective coping strategies and continues to write in her diary by torch about her fearful ordeal.

Goodnight Mr Tom (Simple chapter book)

Willie, a 9-year-old boy who lives with his mentally ill and abusive mother in London is evacuated to the country during World War II. He lives with a widower 'Mr Tom' who shows him love and caring and helps him to cope. There is also a video version.

VIDEOS

My Dog Skip

In this story, set in 1942, a young boy's relationship with his dog reflects some of his painful experiences of growing up.

Castaway

Tom Hanks stars as a character who is shipwrecked by himself on an island and manages to survive.

SCIENCE/TECHNOLOGY ACTIVITY

The metaphor of the bounce-backer

Students can make a bounce-backer (see Chapter 11 of the *Teacher's Handbook*), a powerful metaphor for how individuals can be knocked down and yet bounce back.

UNIT 3—PEOPLE BOUNCING BACK

CLASS DISCUSSION: BOUNCING BACK FROM PHYSICAL DAMAGE

Use the 'bundling' strategy (see Chapter 10 of the *Teacher's Handbook*) for each student to write down three kinds of common sports injuries. Talk about the kind of support that sports people access to help them to bounce back after injury. Link this to their capacity to bounce back after being injured or ill. Talk about the different parts of the body (muscles, tendons, bones, skin) that need to mend and bounce back. Do some sports stars seem more resilient than others? What may be some of the factors that help some players to bounce back more readily? Are there some injuries from which people can't bounce back? What challenges do people face physically and mentally in such situations (e.g. Christopher Reeve)?

Follow-up activities

- Students read and discuss BLM 3.1, 'AFL star bounces back!'.
- Students read and discuss BLM 3.2, 'If I can't walk I'll fly instead'.
- Students conduct their own research of a sports star who has recovered from injury.
- Make links to RICE (which stands for Rest, Ice, Compression and Elevation after injury).
- Read BLM 3.3, 'Bounceback 2000: an environmental recovery project'. Use the 'ten thinking tracks' strategy (see BLM 1.3) to discuss the project.
- Students read and discuss BLM 3.4, 'The ship was crushed but not their spirit'. (The book *Ice Trap! Shackleton's Incredible Expedition* is a helpful resource.)
- A useful website for biographies of young people who achieve against the odds is www.achievers-odds.com.au.

CLASS DISCUSSION: OTHER PEOPLE CAN HELP IF YOU TALK TO THEM. GET A REALITY CHECK

Introduce this discussion with a 'partner retell' exercise (see Chapter 10 of the *Teacher's Handbook*). Students interview each other to find out who they would talk to for help with their maths homework, for help with friendship or relationship problems, for help when they were sick, for help with sport, and for help in making an important decision.

Discussion questions

- Did people choose the same person for each situation?
- Why do we choose different people to help us in different situations?
- How can other people help if you talk to them?
- What might happen if we don't ask for help or talk to a trusted person when we are distressed or worried?

Follow-up activities

- Students read and discuss BLM 3.5, 'Reality checks'.
- Students read and discuss BLM 3.6, 'Kids Help Line'.

CLASS DISCUSSION: UNHELPFUL THINKING MAKES YOU FEEL MORE UPSET

Students read and discuss BLM 3.7, 'Helpful and unhelpful thinking', as the basis of the discussion. Note that 'catastrophising' (see later) is also an example of unhelpful thinking.

Discussion questions

- What are the main differences between helpful thinking and unhelpful thinking?
- What is an example of (each type of unhelpful thinking)?
- What is the helpful-thinking version of each of these examples?

Follow-up activities

- Students read and analyse the cartoons in BLM 3.8 and then debrief as a class.
- Write each type of unhelpful thinking on a card and place the cards in a container. Write a number of brief general situations on cards and place them in another container. Working in groups of three, students draw two cards (one from each container) and then write a story or develop a dramatic scene around the situation and the unhelpful thinking. They then turn it around so that helpful thinking is used instead.

CLASS DISCUSSION: NOBODY IS PERFECT—NOT YOU AND NOT OTHERS

Play the Mac Davis song 'Hard to Be Humble' from his CD 'The Very Best & More' or use the lyrics as a poem. The lyrics are available at www.bbhq.com/lyrics.htm. Alternatively, use Google and search for 'Oh Lord, It's Hard to Be Humble Lyrics Mac Davis'.

Read the picture book *Super Dooper Jezebel* to the class (see below). Then use the 'pairs rally/pairs compare' strategy (see Chapter 10 of the *Teacher's Handbook*) on 'the perfect parent'. What would the perfect parent say, do and look like?

Discussion questions

- Is it ever possible to be 'perfect', given that perfect people are 'painful' and so probably *can't* be perfect?
- What happens if you expect people such as your parents to always be perfect?
- What are some of the problems that people create for themselves by trying to be perfect?
- What is the difference between trying to do the best you can and aiming for a high standard and trying to be 100 per cent perfect? (Striving to improve and do your best keeps you energised and you don't overreact to mistakes and problems, whereas trying to be perfect stresses you out because it is not possible to achieve perfection.)
- Why are some mistakes and imperfections necessary and useful?
- Is it possible for everyone to agree on the criteria for perfection? Would your mother or father have the same view of what constitutes the perfect kid of your age as you have? Where would you agree? Where would you disagree?

UNIT 3—PEOPLE BOUNCING BACK

Follow-up activities

- In pairs, students talk about the attributes of a good teacher. They then draw or write about a humorous response to 'the perfect teacher' (big ears, eyes in the back of their head etc.)
- The same activity can be used for perfect sibling, pet, friend, daughter or son.
- In pairs, students write and illustrate their own version of *Super Dooper Jezebel* for younger children.
- Students complete BLM 3.9, 'I'm perfect'.
- Read the book *Hating Alison Ashley* as a serial. This is a classic tale of how someone can be misjudged. Alison Ashley seems to be so perfect that she makes the narrator feel ill with envy and dislike. However, she turns out to be nicer than she seems and not so perfect after all and the two end up being friends.

BOOK
Super Dooper Jezebel (Picture book)

Jezebel is painfully perfect. She always does the right thing and obeys the rules and lectures the other children on the need to be as good as she is. But when she insists that it is wrong to run because it is against the rules, she is the one eaten by an escaped crocodile which is in the school corridor.

CLASS DISCUSSION: EVERYBODY EXPERIENCES SADNESS, HURT, FAILURE, REJECTION AND SETBACKS

Everybody experiences sadness, hurt, failure, rejection and setbacks. They're a normal part of life. Try not to personalise them.

Introduce the unit with the 'postbox' strategy (see Chapter 10 of the *Teacher's Handbook*), using BLM 3.10, 'Absolutely everybody'. If you have access to it, play the REM song 'Everybody Hurts'. (Lyrics are at www.letssingit.com/lyrics/r/rem/5.html. Music is at jadedesigns.topcities.com/midigarden/70801.html.)

Discussion questions

- Why do we sometimes think that bad things happen only to us?
- How does it help to know that everybody else has problems, difficulties and hard times too?
- What happens when we take things personally and incorrectly think that a certain kind of setback happens only to us because we are us (i.e. jinxed, a loser etc.)?

Follow-up activities

- Students draw a personal timeline to show the bumpy road of life.
- Students draw a poster with the slogan 'Normalise, don't personalise'.
- Students make a journal reflection on their response to the postbox activity.

CLASS DISCUSSION: BLAME FAIRLY

Blame fairly. How much of what happened was because of you, how much was because of others, and how much was because of bad luck or circumstances?

Introduce the class discussion by reading the children's picture book *Alexander and the Terrible, Horrible, No Good, Very Bad Day*. Prior to the reading ask each student to rule up a page into two columns, one column titled 'Blamed fairly' and the other 'Blamed unfairly'. As students listen to the story, have them write examples from the book of when Alexander blamed fairly and when he blamed unfairly. At the end they compare their responses with a partner.

Discussion questions

- What would happen if we always blamed *ourselves* unfairly when things went wrong in our lives? (we would get depressed, give up and not try)
- What would happen if we always blamed *others* when things went wrong in our lives? (we wouldn't learn from our mistakes; we'd fool ourselves; we'd lose relationships)
- What would happen if we always blamed things on *bad luck* or *circumstances* that were out of our control? (we would think that there was nothing we could do to make things better; we wouldn't learn from our mistakes)
- Can we always know why bad things happen? (No. Sometimes there are reasons that we don't know about.)
- What are some of the things that could be put in the category of bad luck or circumstances? (coincidences, genetics, some family factors, weather, illness, who was there at the time, timing, being in the wrong place at the wrong time)

Follow-up activities

- Students write their own version of *Alexander and the Terrible, Horrible, No Good, Very Bad Day* using themselves or a younger student they know as the main character. They can also read and discuss the story with a younger student.
- Students use a drawn pie chart or make a 'responsibility pie chart' (RPC) (see Chapter 11 of the *Teacher's Handbook* for directions). RPCs are concrete aids that help students to calculate how much of what happened was due to their actions, others' actions or bad luck or circumstances. It is helpful to make one first so that students can see the finished product. They can use the templates or make their own using protractors and the measurements provided.
- Students read BLM 3.11, 'Fair go!'. Using their RPC, students work with a partner and calculate what proportion of what happened in the three stories they think was due to 'what I did', 'what others did' or 'bad luck or circumstances'. Debrief as a class.
- Using the stories in BLM 3.11 as a model, in groups of three students write their own scenarios and then give them to another group to analyse using the RPC.
- Each student can write a choose-your-own-adventure story with two endings, one where the main character blames fairly and the other where the main character blames unfairly.

UNIT 3—PEOPLE BOUNCING BACK

CLASS DISCUSSION: ACCEPT THE THINGS YOU CAN'T CHANGE, BUT TRY TO CHANGE WHAT YOU CAN FIRST

Begin the discussion by asking the following questions:
- What do we mean when we say 'That's the way the cookie crumbles' and 'That's the way the ball bounces'?
- Do we have control over everything that affects our life?
- What is meant by 'accepting things'? (realising that things are as they are and will probably not change and finding ways to live with that fact even if you don't like it)
- What are some of the things we have to accept because we can't easily change them? (illness, parental separation, death, moving house, people who don't like us, being a poor performer at something such as art or sport)
- For each of the things we have to accept, what could we do to make them less likely to occur? Are some of them completely outside out influence?
- What does this saying mean: 'Life is what happens when you're making other plans'?
- How do you know when it is time to stop trying to change a person or a situation and accept them or it?

Follow up with students writing in their journals some of the things in their lives currently and in the past that they have learned to accept because they can't change them.

CLASS DISCUSSION: CATASTROPHISING EXAGGERATES YOUR WORRIES. DON'T BELIEVE THE WORST POSSIBLE PICTURE

Read to the class and discuss any version of the story of Chicken Licken (or Henny Penny or Chicken Little) who thought that a falling leaf from a tree was a sign that the sky was falling and made everyone panic. Then introduce 'catastrophising' by asking one student to gradually blow up a balloon. Before each blow, make a statement that is more and more exaggerated, until eventually the balloon bursts (have a pin handy for the last part). Make the tone of your voice sound more and more panicky with each step. For example:
- I've been asked to go out on a friend's sailing boat.
- I would like to go but it might be a really windy day and the boat might lean over.
- When the boat leans over, I might slide from one side of the boat to another and get hurt.
- Then I might fall in the water and get wet.
- I might be run down by another boat.
- I might start to swallow lots of water and start choking.
- I might drown! (burst the balloon)
- I don't think I'll go sailing.

Discussion questions

- What was happening with each step of the story? (the thinking became more and more exaggerated and focused on the awful things that *could* happen as though they definitely *would* happen)
- How does catastrophising affect what you do? (you probably will avoid doing things because you expect the worst; you will feel worse than you have to)

- What do you think can happen if you start to think in this way? (it can become a habit)
- If catastrophising becomes a habit, can a person break it? (yes, habits *can* be broken but it is never easy)
- How can you break such a habit?
  - Do a reality check and get a second opinion and more information.
  - Say to yourself that you can't tell what is going to happen in the future.
  - Ask yourself 'if the worst *did* happen, could I cope with it?'
  - Stay positive and optimistic.

Follow-up activities

- Students complete BLM 3.12, 'How serious is this worry?'.
- Use the 'Think–Pair–Share' strategy (see Chapter 10 of the *Teacher's Handbook*) and ask students to think of a time when they or someone else worried and worried about something but then it didn't happen.
- Give each group of four a balloon. Give them time to plan a short drama scene. One person is the narrator, one blows up the balloon and the other two act out the scenario, where they increasingly catastrophise, for example:
  - Going to the dentist
  - Giving a speech
  - Going on a plane for the first time
  - Riding a horse.
- Each group can make a thought balloon display using larger and larger balloons with each catastrophising increase.
- Students write their own contemporary version of 'Chicken Licken'.

CLASS DISCUSSION KEEPING THINGS IN PERSPECTIVE

Read to the class and discuss the chapter book *It's Not the End of the World* (see below). Also read and discuss the picture book *Jenna and the Troublemaker* (see below).

Discussion questions

- Can anyone think about something bad that happened to them, and when it first happened it seemed like the worst thing that could possibly happen but it wasn't as bad as it seemed?
- If one thing goes wrong in your life, what happens to the rest of your life? (Sometimes it has a small impact on other parts of your life, but mostly the rest of your life is just as good as it was before, although it may not feel like this at first.)

'Perspective' newspaper search

You will need for each group of 3:
- One newspaper
- Scissors
- A metre of masking tape.

- In groups of 3, students search for and cut out 6 articles of events that most people would find devastating, upsetting, sad etc.

- They stick their masking tape to the floor and write on one end '10: most terrible' and on the other end '1: least terrible'. Then they rank the 6 articles in terms of these criteria and place them on the line.
- In each group each student then shares a problem that someone they know has had (no names rule), or one of their own they feel comfortable talking about. Each group together then decides where that problem would sit on the masking tape in relation to the newspaper stories they have read.

Follow up discussion:
- Did you find it easy or hard to rank the newspaper articles on the masking tape continuum?
- Was it easier or harder to rank the real problems (others or your own) compared to the newspaper ones?
- Did the activity help you to put your own problems in perspective?
- What might be some negative consequences of not putting problems in perspective? (over-reacting; becoming depressed; feeling a lack of hope about dealing with a problem; feeling sorry for yourself)
- Students use the notion of ranking their own situations and events from 1 (mildly distressing) to 10 (completely terrible) with personal situations they write about in their journal.

Each group of four students makes a 'perspective' cube using the cube pattern in BLM 11.3 in the *Teacher's Handbook*. On each side of the cube they write one of the following: Schoolwork, Friends, Health, Family, Sport/Leisure, Classmates. They take turns at rolling the dice. They nominate one concern or problem a person could have in the category that is rolled, and then go through each of the other five categories and say whether or not the nominated problem would make a difference to the other parts of the person's life, represented by other categories on the cube.

BOOKS
It's Not the End of the World (Chapter book)

Two children in a family react very differently to their parents' impending separation. The ending is realistic and not glib. They just come to terms with it, despite a lot of negative reactions along the way, including the older brother running away.

Jenna and the Troublemaker (Picture book)

Jenna grizzles constantly about her dreadful troubles, especially having freckles. This attracts the attention of the Troublemaker, an eccentric man who gives troubles to people at random. Taking pity on Jenna, the Troublemaker lets her swap her troubles for someone else's. The result helps her keep things in perspective.

CONSOLIDATION
Practising the acronym

Students use the scenarios on BLM 3.13, 'How can they bounce back?', as the focus for discussion or written practice of the acronyms.

Wallet card

Students make a BOUNCE BACK wallet card (see Chapter 11 of the *Teacher's Handbook*).

BOUNCE BACK advertisement

Students choose one coping statement to advertise its advantages. It may be a 30 second TV commercial, a radio jingle, a newspaper advertisement, stickers, bumper stickers, badges or a poster.

Class recommendations

Students search for and record in a class book, songs, videos, poems and books that fit in with the theme of people bouncing back and being resilient or with any one of the coping statements in the acronym. One such song is 'Keep on Moving' by Five, a 90s song. Lyrics are at www.thelyricarchive.com. Performed versions can be found on many 90s compilation CDs.

Media activity

Give students newspapers and ask them to locate and respond to or display stories about resilient behaviour.

Rewriting BOUNCE BACK statements

In groups of three, students rewrite the coping statements in the acronym:
- In their own words
- In another language
- As if they were hip-hoppers or rap artists
- As if they were poets.

The BOUNCE BACK card game

Make a card game using 150 cards. Make 15 sets of ten BOUNCE BACK cards (one set = 10 cards = one letter per card). (Remember to use B1 and B2 and C1 and C2.) You'll need five or six ice-cream containers as 'discard containers' for each group.
- Allocate students to groups of five.
- Give them five minutes to practise the BOUNCE BACK statements.
- Give each group three shuffled sets of BOUNCE BACK letter cards (i.e. 30 cards in total).
- The dealer deals out five cards (face down) to each student. The rest of the cards are placed face-down in the discard container. No one looks at their cards.
- Students take it in turns to turn over their top card and say the statement that goes with the letter on that card.
- If the player can correctly make the statement, they place that card in the discard container. If they can't, they get an extra penalty card from the discard container.
- The first group to get rid of all its cards is the winner. Students may not help each other.

BOUNCE BACK golf ball quiz

Have two teams of 10 students. You'll need 20 plastic 'practice' golf balls or ping-pong balls. You'll also need two ice-cream containers and two strips of flat wood with ten blobs

UNIT 3—PEOPLE BOUNCING BACK

of blu tac *or* ten velcro dots on each strip (with corresponding velcro bits on the balls). Make two different-coloured sets of ten balls, one set for each team, with the letters from BOUNCE BACK written on them (one letter per ball). Use B1, C1 and B2, C2.

The aim is to be the first team to correctly answer and then fill all of their ten 'slots'. This is done by correctly making the statements that go with the letters BOUNCE BACK. Place each team's 'set' of balls in a separate ice-cream container. Number the players 1 to 10. Dip into each container and remove one ball. Call out a number. The two students with that number come out to the front. They take the ball for their team and try to give the correct statement. If the two drawn balls are the same, they can write their answer on the board.

Making a life maze

Students design a maze where the roadblocks are typical everyday setbacks and worries for students their age. Make copies and they can then complete each other's mazes.

Bouncing and not bouncing

Groups of three or four students (including one 'coach') are given (or draw from a container) a scenario to plan and act out in two different versions. In the first version they *don't* bounce back. In the second version they *do* bounce back by using the strategies associated with one or more of the ten BOUNCE BACK statements. Debrief after each, using the acronym.
- You have a terrible fight with your parents and they are furious with you and send you to your room. They tell you that you can't go to the party on Saturday because of your behaviour.
- Your best friend tells you that he/she is moving interstate next month and you feel both sad and angry about it.
- Your parents tell you that they are going to separate and move into separate houses. You feel very upset and apprehensive.
- You have been in a bad car accident and it has left you feeling anxious and shaken.
- Your teacher returns test papers and you get a lower mark than you expected. You feel like you have been kicked in the stomach.
- You lose your favourite sunglasses at a football match/shopping centre etc. You can't believe it.

Balloon burst quotes and proverbs

X See Chapter 11 of the Teacher's Handbook
- A trouble shared is a trouble halved.
- Fall seven times, stand up eight. (Japanese proverb)
- The only perfect people are those that you don't know very well.
- He knows not his own strength who hath not met adversity. (Samuel Johnson)
- Nothing is terminal. Everything is transitional. What looks like the end of the road will turn out to be a bend.
- Pain is inevitable, but misery is optional.
- A fall in the ditch makes you wiser. (Chinese proverb)
- The first step is always the most difficult.
- The night is darkest just before dawn.
- There's no use crying over spilt milk.
- Time heals all wounds.
- Tomorrow is another day.

Cross-offs

Have students complete BLM 3.14. The message is: It's not how often you get knocked down that matters but how often you get up.

RESOURCES

Books

J Aldridge, 1984, *The True Story of Lilli Stubeck*, Puffin, Ringwood, Victoria.
Judy Blume, 1979, *It's Not the End of the World*, Pan Books, London.
Janeen Brian, 1991, *Tomorrow Is a Great Word*, Era Publications, Adelaide.
Felice Holman, 1989, *Slake's Limbo*, Aladdin Books, New York.
Meredith Hooper & M P Robertson, 2000, *Ice Trap! Shackleton's Incredible Expedition*, Frances Lincoln, London.
John King (illustrator), (traditional song) 1984, *Farewell to Old England Forever*, Collins, Melbourne.
Robin Klein, 1984, *Hating Alison Ashley*, Penguin, Ringwood, Victoria.
Michelle Magorian, 1987, *Goodnight Mr. Tom*, Harmondsworth, Kestrel.
James Moloney, 1993, *Dougy*, University of Queensland Press, St Lucia.
Hiawyn Oram & Tony Ross, 1986, *Jenna and the Troublemaker*, Andersen Press, London.
Gary Paulsen, 1987, *Hatchet*, Bardbury, New York.
Tony Ross, 1988, *Super Dooper Jezebel*, Andersen Press, London.
Louis Sachar, 2000, *Holes*, Bloomsbury Publishing, London.
Dr Seuss, 1990, *Oh, the Places You'll Go*, Collins, New York.
Judith Viorst, (1972) (2001 reprint), *Alexander and the Terrible, Horrible, No Good, Very Bad Day*, HarperCollins, Pymble, Sydney, NSW.
Judith Viorst, 1987, *If I Were in Charge of the World and Other Worries*, Ashton Scholastic, Sydney.
Adeline Yen Mah, 2001, *Chinese Cinderella: The True Story of an Unwanted Daughter*, Puffin, Ringwood, Victoria.

Videos

My Dog Skip, 2001 Warner Brothers (PG)
Castaway, 2000 Fox Home Entertainment (PG)

CD

Mac Davis: 1984 'The Very Best and More'

AFL STAR BOUNCES BACK!

BLM 3.1

When James Hird first played AFL football for Essendon in 1992, it was obvious that he had the ability to become one of the game's greats. He was blessed with great skill, fitness and courage and was considered one of the most exciting players in the league. The following year he played in Essendon's 1993 premiership team.

In 1996 James earned the AFL's highest honour when he won the Brownlow medal. Still in his early 20s, it was expected that he would continue to be one of the game's greatest players for many years to come.

In 1997, however, James suffered a stress fracture to one of his feet. Rather than playing his best football, he was forced to watch from the sidelines as his team finished 14th in his absence. The following year was not much better; while he did everything he could to help his team, he was unable to play his best football because of more injuries, and his team had another disappointing season.

In 1999 James appeared to have made a full recovery. He thought that this would be the year that he made up for all his injury problems and proved to his fans just how good he was. But in only the second game of the season, James discovered that his foot problems had returned. He was forced to watch the rest of the year from the sidelines and it appeared that he might never play football again.

But James refused to give up. He devoted all his time and energy to giving his football career one last shot. He trained longer and harder than ever before to make sure that he was as fit as possible for the year ahead. He was able to play most of the season and captained his team to the 2000 Grand Final, where they defeated Melbourne by 60 points. James was also awarded the Norm Smith Medal as the best player on the field.

In 2002 James suffered further injuries when his face was broken in nine places, including his eye socket. Again, his fierce determination resulted in his returning to play in a matter of months. He now has to wear a helmet when he plays.

- What sports' injuries did James experience?

- What did he do to 'bounce back'?

- How important do you think his mental attitude was in helping him to recover?

- How much would his early successes have helped him to not give up?

© Helen McGrath and Toni Noble, 2003. This page from Bounce Back!® may be photocopied for classroom use.

IF I CAN'T WALK, I'LL FLY INSTEAD

Janine Shepherd had always been good at sport. By the time she was ten, she'd won a number of national athletics titles, as well as excelling in a host of other sports. Eventually she settled on cross-country skiing. She became a national champion and set her sights on the 1988 Winter Olympics to be held in Calgary.

However, while training for the Games, Janine was involved in a terrible accident. She was riding a bike in the Blue Mountains when a truck hit her, shattering her dream of competing at the Olympics. Janine was lucky to survive the accident and was told that she would never walk again and would never have children.

But Janine refused to accept this. One day, watching planes fly overhead, she said to herself, 'If I can't walk, I'll fly.' Instead of giving up, Janine decided to overcome the obstacles that confronted her and she took flying lessons.

It wasn't long before Janine received her pilot's licence. Soon after, she received an instructor's permit, which allowed her to teach others to fly. Later Janine was married and, despite the advice of her doctors, she was able to become a mother.

In 1995 Janine wrote a book titled *Never Tell Me Never* which tells of her struggle with the injuries caused by her accident and her fight to overcome those injuries. A film was also made about her life.

These days, when Janine isn't looking after her children, she's giving motivational speeches, inspiring others to overcome the problems in their lives.

- What personal characteristics might have enabled Janine to bounce back from her difficulties?

- What kind of helpful thinking would also have helped her bounce back?

- Write about someone else you know or have heard about who bounced back from a serious injury or illness.

BOUNCEBACK 2000: AN ENVIRONMENTAL RECOVERY PROJECT

Bounceback 2000 was one of the most ambitious environmental repair jobs ever undertaken in Australia. The aim was to try and restore parts of the Flinders Ranges in South Australia to their original native state.

Until recently, rabbits were eating up to 80 per cent of the edible vegetation. Feral animals such as cats, goats and foxes were eating and eliminating many small native animals. Half of the 50 mammal species known to have lived in the Flinders Ranges were no longer found there. Many other plant species had been almost destroyed by farm animals grazing on them.

The first step in the program was to greatly reduce the rabbit population. Rabbits were caught, deliberately infected with the rabbit calicivirus disease (RCD), and then released. Flies, fleas and mosquitoes then carried the virus to other rabbits and infected them. Bulldozers ripped up the rabbit warrens and the seeds of native plants were sown in the churned-up soil. Rabbits were the chief food source of foxes. Without rabbits to eat, the hungry foxes were more eager to take poisoned baits. National parks were closed so that the Sporting Shooters Association of Australia could hunt and kill the goats. Mammals that are native to the area, such as sandy inland mice and brush-tailed bettongs, were trapped elsewhere and taken back to the area to live.

Now, kangaroos and wallabies are thriving because they are not being eaten by predators such as foxes and they do not have to compete for food with rabbits and farm animals. There has been a phenomenal recovery in the vegetation. Plants that are slowly recovering include the prickly wattle, saltbush, and pearl bluebush.

The adopted mascot of the Bounceback 2000 project is the yellow-footed rock-wallaby, which was headed for extinction after being hunted by sporting shooters. It was unable to compete with goats and rabbits for food and was unable to flee from attacking foxes. There are now 300 of them in the Flinders Ranges.

At the other end of the food chain, the brown goshawk and twelve other native raptors who once thrived on rabbits, are facing an uncertain future without their chief food source.

© Helen McGrath and Toni Noble, 2003. This page from Bounce Back!® may be photocopied for classroom use.

THE SHIP WAS CRUSHED BUT NOT THEIR SPIRIT

BLM 3.4

Sir Ernest Shackleton, a famous Antarctic explorer, wanted to lead an expedition across the Antarctic Continent. He set off from Buenos Aires in August 1914, with a crew of twenty-seven men. He had deliberately chosen crew members who could play music, sing, act, and tell jokes. He believed that these qualities would be useful if they ran into trouble.

The ice conditions on the trip were unusually harsh, and his wooden ship, *The Endurance*, became trapped in pack ice in the Weddel Sea in January 1915. He and his crew were trapped in the ice for 10 months and the ship just drifted. If a crewmember became gloomy or 'down', Shackleton moved them to better quarters which were further away from the others. Shackleton wanted to prevent the spread of pessimism to the whole crew. The crew occupied themselves with games of football and hockey played on the huge ice floes beside the ship. Shackleton reported in his diary that there was much laughter during this time, despite the seriousness of their circumstances.

Eventually, after ten months, the pressure of the pack ice completely crushed the ship and they had to abandon it completely. They were able to take only a few items of warm clothing, shelter, and food with them. They camped on the ice floes for five months. The ice floes drifted further into the open sea and they found themselves near an island called Elephant Island. They managed to sail to the island in three small lifeboats that they had rescued from their ship.

There were enough seals and penguins on the island for them to live on. However they were not on a shipping lane and no one lived on the island. Shackleton decided that their only hope of rescue was for some of them to sail to a whaling station on Georgia Island to get help. Shackleton and five of his men set off in one lifeboat. They sailed through the world's most dangerous seas to Georgia Island. Unfortunately, they could only land on a part of the island where nobody lived. Then they had to leave their boat and climb 26 miles over rocky and dangerous icy crevices and snow to get to the other side of the island where the whaling station was. They were frostbitten, starving, and exhausted, but Shackleton and two of his five men kept going and eventually made it.

Shackleton made three unsuccessful attempts to return to Elephant island and rescue the rest of the crew but his boat was stopped by ice. Finally, in August 1916, two years after he had first set sail, Shackleton was able to rescue the men he had left behind. Despite extraordinary hardship, not one member of the 28-man crew perished. Shackleton is remembered by history for his leadership, optimism, endurance, and courage.

- Why did Shackleton pick crew members who could tell jokes and entertain?
- What were some of the things the crew did to cope with their hardship and stay positive?
- What kind of helpful thinking might have helped the explorers to keep going in these impossible circumstances?

© Helen McGrath and Toni Noble, 2003. This page from Bounce Back!® may be photocopied for classroom use.

REALITY CHECKS

BLM 3.5

Double checking: Have I got my facts right? Have I made mistakes?
This means going over things to make sure you've got things right (e.g. re-checking your answers in a maths test, re-checking the motel room where your family stayed before you leave in case you've left something). It can also mean getting someone *else* to check for mistakes you might have made (e.g. getting someone to proofread your work, scuba-diving partners cross-checking each other's diving equipment).

Looking for new information
This means getting more facts to help you deal with something. For example, you could read books, documentaries or access the Internet or talk to experts (e.g. to check the incidence of shark attacks in the area in which you plan to swim).

Looking for evidence to confirm or contradict what you are thinking
This means trying to find supportive evidence to check out your belief or perception about a situation (e.g. if you thought a coach was being unfair to you, you might ask players in his former team about what he was like with them).

Getting a second opinion
This means talking to someone you trust in order to hear how they see things and to find out whether or not they agree with your thinking (e.g. talking to a parent, friend, teacher or counsellor about your career plans or a relationship problem you have).

Testing it out
This means checking out your assumptions by having a go and seeing what happens (e.g. if you are not sure whether a new classmate will want to come to your home, you check it out by asking them rather than spend lots of time worrying about it).

Write down one example of a time when you have used each type of reality check.

Double checking _____

Looking for new information _____

Looking for evidence _____

Getting a second opinion _____

Testing it out _____

© Helen McGrath and Toni Noble, 2003. This page from Bounce Back!® may be photocopied for classroom use.

KIDS HELP LINE

BLM 3.6

Kids Help Line was founded in 1991 by Brother Paul Smith. He realised that there needed to be a place where troubled students and teenagers could turn to when they felt they were unable to help themselves. Since that time, Kids Help Line has helped young people aged between 5 and 18 in a variety of situations.

Kids Help Line receives most of its funding from the fundraising activities of Boys Town Family Care and the De La Salle Brothers in Australia. It also receives a small amount of financial support from corporate sponsors, and depends on a small amount of money from donations and the government.

Kids Help Line helps young people who are having problems with friends, being bullied, suffering child abuse, going through pregnancy, in need of advice about sex, having problems with their families, having problems with drug use, having problems with their boyfriend or girlfriends, and so on.

The main aim of Kids Help Line is to provide professional counselling to all Australian students who need it. When students who need counselling call Kids Help Line, they are sometimes referred to other professionals, such as doctors and psychologists who are also able to help them.

Kids Help Line is staffed by over 80 qualified and paid counsellors. Each year, the Line responds to around 15 000 calls.

The Kids Help Line is open 24 hours a day, 7 days a week. The phone number is

1800 55 1800.

- To what age group does Kids Help Line offer support?

- How could talking to a counsellor at Kids Help Line help someone who was upset or worried?

- What might make it a bit difficult for some students to use Kids Help Line?

© Helen McGrath and Toni Noble, 2003. This page from Bounce Back!® may be photocopied for classroom use.

HELPFUL AND UNHELPFUL THINKING

BLM 3.7

- **Unhelpful thinking** makes you feel more upset and less hopeful. It stops you from solving problems well. It is not based on facts.
- **Helpful thinking** makes you feel calmer and more hopeful. It helps you to solve problems well. It is based on what is real and known.

Types of unhelpful thinking

Trying to read people's minds
This means guessing and imagining what someone else might be feeling or thinking. One example would be 'guessing' that someone is angry with you by just watching them or what they do and looking at the expression on their face. You may be right, but if you were using *helpful thinking* you would say to yourself, 'There's no point in trying to guess. I might be worrying about nothing.' Then you could do a reality check and ask the person if they are angry with you.

Exaggerating your facts
Making a small problem into a big problem is an example of exaggerating. Thinking that something is the end of the world when it is really just annoying is another example. Using words like *never*, *always*, *everyone* and *no one* usually signal that you are exaggerating things (e.g. I *never* get good presents; *everyone* hates me; I *always* get bad luck; *no one* ever cares about me). If you were using *helpful thinking*, you would ask yourself, 'Am I exaggerating things here?' and then you would do a reality check to find out the real facts or talk to someone else to get a second opinion.

Jumping to conclusions
One example of jumping to conclusions would be thinking that someone must have had an accident because they are a bit late picking you up. If you use *helpful thinking* instead, you would remind yourself that you don't have any evidence that there has been an accident and that there are lots of other possible explanations. You would think, 'It would be better to stay calm because I don't have enough facts here. It will probably be okay. Sometimes they run a bit late.'

Overgeneralising
If you never want to go in a swimming carnival again because you once lost a race, you are using 'overgeneralising'. You think that because it happened once it will definitely happen again and again. When you use *helpful thinking*, you say to yourself, 'Things *can* happen just *once* and then never happen again. This time could be different.

Oversimplifying
This happens when you think that someone or some situation is either *all* good or *all* bad. *Helpful thinking* means reminding yourself that most people have good and bad qualities and that most situations, even if they are bad ones, still have some good aspects. It also means acknowledging that some situations are complex and not black and white.

© Helen McGrath and Toni Noble, 2003. This page from Bounce Back!® may be photocopied for classroom use.

HELPFUL AND UNHELPFUL THINKING CARTOONS

BLM 3.8

Write an explanation about how each cartoon relates to the BOUNCE BACK statements and/or helpful/unhelpful thinking. Write your answers on a separate sheet (and number them).

1.
   - "I've just had the worst day of my life!"
   - "My bike got a puncture, I was late for school and I got into trouble. My computer crashed and I lost my English essay, my mum yelled at me for leaving a messy room!"
   - "I didn't achieve anything all day!" / "Sure you did."
   - "You got through it!"

2.
   - "This zit is so bad! Everyone's going to notice!!" / "No they won't."
   - "But it's so humungous it's embarrassing." / "Nah, you can't even see it."
   - "Can't even see it! It's as big as Everest! Massive elephant-size pus-filled mountain growing off the side of my head!"
   - "The more you worry about it the worse it seems!" / "Tell me about it!"

3.
   - "Do you want to play pool?" / "Yeh that would be great..... if I could win."
   - "But I lost last time so I'll probably lose again. No thanks!"

4.
   - "Why does she swim with all that stuff?"
   - "Cos she nearly drowned when she was 3 years old."

5.
   - "Hey! You wanna play?" / "Nah."
   - "See! I was right... nobody likes me."

© Helen McGrath and Toni Noble, 2003. This page from Bounce Back!® may be photocopied for classroom use.

I'M PERFECT

BLM 3.9

Perry liked everything to be perfect. He hated making mistakes. He would spend absolutely ages working on his school assignments and projects and he always got very high marks. Once his little sister accidentally spilt water on one of his projects and he was so angry with her that he hit her and told her never to go near any of his things again. Another time Perry stayed awake worrying for most of the night because he wanted to get perfect marks in a class test the next day. When the teacher handed back the test and he hadn't got 100 per cent, he was so disappointed that he nearly 'lost it' in front of his classmates.

Perry also had to be the very best at basketball. He spent hours practising shooting goals at home and got really angry with himself when he missed the goal. When he played with his team, he expected everyone to do well and shouted angrily at any team-mate who did something that Perry thought was stupid. Not surprisingly, his team-mates didn't really want him in the team, even though he played well.

Perry also took his ideas of being perfect into class groups. Once when his group was working on a technology task, Perry took over and wouldn't let other people contribute ideas or share the work because he thought that their ideas weren't as good as his ideas. He worried that if the group did what the others wanted the whole project would be a disaster. The other kids ended up letting him do all the work but didn't want to work with him again.

- What were some of the ways in which Perry liked things to be perfect?

- In what ways was Perry 'his own worst enemy'?

- How did Perry's 'perfectionism' affect his relationships with others?

- How could Perry change his thinking so that he was less worried about trying to be perfect?

© Helen McGrath and Toni Noble, 2003. This page from Bounce Back!® may be photocopied for classroom use.

ABSOLUTELY EVERYBODY

BLM 3.10

Circle 'Yes' or 'No' for the following questions and then complete the rest of the question. You may have more than one example for each question.

1. Have you ever felt rejected?   Yes ☐   No ☐

   If yes, then tick any of the boxes where this happened to you (or write 'other').

By someone I wanted to be a friend	By someone with whom I wanted a romantic relationship	By a group

2. Have you ever made a very big mistake related to any of the following things?
   Yes ☐   No ☐

   If yes, tick any of the boxes below where this has happened to you (or write 'other').

School work mistake	Sporting mistake	Money mistake	Friendship mistake	Relationship mistake

3. Have you ever had to do something you didn't want to do and just put up with it?
   Yes ☐   No ☐

   If yes, tick any of the boxes below where this has happened to you (or write 'other').

Doing a test	Performance in a show	Going to a social function	Taking part in a family outing

4. Have you ever wanted something a great deal but you weren't able to have it?
   Yes ☐   No ☐

   If yes, tick any of the boxes where this has happened to you (or write 'other').

A new item of clothing	A new CD	A new game	Not able to go out	Not able to go on a holiday

5. Have you ever lost something or someone you loved?   Yes ☐   No ☐

   If yes, tick any of the boxes where this has happened to you (or write 'other').

A pet	A friend	A family member

6. Has anyone given you a hard time that really was unfair and really upset you?
   Yes ☐   No ☐

   Tick any of the boxes where this has happened to you (or write 'other').

Other students	A teacher	A brother or sister	A parent	A friend

© Helen McGrath and Toni Noble, 2003. This page from Bounce Back!® may be photocopied for classroom use.

FAIR GO!

BLM 3.11

Using your Responsibility Pie Chart, calculate how much of what happened in the stories below was due to:
- What I did (pretend you are the main character)
- What others did
- Bad luck or circumstances.

Sunglasses down the drain
Simon's mother was watching him as he packed for the school camp and she saw him pack his best sunglasses. They were a very expensive pair which he had bought with his paper-round money. His mum suggested that he leave them at home in case they got stolen or broken on the camp. But Simon insisted on taking them. When he returned from camp, his mother was waiting for him in the car in the '5 minutes only' parking zone because it was raining. As soon as he got off the bus, she signalled to him to hurry so she wouldn't be booked. He hurried over, laden down with his backpack, his boots and his favourite pillow. As he ran up to the door of the car, his sunglasses fell out of his jacket pocket and dropped into the stormwater drain on the side of the road. Simon was devastated. His mother said, 'I told you not to take them!'
- My (Simon's) percentage is _____
- Mum's percentage is _____
- Bad luck/circumstances percentage is _____

The CD
Christa's friend Alisha lent Christa her favourite CD for the weekend, on the condition that Christa would return it first thing on Monday morning. On Sunday night Christa put the CD on top of her schoolbag near the front door so she wouldn't forget it. Unfortunately, Christa's little brother got up really early on Monday morning and found the CD on the bag. He tried to put it in the CD player and wrecked it.
- My (Christa's) percentage is _____
- Little brother's percentage is _____
- Bad luck/circumstances percentage is _____

Oh for some cash!
Jackie was having a barbecue luncheon for some friends in her new house on a public holiday. She had been very busy at work and she didn't get home until 9 pm the night before. Her flatmate Kieran suggested that, instead of going out to the supermarket so late, she get up early the next morning and do her shopping then. When she arrived at the supermarket the next morning to buy the meat, the salad and the bread rolls, she discovered that all supermarkets were closed till 1 pm. This hadn't happened on the same public holiday last year. She rushed to a small mini-mart near her flat that was open, only to discover that the shop didn't take credit cards and she had only $5 in cash.
- My (Jackie's) percentage is _____
- Kieran's percentage is _____
- Bad luck/circumstances percentage is _____

© Helen McGrath and Toni Noble, 2003. This page from Bounce Back!® may be photocopied for classroom use.

HOW SERIOUS IS THIS WORRY?

BLM 3.12

For each problem draw a cross on the line to show how serious the problem is. Then rank the eight problems from the MOST SERIOUS to the LEAST SERIOUS problem.

1. Brent is worried about going on a family holiday to Queensland, because another kid told him that there are stingers in the sea that are venomous. Is what he's worried about:

   _____
   Almost impossible   Possible but unlikely   Possible

   What could Brent do to make himself feel less worried?

2. Jack's friend from the gym club has asked him to his party. Jack is worried that he won't know anyone and will be left out. Is what he's worried about:

   _____
   Almost impossible   Possible but unlikely   Possible

   What could Jack do to help himself feel less worried?

3. Tony's father is very late picking him up from footy practice and Tony is sure that his dad has forgotten him. Is what he's worried about:

   _____
   Almost impossible   Possible but unlikely   Possible

   What could Tony do to help himself feel less worried?

4. Kim lives near a bank and often can't sleep at night because she is worried that bank robbers will break into the bank. She thinks that the robbers might try to escape through her house and her family might be hurt. Is what she's worried about:

   _____
   Almost impossible   Possible but unlikely   Possible

   What could Kim do to help herself feel less worried?

5. Lisa really wants to be in the school concert but she is worried that she won't be selected. Is what she's worried about:

   _____
   Almost impossible   Possible but unlikely   Possible

   What could Lisa do to help herself feel less worried?

6. Stephen is really worried about being bullied at his new high school because he has heard that it has a reputation for bullying. Is what he's worried about:

   _____
   Almost impossible   Possible but unlikely   Possible

   What could Stephen do to help himself feel less worried?

7. Shannon is worried that she will get lost when she has to travel by public transport for the first time to her new school. Is what she's worried about:

   _____
   Almost impossible   Possible but unlikely   Possible

   What could Shannon do to help herself feel less worried?

8. Jenny lives in a city flat, on the edge of a bushy park. When bushfires are close to the city she gets really worried that her flat will be burned. Is what she's worried about:

   _____
   Almost impossible   Possible but unlikely   Possible

   What could Jenny do to feel less worried?

© Helen McGrath and Toni Noble, 2003. This page from Bounce Back!® may be photocopied for classroom use.

HOW CAN THEY BOUNCE BACK?

BLM 3.13

It was SO embarrassing!

Sarah has always been a well-liked student who is fun to be with, but recently she has become very withdrawn and untalkative, after an embarrassing experience three weeks ago. Her teacher, Mrs Symons, asked her to thank a guest who had come to the school to talk to the students at assembly. While standing in front of the entire school, she forgot the speaker's name and blushed bright red. When Mrs Symons prompted her, she recovered. But when she turned to leave the stage, she got her directions confused and walked smack bang into the microphone, which made a terrible piercing noise. The entire school burst out laughing. Sarah has been very withdrawn ever since.

Nick's comic disaster

Nick always makes the other kids laugh. Mr Cleary reckons that Nick will be a comedian when he finishes school. Nick gets reasonable grades, even though he fools around in class a lot. But ever since the school concert a few weeks ago, Nick hasn't finished any of his work and he isn't mucking around with the other kids or making jokes in class. For the school concert, Nick was asked to do a comedy routine. He practised it for weeks, and tested out the jokes on some of his mates. On the night of the concert, no one laughed at the first couple of jokes, which made him lose confidence and muck up the rest. Then on his way down the stairs at the side of the stage he slipped and fell. Normally he'd do this for a laugh, but in front of his parents and the whole school he felt so terrible that he burst into tears. The next day at school his mates laughed at him for crying, and he got into a fight with them.

Bad hair day!

Hannah, a young hairdressing apprentice, won the State championship award in hair colouring and was given an all-expenses-paid trip to a capital city in another state to compete in the national championship. On the Friday she was due to fly, the airline went bankrupt and all their planes were grounded. She couldn't get a ticket on any other flight and there wasn't enough time for her to go by car or train. She missed the competition.

© Helen McGrath and Toni Noble, 2003. This page from Bounce Back!® may be photocopied for classroom use.

CROSS-OFFS

BLM 3.14

storm	carrot	couch	lightning	Pacific	division	centenary
it's	igloo	chair	addition	slowly	not	table
mutiplication	Zambia	how	often	sailing	Egypt	you
softly	heatwave	soccer	Arctic	subtraction	basketball	snorkling
get	Nigeria	apartment	knocked	down	hut	that
matters	Indian	but	cleanly	cupboard	house	how
thunder	often	scuba diving	Atlantic	centipede	centurion	radish
you	netball	potato	Morocco	baseball	Ethiopia	get
back	speedily	swimming	centimetre	up	tent	parsnip

To find the message, cross off these words:
5 words that are African countries
5 words that are types of dwellings
4 words that relate to the number 100
4 words that are furniture
4 words that are oceans
4 words that are water sports
4 words about weather
4 words that are vegetables that grow in the ground
4 words that are math terms
4 words that are adverbs
4 words that are non-contact sports

The secret message is _____

© Helen McGrath and Toni Noble, 2003. This page from Bounce Back!® may be photocopied for classroom use.

UNIT 4
COURAGE

KEY POINTS

What is courage?
Courage is not about lack of fear. It's about facing and overcoming fear. Courage is the quality that enables people to face difficulties, danger and adversity without completely giving way to fear or distress. You show 'courage' when you do something because you believe that doing it is more important than your fear, pain or discomfort. You can't be said to be brave if you aren't afraid.

Everyone is frightened and anxious at times.
Fear is a normal and necessary human response to situations where there is potential harm. It places you 'on alert' so that you can deal with the threat. 'Anxiety' is anticipatory fear (i.e. you feel anxious or nervous just thinking about danger that *could* happen). These feelings signal to you that you *might* have a problem to deal with. You can make yourself more nervous or anxious by exaggerating what *could* happen in your mind.

Some people are more prone to anxiety than others.
Everyone has a 'fear centre' in the brain that acts as an alarm, but this alarm goes off more quickly and intensely in the brains of some people than in others. They often inherit this tendency. This makes it harder for them, as they have to deal with fear and anxiety more often.

We don't all get frightened or nervous about the same things.
What scares one person may not frighten someone else. One person may be scared of horses, but not scared on a roller-coaster, and the opposite may be true for someone else. An act of courage for one person may not be an act of courage for another, because of their different fears.

You will need a lot of 'everyday courage' in your life.
Everybody has many chances each day to show 'everyday courage'. This is the courage to do something that is ordinary but still makes *you* feel a bit nervous or anxious. It might be trying something new (because you fear making a fool of yourself), giving a talk, meeting people, taking a test or standing up for others who are being mistreated.

Sometimes you may need to find courage to deal with misfortune.
Unpleasant and unwanted events (e.g. accident, family loss, illness, violence, burglary, breakups) occasionally happen and it takes courage to face them and deal with them.

Sometimes you need to stop and think for a while before you decide to be courageous.
Deciding to be courageous is sometimes spontaneous, but sometimes it requires time to think, to do some reality testing, and encouragement to deal with fear.

Being a hero is a different kind of courage.
Heroism is self-sacrifice. A hero is someone who is scared but is also prepared to risk danger to himself or herself to ensure the wellbeing of someone else. Sometimes it can be foolish to try to save someone if you do not have the skills or resources to do it. You could both get hurt. The best thing might be to run and get help.

Foolhardiness is not the same as courage.
Being foolhardy (e.g. diving into shallow water) is a dangerous and stupid form of courage, because skills and experience are lacking, the possibility of harm is very high, and the risk simply isn't worth it.

Thrill-seeking is different to foolhardiness.
Some people are thrill-seeking but not foolhardy. They engage in extreme sports but they have skills, experience, good equipment and safety rules to minimise harm.

UNIT 4—COURAGE

Class discussion—What is courage? *81*
- BOOKS
  - *The Boy Who Was Afraid* 82
  - *Rose Blanche* 82
- ARTS/TECHNOLOGY ACTIVITIES
  - Courage mobile 82
  - Fearful ladder 82

Class discussion—Courage and fear are different from one person to the next *82*
- ACTIVITY
  - Predictor cards 83

Class discussion—Brave, stupid or thrill-seeking? *83*
- ACTIVITIES
  - Media activity 84
  - Classroom collective research 84

Class discussion—What's a hero? *84*
- ACTIVITY
  - Heroes 85
- ARTS ACTIVITIES
  - Collective classroom research 85

Class discussion—Finding your own courage *85*

Consolidation *87*
- Class recommendations 87
- Balloon burst quotes 87
- Choose-your-own-adventure 87
- Categorising courage 87
- Curriculum integration 87
- Working with younger children 88
- TEAM coaching 88
- Graphical story 88
- Quick quotes 88
- Before or after? 88
- Cross-offs 89

Resources *89*

BLM 4.1—Would you rather . . .? *90*

BLM 4.2—Edward 'Weary' Dunlop *91*

BLM 4.3—Nancy Wake *92*

BLM 4.4—Mahatma Gandhi *93*

BLM 4.5—Simpson and his donkey *94*

BLM 4.6—Finding your own courage *95*

BLM 4.7—You and courage *96*

BLM 4.8—How to give a great class presentation *97*

BLM 4.9—What kind of courage and where? *98*

BLM 4.10—Cross-offs *99*

UNIT 4—COURAGE

CLASS DISCUSSION WHAT IS COURAGE?

Note: it is important to make sure students understand that *everyone* experiences fear, pain and anxiety and that students (especially boys) should not pretend that they are fearless or that nothing upsets or distresses them. Talk about how boys tend to 'minimise' fear and anxiety in front of others.

Begin the topic of courage with a 'bundling' activity (see Chapter 10 of the *Teacher's Handbook*) where each student writes:

- Five examples of different ways people can show courage *or*
- Three well-known people they can think of who have shown courage. Use their information to follow up with a discussion of what courage is and what its key features are.

Discussion questions

- What is courage?
- What are the different kinds of courage that people demonstrate? What well-known people have shown courage?
- What does courage mean? What are other words we use for courage? Why do we say that a person 'has guts'? What do people have to 'face' when they are brave? (fear, and sometimes truth, opponents, illness)
- Can you say that a person is courageous if they don't feel scared?
- Will people be scared or nervous about the same kinds of things?
- Are people such as fire officers or lifesavers courageous? (Not usually when they are doing their everyday job that they are trained for; they have skills, equipment, safety procedures and back-up. However, they have a slightly higher risk of danger in their job and *may* need to be brave at some point.)
- Is someone who saves a person from a burning house or car (but who isn't a fire officer) courageous? (yes) How likely is it that we would be in a position to be courageous in this way? (highly unlikely)
- Is taking great risks, like diving from a bridge into a shallow river or train surfing, courageous? (No. This behaviour is foolhardy. It is highly dangerous and not worth the risks. There are no skills, equipment, experience or safety procedures.)
- Are people who engage in extreme sports courageous? (Not necessarily. They may not be scared.) Are they foolhardy? (No, they rely on equipment, safety procedures and skills.)
- What happens if you let your anxiety or nerves take over? (you end up not doing what you want to do and feeling disappointed with yourself)
- What can help you overcome your nervousness? (the best antidotes to fear are developing skills and using positive self-talk)
- What is everyday courage? (This is the courage to do something that is ordinary but makes us feel a bit nervous or anxious. Sometimes it is the courage to bounce back after difficult times.)
- How is everyday courage different to courage in misfortune?
- What images of courage are portrayed in the movies? Is fear shown or are people presented as being brave but with no realistic fear? Are there gender differences?

Follow-up activities

- Use the 'partner retell' strategy (see Chapter 10 of the *Teacher's Handbook*) and ask each student to share one example of something that makes them nervous (or used to) but they do it (or did it) anyway. Make a board list of situations that require everyday courage. Students can follow up with a journal entry.

- Read to the class and discuss books such as *The Boy Who Was Afraid*, *Rose Blanche* (see below), *Dougy* (see Unit 3), *Stargirl* (see Unit 1) or *The Gizmo* (see Unit 1). Also discuss courage in relation to class novels. Consider showing the movie *Gallipoli*.

BOOKS
The Boy Who Was Afraid

Mafatu, the son of a Polynesian chief, was afraid of the water, after he and his mother nearly drowned when he was a baby. He is called a coward by the tribe. To prove himself, he and his dog go to sea, but they are swept off course and end up on an island that is regularly visited by head-hunters. He eventually develops more confidence and overcomes his fears.

Rose Blanche (Picture book)

This story, set in World War II, has beautiful, detailed, symbolic illustrations. Rose Blanche lives in a small town in Germany and witnesses the changes in the town and country without fully realising what is going on or understanding some of the things she sees. By accident she stumbles on the outskirts of a concentration camp. Appalled by the starvation of the Jewish adults and children she speaks to through the fence, she brings them food on a regular basis. The ending is sad but offers great scope for discussion.

ARTS/TECHNOLOGY ACTIVITIES
Courage mobile

Students construct a mobile that features boxes of many different sizes (see cube pattern in Chapter 11 of the *Teacher's Handbook*). Inside each box they place a piece of paper on which they have written or drawn an example of different types of courage.

Fearful ladder

Students draw or design their own version of a ladder (e.g. with paddle pop sticks) and then sort the family of emotions associated with fears or nervousness into levels of intensity, with the most intense at the top of the ladder: worried, fearful, scared, frightened, concerned, anxious, nervous, terrified, vulnerable, intimidated, insecure, apprehensive, watchful, dreading, cautious.

CLASS DISCUSSION: COURAGE AND FEAR ARE DIFFERENT FROM ONE PERSON TO THE NEXT

Begin with students completing the postbox questions (see Chapter 10 of the *Teacher's Handbook*) on BLM 4.1, 'Would you rather . . .'.

Discussion questions

- What do the results of the postbox survey show us? (That courage is relative. What is scary for one person is not necessarily scary for another person.)

UNIT 4—COURAGE

- Do some people naturally feel more fear or anxiety in situations than others? Why? (Yes. Some people are genetically predisposed to feel more anxiety.)
- Is the reverse also true? Do some people feel little fear in very difficult situations, such as people regularly engaged in extreme sports? (Yes. Some may hurt themselves, because fear can be protective.)
- Do you think that people who have high-risk professions, such as a high-rise window cleaner or someone in the rescue services, feel the same level of fear as the majority of us would in their situation?
- What helps these people to do their job without too much fear? (They are trained in their job and have the right equipment; they may have less fear in *that* situation.)
- Are people such as Edmund Hilary brave or just personally ambitious? (Some people who set out to achieve a personal goal are persistent and determined but not necessarily brave. They sometimes encounter an unexpected situation or misfortune that requires courage and then we are more likely to hear their story.)

ACTIVITY
Predictor cards

(See Chapter 10 of the *Teacher's Handbook*.) The survey question is: Which one of these would make you feel most nervous?
- Speaking in front of an audience
- Standing up against a school bully who is giving another kid a hard time
- Sitting for an important test that will determine what school you go to
- Saying no to a group of friends who want you to do something you don't want to do.

CLASS DISCUSSION BRAVE, STUPID OR THRILL-SEEKING?

Introduce the topic of the foolhardy behaviour that some young people engage in by using the 'pairs rally/pairs compare' strategy (see Chapter 10 of the *Teacher's Handbook*) to have students write some examples. Stress that behaviour is stupid or foolhardy if the danger is very high, if their skills, safety procedures and resources are very low, and if what they stand to get out of it isn't worth the risk. Examples of foolhardy behaviour include:
- Train surfing
- Jumping into shallow water off bridges or cliffs
- Driving while drunk
- Taking unknown drugs
- Making explosives
- Shoplifting.

Discussion questions

- What is the difference between foolhardy behaviour and courage? (see above and key points)
- Why do some kids engage in foolhardy behaviour? (they want bragging rights, to get an adrenalin rush, to show off and look tough, peer pressure)
- What are some of the extreme sports? (bungy jumping, white-water rafting, sky diving, base jumping, aerial skiing)

- What is the difference between foolhardy behaviour and the thrill-seeking that is involved in these extreme sports? (In extreme sports people learn skills, use safe equipment and follow safety precautions. There is also back-up.)
- Are boys or girls more likely to do foolhardy things? Why? (Boys may feel more pressured by peers to show off and impress each other.)
- Are people more likely or less likely to engage in foolhardy behaviour in groups? Why? (In groups they are more likely to give in to peer pressure and dares.)
- What kinds of kids are most likely to engage in risky behaviour such as drug taking? (Those who are foolhardy in that they don't think through the consequences; those who are more likely to give in to peer pressure; depressed young people who may not care much at the time about their own wellbeing.)

Follow-up activities

Use 'multiply and merge' (see Chapter 10 of the *Teacher's Handbook*) to decide on the three most dangerous jobs (e.g. deep-sea welder, stuntman, high-rise window washer, fire officer, lion tamer, astronaut, miner, helicopter rescue service, lifesaver, police officer).

ACTIVITIES
Media activity

Give students newspapers and ask them to work with a partner to find and display or discuss stories and pictures that feature courage. Make a display. During the debriefing, ask the class, 'What was the fear the people in the story were facing?'

Classroom collective research

X   See Chapter 10 of the Teacher's Handbook.

- People who have shown courage (e.g. Stuart Diver, Lance Armstrong).
- Research the training, skills, equipment and procedures that reduce the danger in specific high-risk professions or extreme sports to a very low level.
- Research International, National and State awards for courage or valour.
- Research people who have won awards for courage or valour.

CLASS DISCUSSION   WHO'S A HERO?

Introduce the term 'hero'. The term is often incorrectly used to mean someone who is much admired by society for their achievements. Discussion questions could include:
- Who do you admire? Are these people really heroes or just people who have admirable qualities? Have any of them really shown courage?
- What is a real hero? How is the term 'hero' sometimes misused in the media?
- Can anybody become a hero?
- What is the 'courage of your convictions'? (This is usually shown in actions taken repeatedly and over a long time in order to stand up for a principle or a 'cause' that is important to the individual and the community.)

Follow-up activities

- Students look for any reference to the term 'hero' in the media. Is the term being used correctly or incorrectly? Discuss how many of these references are related to sport and is this realistic? Why is sport so highly valued in Australia while many kinds of courage are overlooked?
- Students undertake research and give class presentations or prepare PowerPoint displays on a person whose life reflects great heroism or the courage of their convictions. For example: Nelson Mandela, Sister Elizabeth Kenny, Aung San Suu Kyi and Eddie Mabo.

ACTIVITY
Heroes

Students complete the following worksheets. Alternatively, remove the questions and use them with the 'jigsaw' teaching strategy (see Chapter 10 of the *Teacher's Handbook*):
- BLM 4.2, 'Edward "Weary" Dunlop'
- BLM 4.3, 'Nancy Wake'
- BLM 4.4, 'Mahatma Gandhi'
- BLM 4.5, 'Simpson and His Donkey'.
  Follow up with biographies such as *Woman in Arms* (the story of Nancy Wake).

ARTS ACTIVITIES
Classroom collective research

X See Chapter 10 of the Teacher's Handbook.

- Heroic acts have been depicted in many forms of artwork, for example the paintings of martyrs such as Saint Sebastian and Saint Joan. Artwork has also been used for political propaganda, as in the paintings of Chairman Mao and Che Guevara, and the Russian constructivist paintings of Stalin, and in sculptures such as the Statue of Liberty. War memorial artwork celebrates heroic deeds, as does Mombasa's Millennium Torch for Olympics 2000.
- Students create their own artwork, photographic display, PowerPoint presentation, sculpture or collage on courage.

CLASS DISCUSSION — FINDING YOUR OWN COURAGE

Introduce the discussion by asking students to decide in pairs on 'Fears that everyone has'. Then debrief and sort the fears into the Five Universal Fears (rejection, pain/death, embarrassment, disapproval, failing/mistakes). Students can then think of more examples of the five fears or situations in which they often occur. Alternatively, use the 'partner retell' strategy (see Chapter 10 of the *Teacher's Handbook*), with students sharing a time when they (or someone they are close to) had to show courage.

Discussion questions

- What helps to reduce fear and nervousness? (experience, learning skills, taking sensible risks, talking to others, getting a reality check, using positive self-talk, remembering previous successes, focusing more on the benefits you'll get from it than on the threats)

- When are we most likely to be nervous or scared? (when we haven't used some or all of the above strategies)
- What kinds of 'unhelpful thinking' can exaggerate your nervousness or fear? (refer to Unit 3, 'People bouncing back', and the Bounce Back acronym, e.g. unhelpful thinking and catastrophising)

Follow-up activities

- Students write in their journals about where they have shown courage and/or where other members of their family have.
- Work with students on developing a Do's and Don'ts for 'Finding your own courage'. Then work through BLM 4.6.
- Students complete BLM 4.7, 'You and courage'. (you will need to enlarge it)
- Students learn the Do's and Don'ts of giving a good classroom presentation from BLM 4.8. Use TEAM coaching (see Chapter 10 of the *Teacher's Handbook*) with this BLM. Then provide many opportunities for each student to practise this skill with increasingly 'threatening' audiences and assess their performance.
- Students make a fridge magnet (see Chapter 11 of the *Teacher's Handbook*) or a poster with a message or quote (see page 87) about courage, for example 'Feel the fear and do it anyway!' or 'The antidote to fear is skill and positive self-talk'.
- Teach students to use the cognitive prompt 'BAD is good' when faced with something that takes courage.

BAD is good!

Briefing
- Stop and clear your mind.
- Remember what you did last time.
- Imagine what you will do now that will be better than last time.

Action
Do it.

Debriefing
- What went well? What didn't?
- What will you do to make it work better next time?

UNIT 4—COURAGE

CONSOLIDATION

Class recommendations

Students record in a classbook their recommendations for:
- Best song/poem/novel/picture book about courage.
- Best movie/web site/TV show/artwork about courage.

Balloon burst quotes

✗ See Chapter 11 of the Teacher's Handbook.

- Courage is not the absence of fear but the judgment that something else is more important than fear. (Ambrose Redmoon)
- Courage is what it takes to stand up and speak; courage is also what it takes to sit down and listen. (Winston Churchill)
- He has not learned the first lesson of life if he does not every day surmount a fear. (Ralph Waldo Emerson)
- Never bend your head. Hold it high. Look the world straight in the eye. (Helen Keller)
- The courage of being one's genuine self, of standing alone and of not wanting to be somebody else. (Lyn Yutang)
- The distance is nothing, it is only the first step that is difficult. (Mme du Deffand)
- The greatest test of courage on earth is to bear defeat without losing heart. (Robert G Ingersoll)
- The human brain starts working the moment you are born and doesn't stop till you stand up to speak for the first time in public. (Sir George Tessell)
- The ultimate measure of a person is not where they stand at times of comfort and convenience but where they stand at times of conflict and controversy. (Martin Luther King Jnr)

Choose-your-own-adventure

Students use the courage quotes above as the basis for a writing exercise or a 'choose your own adventure' story. The story can have two choices—having courage or giving in to fear and then two different endings. Another story could be about being tempted to engage in foolhardy behaviour choices and endings—doing it and suffering the consequences or being sensible.

Categorising courage

Enlarge BLM 4.9, 'What kind of courage and where?', to A3 size and ask students to work in pairs to add more examples and detail to it. Follow with a class discussion.

Curriculum integration

The concept of courage can be applied to many topics, such as:
- Wars and prisoners of war
- Explorers
- Antarctica
- The Holocaust
- Aboriginal land rights
- The gold-rush.

Working with younger children

Students work with younger children by reading and discussing a book on courage, such as *The Inch Boy* or *The Inch High Samurai*, *Hansel and Gretel*, *Crow Boy* or *The Tunnel*. They could also prepare activities for younger children based on their chosen book.

TEAM coaching

X See Chapter 10 of the Teacher's Handbook.

Students practise the meaning and spelling of words and phrases about fear and courage.

Graphical story

Students prepare a graph. On the vertical axis they put the number of heartbeats per minute (from 80 to 160 in gradations of ten). On the horizontal axis they put the following times plotted against the stated number of heartbeats per minute:
- 9 am (85)
- 10.35 am (100)
- 10.43 am (90)
- 11.30 am (110)
- 11.34 am (90)
- 12.50 pm (115)
- 2.10 pm (85)
- 3.20 pm (100)
- 3.35 pm (90).

Students then write a story with a partner that explains why this student's heart rate goes up and down on this school day. Assume that the student's resting heart rate is 80–85 and that the increases reflect fear and the reductions reflect courage or positive self-talk etc.

Quick quotes

X See Chapter 11 of the Teacher's Handbook.

I need courage when I have to . . .

Before or after?

X See Chapter 10 of the Teacher's Handbook.

adversity	endurance	nervousness
anxious	facing	pain
audacity	failure	profession
bold	fear	protest
bravery	foolhardiness	punishment
challenge	fortitude	risky
courageous	grit	scary
dangerous	guts	sensible
daring	idiocy	stupidity
difficult	misfortune	survival
embarrassment	mistakes	valour

UNIT 4—COURAGE

Cross-offs

Have students complete BLM 4.4. The message is: Feel the fear and do it anyway.

RESOURCES

Books

Armstrong Sperry, 1968, *The Boy Who Was Afraid*, Macmillan, New York.
Junko Morimoto, 1984, *The Inch Boy*, Collins, Melbourne.
Shiro Kasamatsu & Ralph F McCarthy, *The Inch-High Samurai*, Kodansha International.
Roberto Innocenti, 1985, *Rose Blanche*, Jonathan Cape, London.
Russell Braddon, 1989, *Woman in Arms*, Collins, London.
Taro Yashima, 1976, *Crow Boy*, Viking Press, New York.
Anthony Browne, 1989, *The Tunnel*, Walker Books, London.
Anthony Browne, 1990, *Hansel and Gretel*, Little Mammoth, London.

Video

Gallipoli, 1981, Paramount, PG rating.

WOULD YOU RATHER . . . ?

BLM 4.1

Tick the box to show which one you would find more scary:
Cut each answer along dotted line and post it.

1. Would you rather be interviewed on TV ☐ or bungy jump ☐?

2. Would you rather ski down a steep icy ski run ☐ or give a class talk ☐?

3. Would you rather donate blood ☐ or stand up for a kid being mistreated by your friends ☐?

4. Would you rather stand for election for class captain against a popular person ☐ or compete on a TV quiz show ☐?

5. Would you rather sing a solo in a school concert ☐ or pick up a spider in your bare hands ☐?

6. Would you rather ride a horse ☐ or swim in a big surf with no lifesavers around ☐?

7. Would you rather make a brief speech at school assembly ☐ or go to a party where you didn't know anyone ☐?

8. Would you rather abseil down a cliff ☐ or hang-glide ☐?

© Helen McGrath and Toni Noble, 2003. This page from Bounce Back!® may be photocopied for classroom use.

EDWARD 'WEARY' DUNLOP

BLM 4.2

Edward 'Weary' Dunlop was born in a Victorian country town in 1907. When he left school, Weary took a job in a pharmacy. In 1927 he became bored with country life and moved to Melbourne. Once in Melbourne, he decided that he wanted to be a doctor and began studying medicine.

As soon as he'd graduated, Weary became a ship's surgeon and sailed to London. Although he enjoyed life at sea, he didn't know exactly what he was going to do with his life—until World War II broke out in 1939.

Weary knew that his medical skills would be needed during the war and he decided to enlist in the army. He was sent to Indonesia where Australian soldiers were fighting the Japanese. His days were spent treating the sick and wounded.

In 1942 the Japanese captured Weary and many Australian soldiers. They were taken to Burma, where they were forced to build the 'Burma Railway' which was over 400 kilometres long. The Japanese treated the Australian prisoners very poorly. They were made to work extremely hard and given little food. Many of the prisoners suffered from malnutrition and tropical diseases. The Japanese had no sympathy and threatened to kill those prisoners who were unable to work.

However Weary stepped in and stood up to the Japanese. As well as treating and operating on the sick and injured, Weary demanded better conditions for the prisoners. He protected those who were unwell, sometimes risking his own life to save someone else's. He was often beaten for doing this, and at one stage he nearly died himself from illness. By the end of the war, Weary had saved a great number of lives and had become a legend.

After the war, Weary was knighted for his contribution to medicine and was named Australian of the Year in 1977. Sir Edward 'Weary' Dunlop died in 1993 aged 85.

- In what ways did Weary demonstrate courage?

- Why would someone risk his own life and wellbeing for others in this way?

© Helen McGrath and Toni Noble, 2003. This page from Bounce Back!® may be photocopied for classroom use.

NANCY WAKE

BLM 4.3

Nancy Wake grew up in Sydney. She was the youngest child in the family and became very independent. In her early 20s, Nancy left Australia for Paris where she worked as a journalist.

In the beginning, Paris was fun. There were lots of parties and she met and fell in love with a Frenchman named Henri. However, Hitler and the Germans had begun to make war on Europe and Nancy knew that the Germans would soon invade France. Nevertheless, Nancy married Henri in 1939. War broke out soon after.

Germany invaded France in 1940 and Nancy joined the French resistance. The aim of the French resistance was to work secretly to weaken the German army in France so that any attack by the Allied troops would be more successful. Nancy also helped hundreds of French people escape capture by the Germans.

The Germans soon became aware of Nancy's activities and nicknamed her 'The White Mouse' because she was so difficult to catch. Nancy knew that she would be killed if she was caught, but she always managed to escape capture.

In 1943 Nancy moved to England where she worked as a British agent. A year later she decided to go back to Paris to continue the fight. She was able to raise money and obtain weapons and a radio for the resistance movement. By sabotaging various targets, she and the resistance played a vital role in the success of the D-Day invasion by the Allies in June 1944. Germany was defeated a year later.

Victory celebrations were cut short for Nancy when she learned that her husband had been killed by the Germans in 1943. After the war Nancy Wake was awarded medals for bravery from Great Britain, France and the United States.

She will be remembered for her courage and bravery at a time when women were expected to stay at home in a supportive role while men fought the war.

- Who were the Allied troops?

- What different kinds of courage did Nancy demonstrate?

- What do you think motivated her to do what she did?

© Helen McGrath and Toni Noble, 2003. This page from Bounce Back!® may be photocopied for classroom use.

MAHATMA GANDHI

BLM 4.4

Mahatma Gandhi was born in India in 1869. He was married when aged only 12 and finished high school when he was 18. Three years later he moved to South Africa, where he became a legal advisor. It was in South Africa that Gandhi first witnessed *apartheid*. Under this system, blacks and Indians were treated by whites as second-class citizens.

Gandhi decided to do something about this problem. Through *passive resistance*, Gandhi and his supporters showed their unhappiness to the South African government with a series of protests. They were constantly beaten, but they didn't fight back. They were put in jail, but as soon as they were released they went straight back to protesting. After 20 years of this sort of protest, the South African government began to listen. Life in South Africa improved for its Indian citizens.

By the end of World War I Gandhi had moved back to India. He had decided that life also needed to improve for Indians in India. At that time India was under British rule and the British treated the Indian people very badly. Gandhi soon had a large following and, using passive resistance, he began protesting against some aspects of British rule.

The British usually *retaliated* with violence. Gandhi's response was to encourage Indian citizens to withdraw their children from British schools and to squat in the streets to protest against unfair treatment.

The British didn't know how to handle Gandhi. When they put him in prison, Gandhi would refuse to eat. When they released him, he would organise more protests. In 1930 Gandhi protested against the payment of tax by India's poorest citizens. He led a march of protestors 380 kilometres to the sea. All over the country, Indians followed his example and more arrests followed.

Finally, in 1947, India won its independence from the British. Tragically, Gandhi was assassinated one year later. Gandhi could have lived a wealthy life as a lawyer. Instead, he gave up a life of comfort to improve conditions and fight for justice for millions of others. His method of passive resistance was later used successfully by Martin Luther King in America.

- What is meant by the terms 'apartheid', 'passive resistance' and 'retaliate'?

- What characteristics of Gandhi enabled him to do what he did?

- What do you think motivated him to do what he did?

© Helen McGrath and Toni Noble, 2003. This page from Bounce Back!® may be photocopied for classroom use.

SIMPSON AND HIS DONKEY

BLM 4.5

John Simpson Kirkpatrick was born in England in 1892. As a young man, he joined the Marines, before deciding that life at sea wasn't for him. Simpson and a few of his friends left the Marines and arrived in Australia in 1910. Starting in Newcastle, Simpson roamed the cities and towns of Australia, working here and there. When World War I broke out, he enlisted in the Australian army.

Simpson and the rest of the Anzacs arrived at Gallipoli on 25 April 1915. As a stretcher-bearer, Simpson found the early days extremely difficult. Over 750 Australian soldiers were killed on the first day alone, and Simpson had seen men killed all around him. His job involved walking through the trenches and enemy fire to collect and carry wounded soldiers back to the medical tent.

Simpson soon found the weight of the injured men too much for him. Instead of carrying the men, he used a donkey draped with a red cross flag to transport them to safety. This allowed him to move more quickly and rescue more injured men. However, it also meant that he risked death more often than before.

Despite the risks, Simpson fearlessly patrolled the battlefield for wounded men. Each time, he would brave the deadly Turkish snipers and the constant shrapnel fire that swept the area. Simpson's only concern was the rescue of wounded soldiers. The fact that Simpson wasn't killed each time he entered the battlefield was a miracle in itself.

Simpson's luck finally ran out on 19 May. Attempting to rescue yet another wounded soldier, Simpson was shot in the back by a Turkish machine-gunner and killed instantly. He died saving the lives of others.

News of Simpson's death was met with great sadness by the Anzacs. Although Simpson had been at Gallipoli for only 24 days, his courage during that time had saved a great many lives and he had earned the respect of his fellow soldiers.

A statue of Simpson and his donkey was erected near Melbourne's Shrine of Remembrance.

- What risks did Simpson face?

- What do you think motivated him to do what he did?

- What does ANZAC stand for?

© Helen McGrath and Toni Noble, 2003. This page from Bounce Back!® may be photocopied for classroom use.

FINDING YOUR OWN COURAGE

BLM 4.6

Do's	Don'ts
Do a reality check. Think about the risks and dangers. Think carefully. What part makes you feel nervous? Are your fears justified or exaggerated? Is it worth taking this risk?	Don't do it without thinking about the risks first. Don't do something potentially dangerous just to impress others or to get bragging rights.
Concentrate on the positives. Think about the good things that could come from overcoming your fears (e.g. more self-respect, confidence, respect from others, progress). Use positive self-talk.	Don't use negative self-talk such as 'This will be awful' or 'I can't do this'. Don't focus only on the threatening bits.
Believe in yourself. Remember other times when you have acted with courage or overcome your nerves. Remember all the things you have done well. Tell yourself that you can do this even though you are a bit nervous. Most people would feel a bit nervous, not just you.	Don't think too much about any previous times when things went wrong. Don't focus on your weaknesses. Don't assume that everyone else does it perfectly and isn't nervous.
Go slowly, one step at a time. Tell yourself that sometimes it takes a while to access courage.	Don't rush in. Don't lose your confidence just because it may take you a while to feel ready to do a difficult thing. The end result is what matters.
Talk to people who care about you. Get a reality check, support and encouragement. Express your concerns and nervousness.	Don't think that others don't care about you or won't help you.
Know that you might make a mistake. Even when you do access courage, sometimes things are still too hard to do. Be prepared to try again in some cases.	Don't think that you have failed if you can't do something. Just having a go at something that was difficult for you was courageous.

© Helen McGrath and Toni Noble, 2003. This page from Bounce Back!® may be photocopied for classroom use.

YOU AND COURAGE

BLM 4.7

Think hard about the different types of courage you have demonstrated at some time in your life. Fill in the boxes that apply to you.

Type of courage The courage to . . .	An example of when you have showed this type of courage	What were the good outcomes for you?	What did you say to yourself or do that helped you to access courage here?	What fear made it hard to demonstrate this kind of courage?
voice your own opinion				
perform when anxious				
stand up for yourself				
be yourself				
try something new				
make a difficult decision				
stand up for others				
reach out in friendship				
try again				
stand up for what you believe is right				
admit when you are wrong				
say 'no'				
do something that could hurt you				
endure a distressing situation that can't be changed				

© Helen McGrath and Toni Noble, 2003. This page from Bounce Back!® may be photocopied for classroom use.

HOW TO GIVE A GREAT CLASS PRESENTATION

BLM 4.8

Do's	Don'ts	How did you go? Use a 1 to 5 rating (with 5 being excellent)
Plan Make a plan of what you will say. Write only five points on a card, to help you remember them.	Don't have more than five main things to say. Don't have too much information on your card.	
Be positive Take deep breaths and say to yourself, 'This will be fine. I can do this.' Remember when you have been successful before.	Don't use negative self-talk. Don't say things to yourself like 'I will muck this up'.	
Look and sound confident Stand tall. Smile. Look people in the eye. Use a reasonably loud voice.	Don't use nervous behaviour such as fidgeting. Don't look down or use a soft voice.	
Involve the audience and take the attention off yourself at the start Start by getting the audience to DO something, such as: • Look at an overhead transparency • Answer a question • Look at something you have shown.	Don't read lots of notes. Just speak naturally from the main points on your cue card.	
Be both serious and funny Treat the topic with seriousness but use a bit of humour when you can. It relaxes the audience and it relaxes you.	Don't be silly and show off. This can result in a loss of audience respect.	
Use different ways to keep their attention • Tell brief stories or show things. • Get them to do or write things. • Ask if they have any questions. • Ask them to discuss something with the person next to them.	Don't just talk to them and don't give lots of unnecessary detail.	
Use good time management Stick to your time limit. Use a clock or timer. Thank them at the end for listening to your talk.	Don't go over time. Your audience will lose interest.	

© Helen McGrath and Toni Noble, 2003. This page from Bounce Back!® may be photocopied for classroom use.

WHAT KIND OF COURAGE AND WHERE?

BLM 4.9

Write in any more information that you can think of in each section.

	Everyday courage	Heroism	Courage of one's convictions	Courage in misfortune	Risky professions	Thrill-seeking	Personal goal-seeking that may have risky elements	Foolhardiness
Examples	Performing on stage	Saving someone from a burning car	Mahatma Gandhi	People trapped in mines	Police officer	White-water rafting	Ernest Shackelton	Diving into shallow water
What is the usual fear to be faced?	Embarrassment; Failure	Physical harm or death	Punishment	Physical harm or death	Usually none, but things can go wrong and then it would be physical harm	Usually none, but things can go wrong and then it would be physical harm	Usually none, but things can go wrong and then it would be physical harm	Physical harm, death and punishment
What are the positive outcomes that make using the courage required worth it?	Self-respect and confidence. Progress and growth	Saving a life or ensuring the wellbeing of another	Making a difference to the lives of others	Personal survival	Personal survival (if things go wrong). Sometimes saving a life (if things go wrong)	Excitement	Achievement and satisfaction. Respect from others. Personal survival (if things go wrong)	Impressing others 'Bragging rights'
Are there any features that help them to reduce the danger?	Skills can be practised in advance. Positive self-talk can be used	None	Usually not	Police and emergency services may be available	Safety equipment. Skills. Procedures. Trained back-up	Safety equipment Trained back-up	Skills. Equipment. Back-up	None

© Helen McGrath and Toni Noble, 2003. This page from Bounce Back!® may be photocopied for classroom use.

CROSS-OFFS

BLM 4.10

brooch	feel	truck	mission	drum	script	bracelet	train
macadamia	truck	flathead	the	snapper	saucepan	flute
piano	director	earring	herd	donuts	almond	station
decision	fear	whiting	chips	bus	producer	pride
and	camera	frypan	do	blue	grey	trout
fawn	walnut	it	division	yellow	griller	hazelnut
necklace	anyway	guitar	meat pie	actor	car	barbecue

To find the message cross off these words:

- 5 words that are to do with making movies
- 4 words that are types of nut
- 4 words that are colours
- 4 words that end in –ion
- 4 words that are musical instruments
- 4 words that are items of jewellery
- 4 kinds of vehicles
- 4 words that are types of fish
- 4 words that are things you cook with
- 3 words that are high fat junk food
- 2 words which are about collections of animals

The secret message is _____

© Helen McGrath and Toni Noble, 2003. This page from Bounce Back!® may be photocopied for classroom use.

UNIT 5
THE BRIGHT SIDE

KEY POINTS

Some people are 'positive trackers' and others are 'negative trackers'.
Imagine that everyone has both a positive and a negative antenna on their head. Positive trackers have their positive antenna turned up to VERY HIGH so they mostly look for and talk about the good things about themselves, others and life. Their negative antenna is turned right down to LOW, so they only occasionally find and comment on the negative aspects. On the other hand, negative trackers have their negative antenna turned up to VERY HIGH and their positive antenna down to LOW, so they spend most of their time looking for the bad things about themselves, others and life, and only occasionally finding the good things.

Positive trackers tend to have happier and more successful lives.
Compared with negative trackers, positive trackers cope better, are more popular, achieve more of their goals, have higher self-esteem, and are more successful in their work lives and relationships.

You can decide to be a positive tracker.
Being a positive tracker is something anyone can learn to do if they choose to.

Some people are more optimistic than others.
Positive trackers are more likely to be optimistic. Being optimistic means believing that outcomes are more likely to be good. Being pessimistic means believing that outcomes are more likely to be bad. Being optimistic helps you stay hopeful, cope better and bounce back when things go wrong, whereas being pessimistic makes you feel worse and not as hopeful.

Sometimes it is harder to feel optimistic than at other times.
Even the most optimistic person sometimes encounters a situation where it is very hard to be immediately optimistic. Sometimes it can take a while to start thinking optimistically again.

Optimists think differently from pessimists.
Optimists and pessimists think differently in these four ways:
1. Optimists believe that when bad things happen they are only temporary and that things will be better soon. They try to take one day at a time till things improve. On the other hand, pessimists think bad times last forever.
2. Optimists understand that if something goes wrong in one part of their life it doesn't necessarily mean that the other parts of their life will be affected. Pessimists, however, believe that if things aren't going well in one part of their life then everything else in their life will go badly too. When a small mark is found on a new jacket the optimist says 'I don't like it that there is a mark but I think I can cover it up or hide it. I can still wear it'. The pessimist says 'my best jacket is ruined and now I have no decent clothes to wear'.
3. Optimists believe that there are usually many reasons why a bad event occurs, including their own contribution. Pessimists blame themselves and who they are most of the time when things don't go well.
4. Optimists give themselves a lot of the credit for the things they do to create good events in their lives. They do many things to make it more likely that they will get good luck (e.g. try again, look for opportunities). Pessimists think that nothing they do makes any difference to whether or not good things happen and it's just about luck. Pessimists believe they don't get much luck.

UNIT 5—THE BRIGHT SIDE

Class discussion—Positive tracking *102*

BOOKS
Fortunately! *102*
Hooray for Diffendoofer Day *102*

MATHS/ENGLISH ACTIVITY
Survey *102*

GAMES
Fortunately *103*
Positive shapes/Picture/Lego *103*

DRAMA ACTIVITY
Positive and negative skits *103*

MEDIA ACTIVITIES
Positives and negatives *103*

ACTIVITIES
Working with younger students *104*
Classroom organisation *104*

Class discussion—Hope *104*

BOOKS
The Red Tree *105*
The Angel with a Mouth Organ *105*
Prayer for the Twenty-First Century *105*
The Miracle Tree *106*
The Boy Who Painted the Sun *106*

Class discussion—Optimism *106*

Class discussion—Making your own good luck *107*

BOOK
The Duck That Had No Luck *108*

Class discussion—Bad times don't spoil everything *108*

BOOK
Bushfire *109*

Consolidation *109*

'Throw the Dice', 'Inside-Outside Circles' or 'Musical Stop and Share' *109*

Bright side cartoons *110*
Balloon burst quotes *110*
Class recommendations *110*
Quick quotes *110*
Working with younger students *110*
Before or after? *110*
Cross-offs *111*

Resources *111*

BLM 5.1—Become a positive tracker today! *112*

BLM 5.2—What kind of a tracker are you? *113*

BLM 5.3—What would the optimist and pessimist say? *115*

BLM 5.4—Bright side cartoons *117*

BLM 5.5—Cross-offs *118*

CLASS DISCUSSION POSITIVE TRACKING

Ask students to read BLM 5.1, 'Become a positive tracker today!', in preparation for the discussion. Begin the discussion by reading either *Fortunately* or *Hooray for Diffendoofer Day* (see below).

Discussion questions

- What are positive and negative trackers? (see key points)
- What might be some of the effects of being a positive tracker versus a negative tracker?
- How could someone become a more positive tracker?
- Do you know anyone who is a negative or a positive tracker (no names)? How do you react to them?

Follow-up activities

- Students complete BLM 5.2, 'What kind of tracker are you?'. This can be used as a personal reflection activity, a diagnostic measure or a measure of change over time.
- Students work in pairs to make a list of all the good things about their school. Then each pair can write a page in verse that can be compiled into a class book.
- Students draw images or make posters of positive versus negative tracking.
- Students work in cooperative groups of four to plan an advertising campaign to encourage students in the school to become more positive (e.g. using the slogan 'No one ever went blind looking on the bright side!').
- Students make a class 'Positive memories' book. Each student writes a positive memory on one A4 page, and the pages are then collated into a class book.
- Students complete this sentence:
  'I don't like that my mother/father/parents . . . but I also appreciate that she/he/they . . .'
  Then substitute the words 'school' or 'teacher'.
- If you were given $10 for everything you are currently thankful for, how much money would you get? Write out your bank statement.

BOOKS

Fortunately! (Picture book)

Fortunately, one day Ned got a letter that said 'please come to a surprise party'. But unfortunately the party was in Florida and he was in New York. Fortunately, a friend loaned him an aeroplane. Unfortunately, the motor exploded. Fortunately, there was a parachute on the plane. Unfortunately, there was a hole in the parachute. And so on!

Hooray for Diffendoofer Day (Dr Seuss picture book)

The students in this unusual school celebrate the differences in their teachers. They value the support staff and love their school, which is not the case at the school at Flobbertown. This book is also used in Unit 1.

MATHS/ENGLISH ACTIVITY
Survey

Students plan and conduct a survey to find out which of these two statements most people agree with:

- Whatever be your creed, brother, whatever be your goal, keep your eye upon the donut, not upon the hole.
- Expect the worst and you'll never be disappointed and you'll always be ready.

The class can make a giant donut on which they write positive comments.

GAMES
Fortunately

Form two teams. The members of one team are the positives and the members of the other are the negatives. Start a story and let the two teams take it in turns to provide the next sentence. You might end up with something like this: One day when Susie was out walking in the forest, she found a lost dog. Fortunately the dog was very cute and friendly. Unfortunately it was also wild and it started to chase her. Fortunately it chased her into a cave where she found lots of treasure. Unfortunately the pirates who had stored it in the cave arrived just at that moment to collect it. Add some 'realistic' scenarios related to students lives.

Students can also play this game with younger children.

Positive shapes/Picture/Lego

Students work in pairs. One student draws a shape using five triangles, three squares, three rectangles and four circles (or any other combination), all touching in various places. Without showing their partner the shape-drawing, the drawer then instructs them how to draw it but can give only positive feedback. Corrective positive feedback may be given (e.g. 'Yes, that's right and you need to add a line there' or 'You have drawn the circle the correct size'), but students can't use any negative words or phrases, such as 'no', 'not', 'wrong', 'incorrect', 'you've put the circle in the wrong place' etc. This strategy can also be used with drawing a detailed picture (e.g. of a beach scene) or making the same Lego construction.

DRAMA ACTIVITY
Positive and negative skits

Students make rose-coloured and grey-coloured glasses and use them in dramatic skits to see the same situation in two ways, negatively or positively. Alternatively, they could use the two ends of binoculars to magnify the positives and minimise the negatives. Use cardboard cylinders, or op-shop glasses and cellophane.

MEDIA ACTIVITIES
Positives and negatives

- Give students newspapers and ask them to work with a partner to rank five articles in terms of how much negative and positive tracking occurs. They could rewrite one of the newspaper articles more positively.
- Give students the real estate pages and ask them to find a house-for-sale advertisement that uses positive tracking. Rewrite using humorous negative tracking.
- In groups, students record and analyse a television advertisement (aimed at their age group) for positive tracking. Then they can act it out with negative tracking.
- What does a public relations company do? Why are PR people called spin-doctors? Students look through newspapers to see if they can locate the work of a spin-doctor.
- Students can listen to or watch interviewers and talk-back hosts and analyse their positive/negative responses ratio and style (Oprah is especially positive).

ACTIVITIES
Working with younger students

Students can make positive and negative antennae (one of each) on headbands for younger students and develop drama activities for them. They could also ask the children to say all the positive things about their school or class and help them make a poster of the information. They could use inexpensive headbands with pipecleaners attached plus stars, happy faces, sad faces etc.

Classroom organisation

- There are some guidelines on changing classroom negativity in the book *Dirty Tricks* (see resources section).
- Whenever possible, use situations that occur naturally to help students practise positive tracking.' For example, find the small good things in the bad things. If the printer breaks down, say, 'Let's positive track: At least we had managed to print the most important part.'
- Regularly use activities such as 'The ten best things about our class/the school/being a certain age/our city' etc, five good things we did today.

CLASS DISCUSSION HOPE

Ask students to draw 'hope'. Then debrief and collate the categories. You will usually get:
- Lucky charms (four-leaf clover, rabbit's foot, horseshoe)
- Light (candles, stars, sun; connects with the light that dispels darkness and the light at the end of the tunnel)
- Religion (church, cross)
- Nature (because of its continuity, predictability and beauty; flowers, sunrise, spring, rainbows after rain).

Then read to the class and discuss the older picture book *The Red Tree* (see below). You could also read any of these books before or after the discussion: *The Angel with a Mouth Organ, Prayer for the 21st Century, The Miracle Tree, The Boy Who Painted the Sun* (see below).

Discussion questions

- What is hope? (the belief that a positive outcome or a brighter future is possible, sometimes despite the odds)
- What were some of the things that people did after the terrorist attacks on the World Trade Centre buildings in New York and in Bali that helped them to cope better and feel more hopeful? (e.g. lit candles, sent flowers, said prayers, wrote notes about peace and hope)
- How does being hopeful help you to achieve what you want, solve problems or feel better? (it helps you to feel less sad and worried and take actions that might help the situation)
- What happens if you give up hope? (despair and lack of action or problem solving)
- Have you ever experienced a time when you (or someone close to you) lost hope but things turned out well anyway (no names)?
- How is persistence related to optimism and hope? (if you believe it is possible, you keep trying)
- How can music sustain hope? Can you think of any examples?

Follow-up activities

- Students can make a photographic display of symbols of hope. Encourage them to look for symbols and icons of hope in other cultures and in artwork as well.
- Students can research songs that became popular during World War I and World War II, during the convict days of early Australia, and during times of slavery in the United States to help people maintain hope. One example is 'Pack Up Your troubles in Your Old Kit Bag and Smile, Smile, Smile' (1915). (Lyrics and music are at www.melodylane.net/songlist.html or www3.sympatico.ca/cottagecountry//dir-cam.htm.)
- The books *Rose Blanche* (summarised in Unit 3) and *Let the Celebrations Begin* (summarised in Unit 9), both offer messages of hope. In *Rose Blanche*, the image at the end represents hope through nature regeneration.

BOOKS

The Red Tree (Picture book)

This powerful picture book has extraordinary images and few words. Prompt students to look for the red leaf on each page, as it is the symbol of hope. Here are some activity suggestions:
- Use the 'pairs rally/pairs compare' strategy (see Chapter 10 of the *Teacher's Handbook*) and ask students to write down the negative emotions they can identify in *The Red Tree*, and the symbolism of these emotions.
- Use the 'partner retell' strategy (see Chapter 10 of the *Teacher's Handbook*) and ask each student to share one or two situations that people their age might experience that might leave them feeling these negative emotions. How can positive tracking and optimistic thinking help?
- Make a class red tree of hope. Put a stick in a pot of sand or dirt and the other end in a block of florist's oasis. Each student writes one or two messages of hope they have *for their future* on one or two leaves cut out of red card. Using florist's wire, they stick their messages in the oasis. A ball of chicken wire or a branch could also be used for a tree. Red card leaf messages can be tied on the branches with pipe cleaners. You could also spray big leaves red and have students write in texta on the leaves, which can be scattered around the base of the tree.

The Angel with a Mouth Organ (Picture book)

A family are forced from their home during war and become wandering refugees, enduring hardships such as the death of their baby sister and the callous behaviour of some of the people they encounter. Father always has his mouth organ to cheer them up, but he is taken away by soldiers. Finally the war ends, and after much searching they find their father, who has with him not only his mouth organ but also a piece of stained glass from a church window, with an engraving of an angel with a mouth organ. They eventually find a place to live, and forever after the fragment of glass takes pride of place on their Christmas tree.

Prayer for the Twenty-First Century (Picture book)

John Marsden's hopes for peace and wellbeing in the future are illustrated with photos and artwork.

The Miracle Tree (Picture chapter book)

This story of hope for the future of the world is set in Nagasaki after the dropping of the atomic bomb. A pine tree becomes the focus of hope for three people who have been damaged and separated by the war. Charcoal drawings highlight the sadness of the story as well as the optimism. This is a longish picture book with chapters.

The Boy Who Painted the Sun (Picture book)

A young boy has to move from the country to the city with his family, after hard times on their farm. He finds a way to help himself and his family survive the depressing grimness and greyness of the city by painting murals of animals, trees and the sun on the walls of the buildings. The pictures cheer everybody up.

CLASS DISCUSSION OPTIMISM

Use the 'balloon burst quotes' strategy (see Chapter 11 of the *Teacher's Handbook*) as an introduction, using the quotes below. Alternatively, show the video of *The Castle*.
- Every cloud has a silver lining.
- It is better to light a small candle than to curse the darkness. (Confucius)
- It's an ill wind that blows no good.
- If life gives you lemons, then make lemonade.
- No pessimist ever discovered the secret of the stars or sailed to an uncharted land. (Helen Keller)
- Optimist: One who finds an opportunity in every difficulty. Pessimist: One who finds a difficulty in every opportunity.
- Optimists are right and so are pessimists. It's up to you to choose which one you'll be. (Harvey Mackay)
- Some people are always grumbling because roses have thorns. I am thankful thorns have roses. (Alphonse Karr)
- The world belongs to the optimist; pessimists are only spectators. (Francois Guizot)
- There are no hopeless situations in life; there are only people who have grown hopeless about them. (adapted from Clare Booth Luce)
- What seem to us bitter trials are often blessings in disguise. (Oscar Wilde)
- When one door of happiness closes, another opens. Often we look so long at the closed door that we do not see the one that has been opened for us. (Helen Keller)

Discussion questions

- What is optimism? (the belief that things are more likely to turn out well)
- What is pessimism? (the belief that things are more likely to turn out badly)
- How would optimism help you to bounce back from a difficult situation? (you don't feel so sad or worried; it gives you hope; it keeps you trying to solve a problem)
- How would pessimism make things worse? (you feel bad; you give up)
- Can you change the way you think to become more optimistic? (Yes. See the key points and the BOUNCE BACK acronym.)
- Have you ever been in a situation you didn't like and thought it would never improve but it did? (bad times are usually temporary)
- Why don't bad times last? (because situations change; time makes things seem less awful; other people help along the way; time helps you to see things more in perspective; more ways to solve the problem occur to you)

- Why do optimists persist more and not give up?
- When might it be hard to be optimistic?
- Can you be too optimistic? (Yes, blind faith can be dangerous i.e. not doing a reality check.)
- What does the saying 'Confidence is optimism in action' mean?
- What might the expression 'Positive conversion of mistakes' mean? (When something goes wrong you turn it into a good thing, for example, you miss your bus but then you decide to walk instead to keep fit; you try to see 'threats' as 'challenges'.)
- Can anyone think of any examples of 'positive conversion'?

Follow-up activities

- Students complete BLM 5.3, 'What would the optimist and pessimist say?'.
- Students write a story about how optimism saved the day.
- Students research, write and present brief biographies about well-known people who have demonstrated optimism (e.g. Christopher Reeve, the former actor in the movie *Superman*, who persisted and is slowly triumphing over almost total paralysis after a horse-riding accident. He is achieving things that the medical profession did not believe were possible).
- The main characters in the books reviewed in Unit 3, 'People bouncing back', all show optimism in difficult times. Students can review the books in relation to optimism.
- Use the 'partner retell' strategy (see Chapter 10 of the *Teacher's Handbook*) and ask students to talk about where they have a lot of confidence and how that reflects optimism *or* when they have found a way to 'positively convert' a mistake or bad situation.

CLASS DISCUSSION MAKING YOUR OWN GOOD LUCK

Begin with the 'people pie' activity (see Chapter 10 of the *Teacher's Handbook*).
- Do you agree that a good-luck charm can bring you good luck? How? (it can change what you *do*)
- Have you (or a family member) ever had a good-luck charm?
- Have you or any member of your family ever won a prize in a raffle?

Then read the picture book *The Duck That Had No Luck* and/or the poem 'I Found a Four-Leaf Clover' (see below). The books *Holes* and *Chinese Cinderella* (both summarised in Unit 3, 'People bouncing back') also contain elements connected to the issue of 'luck'.

Discussion questions

- What is 'good and bad luck'? (we all get some of each and it is 'random')
- Why do people have lucky charms?
- What are some of the symbols of good luck? (ask students to draw one, for example, a four-leaf clover, a rabbit's foot, a horseshoe with the horseshoe up so luck doesn't run out, blowing out birthday candles and making a wish, a shooting star)
- When have you wished for good luck? Did you get it?
- What are some examples of gambling? What role does luck play in gambling? How do people become addicted to gambling? (they get a payoff every now and then and so they think it can happen again; the casino statistically programs machines to pay off occasionally)
- Is anyone lucky all the time? (no; it is randomly distributed)

- Why do some people think they are 'unlucky' most of the time? (They focus too much on the times when things don't go their way and underplay the times when things go well. That is, they get things out of balance to fit in with their idea that they are unlucky people; because they don't believe they *will* get lucky so they are less likely to put in the work and look for opportunities.)
- What does the statement 'the harder I work, the luckier I get' mean?
- How can we make ourselves luckier? (work harder, get information, find out what might get in the way and try to solve that problem, ask people to help us)
- Use the 'partner retell' strategy (see Chapter 10 of the *Teacher's Handbook*) and ask students to share an example of good or bad luck that has happened to them
- Use the 'partner retell' strategy and ask students to share one way in which they have helped themselves to be luckier (e.g. wanting to get into a team so practising harder; wanting to be friends with someone so making an effort to talk to them; wanting to get better at reading so reading more often; saving up for something they really wanted). Each group reports back on what they have learned from their stories.

Follow-up activities

- Research how poker machines are designed to let people win occasionally, or the random 'luck' factors in other forms of gambling e.g. horse racing.
- Use the 'collective classroom research' strategy (see Chapter 10 of the *Teacher's Handbook*) to collect:
  - Symbols of good luck in different cultures (e.g. Chinese, Irish, Indian)
  - Song titles that feature any of these words: 'hope', 'luck', 'lucky', 'positive'.
- Play the probabilities game in Unit 10, 'Winners' (see page 245).
- Play the 'Four corners probability game' to look at luck and randomness. Put four different-coloured balls or cards into a container. Label each of the four corners of the room a different colour. Every student selects a corner to stand in. Draw a colour. All people at that corner go out. Repeat each step several times till only one person is left.

BOOK
The Duck That Had No Luck (Picture book)

In this wildly exaggerated rhyming tale, a duck oversleeps and misses flying south for the winter with the rest of the flock. He tries to find his way south, but no matter what he does, disaster follows him and he eventually arrives at the North Pole instead! Fortunately there are some very welcoming polar bears and birds there and in a positive way he makes the best of a bad situation. The illustrations are cartoon style.

CLASS DISCUSSION BAD TIMES DON'T SPOIL EVERYTHING

Read to the class and discuss the picture book *The Bushfire* (see below).

Discussion questions

- Have you ever had a fight with someone and thought it was forever but it wasn't? Why? (people forget, their feelings reduce, things change)

UNIT 5—THE BRIGHT SIDE

- When you are at the dentist, does it ever *seem* as if you will be there having treatment forever? Does it help to say 'I'll soon be out of here'?
- Have you ever been in a situation you didn't like and thought it would never improve but it did?
- Why don't bad times last? (because situations change; time makes things seem less awful; other people help along the way; time helps you to see things more in perspective; more ways to solve the problem occur to you; you learn to cope; some good luck might occur)
- When a bad thing happens to you, does it mean other bad things will happen to you? (no, but sometimes one thing can briefly affect another)
- When a bad thing happens, does it mean the start of lots of bad luck? (no)

Follow-up activities

- Students look at how people bounce back after natural disasters such as bushfires, floods and earthquakes. Why do most of the bad effects of these things usually go away in time?
- Students make a fridge magnet with the phrase 'Bad times don't last' or 'One bad thing doesn't have to spoil everything else'.
- Discuss how students in Seattle (an earthquake-prone zone that had an earthquake in 2001) prepare, each year, an earthquake survival pack to take with them if they have to seek shelter or are trapped. Many children in Australia have had to flee from natural disasters threatening their home such as bushfires or floods. What would students put in their survival packs? (food, photos, games etc.)
- Consider reading to the class the book *Tomorrow Is a Great Word* (see Unit 3), a story of a teenage earthquake survivor who thought that things would never improve but they did.

BOOK

Bushfire (Picture book)

This is a rhyming story of a family whose house burns down in a bushfire. As they sift through the remains, they find an intact toy fire truck (humour), see the small positive side of the situation and remain hopeful for the future.

CONSOLIDATION

'Throw the dice', 'Inside–outside circles' or 'Musical stop and share'

X See Chapter 10 of the Teacher's Handbook.

- The best time I have ever had with my family was when . . .
- One thing that has happened recently that has made me feel great is . . .
- A nice thing I did for somebody once was . . .
- A nice thing someone did for me once was . . .
- A time that someone I know lost hope but things turned out well anyway was when . . . (no names)
- I am looking forward to . . .
- One time I was lucky was when . . .
- One thing I'm hoping to do in the future is . . .
- My favourite place/book/lesson/family holiday/movie/song/toy/TV show/game/sport is . . .

- I like it when . . .
- The best thing about the weekend/my house/class/family/pet/grandparent is . . .
- The best thing about bad weather/being at school/going to the doctor is . . .

Cartoons

Students read and analyse the cartoons in BLM 5.4, 'Bright side cartoons', and write in detail what each means and how it relates to 'The bright side'.

Balloon burst quotes

Using the quotes on page 106, students could also choose some to draw as class books, posters, fridge magnets or bookmarks.

Class recommendations

Students record in a class book their recommendations for the best book, poem, film, song, artwork or television show with a theme of hope or optimism or the idea that bad times don't last.

Quick quotes

X See Chapter 11 of the Teacher's Handbook.

'The best thing about school is . . .' *or* 'One thing I am looking forward to about my future is . . .'

Working with younger students

- In groups students can write and illustrate for a younger child a flapper card or a simple picture book of flappers titled 'It could be worse!'. They draw/write about little things that upset small children, such as falling over, someone taking their toy, getting a hole in their jumper etc. on the top and under the flapper they draw an exaggerated version of how it could be worse.
- Students write a story about two children, one who was a negative tracker and one who was a positive tracker, using the younger child as the positive tracker.

Before or after?

X See Chapter 10 of the Teacher's Handbook.

Bright	Optimism
Clover	Optimist
Donut	Pessimism
Future	Pessimist
Hope	Positive
Hopeful	Rainbow
Last	Side
Lemonade	Spoil
Light	Sunny
Luck	Symbols
Lucky	Temporary
Negative	

UNIT 5—THE BRIGHT SIDE

Cross-offs

Have students complete BLM 5.5. The message is: Bad times don't last and things always get better.

RESOURCES

Books

Remy Charlip, 1969, *Fortunately!* Scholastic Books, New York.
Jonathan Long & Korky Paul, 1996, *The Duck That Had No Luck*, Bodley Head Children's Books, London.
John Marsden, 1997, *Prayer for the Twenty-First Century,* Thomas Lothian, Melbourne.
Christobel Mattingly & Astra Lacis, 1984, *The Angel with a Mouth Organ*, Hodder and Stoughton, Sydney.
Christobel Mattingly & Marianne Yamaguchi, 1985, *The Miracle Tree*, Hodder and Stoughton, Sydney.
H McGrath, 1996, *Dirty Tricks: Classroom Games for Teaching Social Skills*, Longman Australia, Melbourne.
Jill Morris & Geoff Hocking, 1983, *The Boy Who Painted the Sun*, Kestrel, Harmondsworth (order from: jillmorris@greaterglider.com).
Dr Seuss (with Jack Prelutsky & Lane Smith), 1998, *Hooray for Diffendoofer Day*, Harper Collins Children's Books, Sydney.
Marguerite Hann Syme & David Cox, 2000, *Bushfire*, Scholastic Australia, Sydney.
Shaun Tan, 2001, *The Red Tree*, Lothian, Melbourne.

Video

The Castle, 1999, Mirimax Home Video, Rated R for language.

BECOME A POSITIVE TRACKER TODAY!

BLM 5.1

Some people are 'positive trackers'.
The key words that describe what a positive tracker does are: 'affirm', 'applaud', 'acknowledge', 'accept', 'respect', 'admire' and 'optimism'. Positive trackers seem to have a positive antenna on their head that is turned up to VERY HIGH and that constantly searches for:
- The things that go right for them and that they like
- Their successes and the best things about their own character and behaviour
- The small good things that happen in their daily lives
- The good bits, however small, in any bad things that happen to them
- Other people's successes and the good parts of who they are.

When they find these good things they talk openly about them. This has a powerful effect on other people. Most people like positive trackers a lot. They think positive trackers are more confident. They feel safer in their company because they know they will be focusing on their good points. This makes people feel good. Because they are always pointing out the good things, positive trackers create a more upbeat and friendly environment where things seem more fun.

Some people are 'negative trackers'.
The key words and phrases that describe what a negative tracker does are: blame and complain, 'bitch and snitch', 'moan and groan', 'doom and gloom', 'reject and disrespect', and 'pessimism'. Negative trackers seem to have a negative antenna on their head which is turned up to VERY HIGH and that constantly searches for:
- The things that go wrong for them and that they don't like
- The bad things that happen in their daily lives
- Their own mistakes and failures and the flaws in their own character
- The mistakes that other people make and the bad side of who they are.

When they find these negatives they speak critically and sourly about them. The effect of negative trackers on other people is a sad one. Most people find it harder to like negative trackers. They don't seem very confident because they act as if they don't like themselves much. This puts people off. People don't feel very safe in the company of negative trackers because they know that they will be looking for their mistakes and flaws. Their negativity is contagious and discouraging, so they don't make good company and tend to create a negative 'downbeat' environment.

Can people change?
Everyone is a 'negative tracker' sometimes because none of us are perfect. We all have both a positive and a negative antenna. We can practise turning our negative antenna down to LOW and our positive antenna up to VERY HIGH. Here are some suggestions:
- At the end of each day think about at least five good things that happened.
- Avoid badmouthing others when they aren't there or putting them down. Remember that bitching comes back to bite you.
- Try not to grizzle, moan or groan when things don't go your way.
- Be less critical of yourself and others.
- Look for all the things you do well, no matter how small.
- Comment genuinely on the positive things about others.
- When a bad thing happens in your life, try to find any small thing about it that is positive (e.g. Did you learn anything from it? What might have been worse? Were there any small good spin-offs from it?)

© Helen McGrath and Toni Noble, 2003. This page from Bounce Back!® may be photocopied for classroom use.

WHAT KIND OF TRACKER ARE YOU?

BLM 5.2

Tick the box that best shows what you think and do.

	Column A	Column B	Column C
1. Do you talk a lot about the things that go well in your day?	Yes, a lot	Sometimes	Not often
2. Do you look for and notice the mistakes that people make rather than what they do well?	Yes, a lot	Sometimes	Not often
3. Do you give yourself a very hard time when you get something wrong or forget something?	Yes, a lot	Sometimes	Not often
4. Do you talk about what you like about people you know?	Yes, a lot	Sometimes	Not often
5. Do you notice and talk about the things you do well?	Yes, a lot	Sometimes	Not often
6. Do you talk about the bad things about other people?	Yes, a lot	Sometimes	Not often
7. Do you pay attention to what you like about how you look rather than what you don't like?	Yes, a lot	Sometimes	Not often
8. Do you focus a lot on the things you can't do well?	Yes, a lot	Sometimes	Not often
9. Do you usually forgive yourself when you get something wrong and see it as an experience that helped you to learn?	Yes, mostly	Sometimes	Not much
10. Do you talk about the things that go wrong in your day?	Yes, a lot	Sometimes	No
11. Do you agree with the statement that you can learn at least one thing from everybody you meet or know?	Yes	Unsure	No
12. When you are having a hard time, do you fear that things will be terrible forever?	Yes, often	Sometimes	Not often
13. When things go wrong for you, do you find one small good thing about the situation to hang on to?	Yes, usually	Sometimes	Not often
14. Do you believe that nearly everyone has some positive qualities?	Yes	Unsure	Not really
15. When things go wrong, do you spend a lot of time agonising about how terrible the situation is?	Yes, a lot	A bit	Not much
16. When you are having a hard time, do you feel confident that things will get better in a while?	Yes, usually	A bit	No
17. Do you believe that some people have absolutely nothing to offer other people because they are complete losers?	Yes	Sort of	No

© Helen McGrath and Toni Noble, 2003. This page from Bounce Back!® may be photocopied for classroom use.

WHAT KIND OF TRACKER ARE YOU? (CONTINUED)

BLM 5.2

Scoring for 'What kind of tracker are you?'
Transfer your ticks to this column to get your scores. Then add up all your points.

Question number	Column A	Column B	Column C
1.	2	1	0
2.	0	1	2
3.	0	1	2
4.	2	1	0
5.	2	1	0
6.	0	1	2
7.	2	1	0
8.	0	1	2
9.	2	1	0
10.	0	1	2
11.	2	1	0
12.	0	1	2
13.	2	1	0
14.	2	1	0
15.	0	1	2
16.	2	1	0
17.	0	1	2

Put a mark on the scale to show your total positivity score. Make a plan to become more positive and get a higher score next time you answer the quiz.

0 |||||||||||||||||| 17 |||||||||||||||||| 34

You need a *lot* more practice at being positive

You need some practice at being more positive but you're on the right track

You're a very positive person. Keep practising!

© Helen McGrath and Toni Noble, 2003. This page from Bounce Back!® may be photocopied for classroom use.

WHAT WOULD THE OPTIMIST AND PESSIMIST SAY?

BLM 5.3

For each situation, write in the thought balloon what the optimist and what the pessimist would say. Remember, the optimist:
- Looks for the positives and stays hopeful
- Thinks that bad times are temporary
- Knows that one bad thing that happens doesn't have to spoil everything else in your life
- Takes credit for their own effort and successes however small.

On the other hand, the pessimist:
- Looks for the negatives and loses hope quickly
- Thinks that bad times go on and on
- Thinks that if one bad thing happens everything is spoiled
- Thinks that good things happen to them just because of freakish good luck not their own efforts.

You are invited to a party where you won't know many people.

The optimist would say   The pessimist would say

You can't find any friends when you first arrive at a new high school.

The optimist would say   The pessimist would say

© Helen McGrath and Toni Noble, 2003. This page from Bounce Back!® may be photocopied for classroom use.

WHAT WOULD THE OPTIMIST AND PESSIMIST SAY? (CONTINUED)

BLM 5.3

| Your grandmother has a sudden heart attack and is in hospital. | The optimist would say | The pessimist would say |

| Your pet dog disappears and can't be found. | The optimist would say | The pessimist would say |

| You nominate for captain and then find that a popular kid has too. | The optimist would say | The pessimist would say |

© Helen McGrath and Toni Noble, 2003. This page from Bounce Back!® may be photocopied for classroom use.

BRIGHT SIDE CARTOONS

BLM 5.4

On a separate sheet, explain why each cartoon is funny and how it demonstrates an aspect of optimism/being positive (or the lack of them).

1. WOW THAT'S MANURE! THERE MUST BE A PONY AROUND HERE!

2. GEE YOU'RE SO LUCKY GETTING EXTRA TIME ON THE COURT!
YEAH, I GOT LUCKY EVER SINCE I STARTED TRAINING 3 NIGHTS A WEEK!

3. IT COULD BE GOOD, BUT THEN AGAIN, IT COULD KILL YOU!
OUTSIDE IS DANGEROUS
BE PREPARED! EXPECT THE WORST
BAD LUCK IS REAL
TRAVEL = DISAPPOINTMENT
Welcome to the PESSIMISTS SOCIETY
NO THE ANNUAL PICNIC IS CANCELLED BECAUSE WE'RE SURE IT'S GOING TO RAIN!

4. ALL I GET IS CAT FOOD FOR CHRISTMAS WHEN EVERYONE ELSE IS EATING TURKEY.
I SUPPOSE IT COULD BE WORSE. I COULD HAVE BEEN BORN A TURKEY!

5. I NEED TO LOSE WEIGHT, GET BETTER MARKS, COOLER CLOTHES AND GET A BOYFRIEND.
CAN'T YOU BE A LITTLE MORE POSITIVE!
OK. I'M POSITIVE I NEED TO LOSE WEIGHT. I'M POSITIVE NO ONE WILL GO OUT WITH ME...

© Helen McGrath and Toni Noble, 2003. This page from Bounce Back!® may be photocopied for classroom use.

CROSS-OFFS

BLM 5.5

leaf	Africa	wool	doberman	tennis	torch	bad
times	gnarled	Antartica	badminton	modem	amusing	helicopter
keyboard	hull	don't	candle	stem	gnome	seagull
squash	last	mast	Europe	pelican	and	fuselage
hilarious	sun	gnu	things	spatula	dalmatian	whisk
poodle	silk	jet	sail	Asia	tongs	cotton
comical	always	wing	parrot	flower	get	software
Australia	screen	gnat	lamp	labrador	better	port hole

To find the message, cross off these words:

5 words that are continents
4 words that have a silent g in them
4 words that are about boats
4 words that are breeds of dogs
4 words that are sources of light
4 words that are about aircraft
4 words that are about computers
3 words that are parts of plants
3 words that mean funny
3 words that are the names of birds
3 words that are natural fibres
3 words that are racquet sports
3 words that are cooking implements

The secret message is _____ _____

© Helen McGrath and Toni Noble, 2003. This page from Bounce Back!® may be photocopied for classroom use.

UNIT 6
EMOTIONS

KEY POINTS

Emotions are useful to you, even unpleasant or uncomfortable ones.
'Emotion' is another word for 'feeling' and it comes from the Latin meaning 'to move'. So emotions 'move' you to act. They energise you. Angry feelings warn you about possible unfairness and 'move' you to act in your own defence. Feelings of fear and nervousness warn you about possible danger and 'move' you to protect yourself. Guilty feelings let you know that you have acted against your own standards and 'move' you to make amends and change.

Unpleasant or uncomfortable emotions are useful, but they also need to be managed.
If your negative emotions control you, they can be very destructive for both you and others. Uncontrolled anger can cause your friendships to break up, get you a bad reputation and result in your being punished. You are responsible for your own anger and how you handle it. One of the most important life skills is to learn to manage your unpleasant or uncomfortable feelings.

Managing your emotions is *not* the same as trying not to have any.
You *need* all of your feelings, even the unpleasant ones. Without them you wouldn't be able to protect yourself, stand up for yourself and what you think is right, or make up for the wrong things you do. However if you don't try to keep your strong feelings under some control, you can become 'emotionally hijacked' and act without thinking and cause yourself or others harm.

It is very important to correctly recognise and name your own feelings.
You can easily make a mistake about what feeling you think you are having. You might think you are feeling angry when you are really feeling scared. The sensations in your body can feel very similar. You can also make a mistake about how strong your feeling is. For example, you may think you are 'furious' when in fact you are only 'annoyed'. They are both words to describe angry feelings but they are different strengths or intensities.

Recognising how other people are feeling helps you to understand them.
Trying to understand how someone else is feeling is called 'empathy', and it is vital for good relationships, for caring and for compassion.

You can have mixed feelings about something.
'Ambivalent' is a word that means having both positive and negative emotions in response to a situation. For example, if someone says, 'I felt ambivalent about winning the prize', they might mean that they were scared by it in some ways but pleased by it in other ways.

Negative and unhelpful 'self-talk' exaggerates feelings and creates overreactions.
No person and no event can *make* you feel a certain way. It may be understandable that you have a certain feeling in response to an event or another person's behaviour, but what exaggerates your feelings is what you say to yourself about what has happened (i.e. your 'self-talk').

Managing negative feelings involves four tools
The four tools for keeping uncomfortable feelings under some control are: calming down what's happening in your *body*, using helpful and calming *thinking*, using *effective non-damaging communication* to say how you feel and why, and finding a strategic way to *solve the problem* so you can still be friendly.

UNIT 6—EMOTIONS

Class discussion—Why do we have feelings? *121*
- ACTIVITIES
  Working with younger students *121*
  Class recommendations *121*
- BOOKS
  Crow boy *122*
  The Red Tree *122*
- SELF-REFLECTION
  My feelings journal *122*
- ENGLISH/ARTS ACTIVITIES
  Feelings ladders *122*
  Colours and feelings *123*
  Draw the sayings *123*
- MEDIA ACTIVITY
  Emotions and the media *123*

Class discussion—Pleasant and enjoyable feelings *123*
- BOOK
  The Happy Hedgehog *124*

Class discussion—Feeling worried or nervous *124*
- ARTS/TECHNOLOGY ACTIVITY
  Making a stress ball *125*

Class discussion—Sadness *126*
- BOOKS
  Modoc: The Story of the Greatest Elephant That Ever Lived *126*
  How Smudge Came *126*
  Passing On *127*
  Brodie *127*
  Nana Upstairs and Nana Downstairs *127*

Class discussion—Anger *127*

Class discussion—When do you feel angry? *128*
- ACTIVITIES
  Four corners *129*
  Ten thinking tracks *129*
  Media activities *130*
- ENGLISH ACTIVITY
  Choose your own adventure *130*
- INTERVIEW
  Managing anger *130*
- DRAMA ACTIVITIES
  Turning things around *130*
  Was it an accident? *131*
- ACTIVITIES
  Predictor cards *131*

Class discussion—Unpleasant feelings *131*
- ACTIVITY
  Four leaders *132*
- BOOK
  The Visitors Who Came to Stay *133*

Class discussion—Ambivalent feelings *133*

Class discussion—Empathy *133*
- BOOK
  Voices in the Park *134*
- ACTIVITIES
  Media activity *135*
  How do you know when someone is feeling . . .? *135*
  Empathic card matching *135*
  What's it like to be . . .? *135*
- DRAMA ACTIVITY
  Chair swapping *136*
- CLASSROOM ORGANISATION
  Community service *136*

Consolidation *136*
  Working with younger students *136*
  Feelings spinner *136*
  'Throw the dice', 'Inside–outside circles' or 'Musical stop and share' *136*
  English activities *137*
  Drama/music activities and games *137*
  Feelings visual display *137*
  Management tools *137*
  Feelings cartoons *138*
  Balloon burst quotes *138*
  TEAM coaching *138*
  Quick quotes *138*
  Cross-offs *138*

Resources *139*

BLM 6.1—How feelings can energise you *140*

BLM 6.2—Feelings quiz *141*

BLM 6.3—How well do you deal with nervousness? *142*

BLM 6.4—In what situations do people often feel angry? *143*

BLM 6.5—What do you do when you're angry? *144*

BLM 6.6—Anger can be dynamite! *145*

BLM 6.7—Managing difficult feelings *146*

BLM 6.8—Try a little understanding *147*

BLM 6.9—Feelings cartoons *148*

BLM 6.10—Cross-offs *149*

UNIT 6—EMOTIONS

CLASS DISCUSSION: WHY DO WE HAVE FEELINGS?

Play the theme music from a number of movies to introduce the topic, and then ask students to try and pick the kind of movie each piece of music might have been used in, based on the feelings the music creates in them. Discuss why film and television producers use music in their shows.

Then ask students to work in groups of three and make two lists of feelings, one pleasant and the other unpleasant or uncomfortable. Debrief as a class and use the discussion to make a class list of feelings. (Also refer to the A–Z list of emotions in BLM 11.1 on p. 189 of the *Teacher's Handbook*.)

Discussion questions

- What are feelings?
- What are other words that mean feelings? (emotions; mood)
- What are some pleasant and desirable feelings?
- What are some unpleasant and uncomfortable feelings?
- Why do we have feelings? (see key points)
- What happens when we become emotionally hijacked? (we lose control; we don't think clearly; we make bad decisions)
- What are some possible bad effects of strong feelings? (distress, harm to self or others, alienation)
- Why do we say we are 'moved' by a piece of music?

Follow-up activities

- Students complete BLM 6.1, 'How feelings can energise you'.
- Students make an electronic quiz (see Chapter 11 of the *Teacher's Handbook*) of different situations and associated feelings for younger students.
- Invite students to play and discuss their own CD tracks of music that 'moves' them, or ask them to associate songs with particular emotions you nominate (e.g. sad, scared, triumphant). They can then analyse why the song has that effect by considering tempo, instruments, beat, words etc.
- Students complete BLM 6.2, 'Feelings quiz', and then share their answers with a partner.

ACTIVITIES

Working with younger students

Students make cartoons about situations and feelings for younger students. They could use the book *Feelings* by Aliki as a reference, or they could read and discuss the book to help the younger students talk about emotions.

Class recommendations

Students nominate and record in a class book their preferred songs, poems, videos, artworks and books that focus on feelings.

BOOKS
Crow Boy (Picture book)

A strange, withdrawn and very short boy is teased at his school in a small village in Japan. He makes no friends for the six years he is there. A new teacher realises that the boy has some talents and gives him the opportunity to demonstrate them to the other children. This is a very moving book, with simple but evocative illustrations. Read it to the class and then ask them to write down their feelings in response to different parts of the story, and all the feelings that are present in the story.

The Red Tree (Picture book)

Summarised in Unit 5. Follow up activities are also provided.

SELF-REFLECTION
My feelings journal

Students keep a record of all their feelings for a week. They use a chart as below:

Time, date and place	The situation	How I felt	How strong the feeling was (from 1 to 10, with 10 being the strongest)	Was the feeling pleasant or unpleasant?	If it was an unpleasant feeling, how did you keep it under control?
Monday 26 July 2004 8.45 am at home	Running late for school and Mum says she won't drive me	Furious	8/10	Unpleasant	• Took some deep breaths • Said to myself that it really wasn't Mum's fault I was late

ENGLISH/ARTS ACTIVITIES
Feelings ladders

Students design and make a ladder and then sort one family of emotions into levels of intensity, with the most intense at the top of the ladder. For example:
- Angry, cross, irritated, annoyed, furious, enraged, livid
- Ecstatic, happy, pleased, delighted, contented, blissful, joyous, satisfied
- Sad, sorrowful, depressed, blue, down, unhappy, grief-stricken, broken-hearted, despairing
- Surprised, shocked, stunned, puzzled, uncertain
- Appalled, horrified, disgusted, scornful, contemptuous, revolted, repulsed.

Use paddlepop sticks for the ladder and write the feelings on cards/paper.

Colours and feelings

Read to the class the simple picture book *My Many Coloured Days* by Dr Seuss. Follow up with students:
- Making their own version for younger children
- Writing an illustrated story using as many feelings and colour expressions as they can think of (e.g. green with envy, purple with rage, red with embarrassment)
- Making mobiles connecting colours and their own feelings.

Draw the sayings

Use the book *A Bee in Ben's Bonnet* which is based entirely on cliches to show students how to draw metaphors such as:
- Anger getting on top of me
- Blowing your top
- Bored out of my brain
- Giving someone a serve
- Green with envy
- Happy as a pig in mud
- Going feral
- Seeing red
- Losing face
- Your blood just boiling
- Spitting the dummy
- The green-eyed monster
- Scared out of your wits
- So excited you couldn't sit still
- So revolted your skin began to crawl
- Being absolutely ropeable
- Like a bull in a china shop.

MEDIA ACTIVITY
Emotions and the media

Provide newspapers and ask students to collect articles that contain 'emotive' words or pictures that are designed to create certain feelings in the reader. Discuss the writer's motivation. Rewrite some without the emotion.

CLASS DISCUSSION
PLEASANT AND ENJOYABLE FEELINGS

Start by reading to the class and discussing *The Happy Hedgehog* (see below). Alternatively, ask students to bring to class a photo of a happy time. Warn them that it will be passed around. Ask each student to introduce their photo by saying why it is connected to happy feelings for them. Alternatively, display them, with each student writing a paragraph to explain, then use the Classroom stroll activity (see Chapter 11 of the *Teacher's Handbook*).

Discussion questions

- What is happiness?
- When have you felt happy?
- How long does happiness last? (Happiness tends to be fleeting because it is an intense feeling. If you were happy for a long time, you probably wouldn't notice it and value it so much.)
- What is the difference between happiness, satisfaction and contentment? (Long-term satisfaction and contentment may be similar to happiness but less intense. They may be less focused or less based on expectations.)
- Eleanor Roosevelt once said, 'Happiness is a by-product not a goal in itself'. What does this mean? Do you agree?
- Ambrose Pierce defined happiness as 'an agreeable sensation arising from contemplating the misery of others'. Do you agree?
- Is happiness in the journey rather than in the arrival?
- What are some of the other pleasant or enjoyable feelings that we all strive to experience?
- When are most people likely to feel proud? Excited? Relieved? Contented? Secure? Satisfied?

Follow-up activities

- Students write about experiences that have led them to feel pleasant and enjoyable emotions and to say why. Ask them to note what they learned about themselves and their feelings each time they felt these emotions.
- Students write a story or plan a dramatic enactment called 'A Perfect Day' that features at least ten different pleasurable emotions.

BOOK

The Happy Hedgehog (Picture book)

The preface quotes Buddha: 'no path leads to happiness: the path itself is happiness'. After being chastised for being lazy by his grandfather Mikko, a young hedgehog leaves his garden where he feels content to talk to various animals about what they are doing to make themselves happy. Ultimately he concludes that he doesn't want to be the busiest, the fastest, the strongest or the cleverest. He has already developed what matters to him, namely his great skill in healing with herbs and his love of the garden in which he grows them.

CLASS DISCUSSION FEELING WORRIED OR NERVOUS

Also refer to Unit 4, 'Courage'.

- What is worry? (Anticipatory fear. That is, the perceived danger is 'potential', in that it has not yet happened and often *won't* happen.)
- What do students your age worry or feel nervous about and why?
- What is stress? (stress is the worry associated with *not* having the skills or resources to deal with a problem or task or meet a deadline)
- Is a little worry or nervousness a good thing? (Yes. Research shows that you need *some* worry before a performance or challenge in order to feel motivated and try hard. Too

little anxiety means that you get too laid-back and feel over-confident. Too much nervousness means that you feel unable to think clearly and keep your mind on the task.)
- What are some good ways to make yourself feel less nervous before a test? (Say to yourself, 'I'm good at this; I've studied hard; when I study hard I do okay'; talk to a friend and test each other.)

Follow-up activities

- Students draw the outline of a person and label the parts that respond when you are worried. For example you may experience the following sensations:
  - Trouble catching your breath
  - Tightness in your chest
  - Feeling as if you are being smothered or are choking
  - Dizziness or feeling light-headed or as though you are about to faint
  - A tingling in your fingertips
  - Hot or cold all over, especially in the face, or sweaty
  - Hot able to think properly
  - Shivering or shaking
  - Like you want to be sick
  - Your heart beating faster than normal and being able to feel it
  - A sense of things being unreal or like in a dream
  - Like something bad might happen or you might be going to die
  - Getting a headache
  - Having a dry mouth
  - Giggling in a silly way
  - Feeling as if there are butterflies in your stomach
  - Hands are clammy
  - Feel like crying
  - Going pale.
- Students complete BLM 6.3, 'How well do you deal with nervousness?'.

ARTS/TECHNOLOGY ACTIVITY
Making a stress ball

Students can make their own stress ball. For each student you will need:
- A shared dessertspoon and sharp scissors
- Three heaped dessertspoons of birdseed
- One heaped dessertspoon of cornflour
- Two small plastic bags (sandwich size)
- Two 25 cm round balloons of different colours.

Instructions

1. Place one plastic bag inside the other to give strength.
2. Place the birdseed and cornflour into the bag and tie a knot.
3. Cut off any leftover plastic above the knot.
4. Cut the neck off the two balloons.
5. Stretch one balloon over the plastic bag of seed and flour.
6. With the scissors cut a small piece off the end of the second balloon.
7. Stretch the second balloon over the first so that the plastic bag does not show.
8. Cut small holes in the second balloon so the colour of the first balloon shows through.

CLASS DISCUSSION SADNESS

There are several ways in which you could introduce the emotion of sadness. In advance, you could read to the class (as a serial) *Modoc: The Story of the Greatest Elephant That Ever Lived* (see below). Or you could read to the class and discuss one of these picture books: *How Smudge Came*, *Passing On*, *Brodie* or *Nana Upstairs and Nana Downstairs* (see below).

Discussion questions

- What is sadness? (feelings of sorrow, grief, and a temporary loss of hope)
- In what kinds of situations do we feel sad? (Usually situations involving loss or potential loss, such as death, loss of a dream, loss of contentment and peace of mind, rejection [loss of acceptance], loss of a lifestyle [e.g. through family separation]. We can also feel sad when someone else experiences a loss or loses their peace of mind, because we 'lose' our sense of security for that person.)
- How is it useful to us to be able to feel sadness? (It tells us about the importance of what has been lost and that we need to find a way to grieve, move on, and if possible replace it in some way.)
- What can you do if you are feeling sad or 'down'?
    - Hang around happy people. Their mood is often contagious.
    - Keep busy with a non-emotional task which is very absorbing.
    - Read a joke book or watch a funny show.
    - Write a long description of why you feel down.
    - Tell someone who cares, so they can support you.
    - Try to solve any problem that is making you feel sad.
    - Remind yourself that things will be better soon.
- What is the best way to handle things if you think a friend is sad and can't get themselves out of it?
    - Have they had a recent loss? They may need to go through some grief stages yet. Show them that you care that they are feeling sad and that you will spend time with them and listen to them if they want you to. Check in a lot.
    - Try to cheer them up with humour, or distract them with an interesting activity (but stop if they don't like it).
- Should you tell a teacher or parent if you are concerned about a friend, even if they ask you not to? (yes, unless it is a brief and recent sadness and seems to be improving)

BOOKS

Modoc: The Story of the Greatest Elephant That Ever Lived (Chapter book)

The ending of this book may reduce many of your students to tears, even the most macho ones! This is the true story of Bram Gunterstein who was born into a family of German circus elephant trainers on the same day as Modoc the elephant was born, in the barn next door. The book is about the intertwined lives of and lifelong bond between the man and the elephant.

How Smudge Came (Picture book)

Cindy is a young woman with an intellectual disability who lives in a group home. She smuggles in a cat, Smudge, and then loses and regains him.

Passing On (Picture book)

In this simple rhyming story, a teenager reflects on the joyous and loving experiences he shared with his beloved grandmother. He passes some of those experiences on to his younger brother.

Brodie (Picture book)

Brodie is an upper primary student with a serious illness. The story tells of his battle against his illness and his eventual death through the eyes of his classmates, who find ways to mourn his loss and celebrate his life.

Nana Upstairs and Nana Downstairs (Picture book)

The story of a boy's relationship with his two, very different grandmothers, and how he copes with their eventual passing.

CLASS DISCUSSION — ANGER

Start with this 'Postbox' on anger (see Chapter 10 of the *Teacher's Handbook*):
1. Describe a situation in which you have felt really angry (no names).
2. When you see someone being really angry and not controlling themselves, what do you think about them?
3. Think about a positive and popular kid you have known. What was their way of dealing with being really angry?
4. What is the best thing that people can say to themselves to *cool down* when they are angry about something?
5. What kind of exercise do you find the best to do when you want to calm yourself down?

Discussion questions

Begin discussion by asking each group to report on their Postbox findings. Then discuss the following questions.
- What is anger? (a strong feeling of annoyance when we think something wrong has been done to us)
- When is anger helpful? (when it warns us to stand up for our rights and protect ourselves)
- When is anger destructive? (when it emotionally hijacks us and controls us so that we don't use helpful thinking and then we act in destructive ways)
- What bad results might happen if anger gets on top of you? (reputation damage, the break-up of friendships, lack of cooperation from other people, guilty feelings, loss of self-respect, getting into trouble with authority [i.e. teachers, police, bosses], looking 'uncool' and not in control of yourself in front of others)
- What other feelings can sometimes be hiding behind our anger? (fear, jealousy, sadness, guilt) Can you think of any examples? (no names rule)

CLASS DISCUSSION WHEN DO YOU FEEL ANGRY?

Start with this 'Predictor card' activity (see Chapter 10 of the *Teacher's Handbook*). The survey question is: In which two of these situations would you feel most angry?
1. If someone made fun of how I looked in front of others, and everybody laughed.
2. If one of my parents told me I couldn't go somewhere and didn't give me a good reason.
3. If I got into trouble from a teacher because the teacher thought I was lying when I wasn't.
4. If I was trying to do something on the computer for a project and no matter how hard I worked at it I couldn't make the computer do it.
5. If another kid my age treated me disrespectfully and as though I was nothing.
6. If another kid tried to start an argument with me without any reason.
7. If my parents decided we had to move and I felt like I had no say in where we lived or where I went to school.

Discussion questions

- What are some other situations in which someone your age might feel angry and why?
- Can a person or situation *make* you angry? (No, no one and no situation can *make* you angry. It is sometimes understandable that you feel angry in some situations, but *you* are responsible for your own anger and how you handle it. What you say to yourself and whether you have good ways to get on top of your anger are what makes the difference.) Discuss the results of the Postbox activity.
- What is the 'fall-out' if you allow angry feelings to hijack you and control you? (damaged relationships; loss of reputation; looking uncool and unable to control yourself; punishment; physical harm to another or to yourself; feeling bad about yourself afterwards)
- Is it true that the best way to deal with angry feelings is to express them and let them out? (No, that makes things worse and you usually feel even more angry. The best way is to calm down and then tell the other person why you are angry. If you are not angry with another *person*, but angry instead because of something that has happened, the best way is to calm down, talk about it to a friend or parent, think the problem through and then problem-solve.)
- Why do we sometimes feel angry towards someone even though they have not done anything wrong and we just don't like the situation? (we find the nearest 'target' because we don't stop and try to think things through after being emotionally hijacked)
- What do people say to themselves that can wind-up angry feelings and exaggerate them? ('She can't do that to me!', 'How dare he!', 'Who do they think they are!', 'They won't get away with this!', 'She's making me look stupid!', 'I'll show them!', 'I must win no matter what the cost')
- What are some of the things that people can think or say to themselves to calm themselves down and let them be more in control of themselves and the situation? ('Stay cool', 'What will losing control cost me?', 'Staying friends is more important than venting my anger', 'I'll probably laugh about this later', 'It won't matter in five minutes', 'The real loser is the person who "loses" it', 'I can't make any difference to this situation so I won't try', 'You win some, you lose some', 'Things are already bad enough', 'I won't sweat the small stuff')
- What are some ways to calm yourself down when you feel angry? (exercise, sport, music, pets, reading, TV, talking to a friend or parent about it, counting backwards from 100 by threes, channelling angry energy into doing a useful task such as cleaning up, trying to relax by alternatively stregching each limb and then flopping)

- What are some of the other ways to handle angry feelings in a helpful way that doesn't harm anyone but gets the problem sorted out? (calmly but firmly telling the person why you are angry and trying together to sort it out)
- What is meant by 'sulking'? (Refusing to talk about something and acting as if you are sad, because you feel angry and you are trying to make the other person feel sorry for you or guilty. It's a kind of punishment as well as a 'plea' for the other person to make amends for what you believe they have done to you.)
- What is the result of sulking? (A loss of respect for you because you are not assertively dealing with the problem and not seeing what has happened from any other point of view but your own. It is better to speak up in a calm and honest way.)

Follow-up activities

- Students complete BLM 6.4, 'In what situations do people often feel angry?'.
- Students individually write down three situations in which they sometimes feel angry. They then work with a partner, swapping lists and offering each other some suggestions about how to stay calm and deal well with their angry feelings for each of the other person's situations.
- Students carry out a survey on people's best 'wind-down' phrase. Each student asks the following question to three adults over 21 and three students of their own age: 'What is your best strategy and self-talk for calming yourself when you feel angry?'.
- Students complete BLM 6.5, 'What do you do when you're angry?'.
- Students complete BLM 6.6, 'Anger can be dynamite!' using a situation of their own.
- In groups of three, students plan an advertising campaign around the theme of 'Those who lose it end up the losers'.
- Teach students to use the 'BAD is good' prompt when they deal with angry feelings (see Unit 4, 'Courage', page 86).

ACTIVITIES
Four corners

Describe an anger-provoking scenario. Ask students for ideas on how best to deal with it. Write the best four ideas they come up with on large sheets of paper (one idea per sheet) and attach one sheet to the walls at each of the four corners. Ask students to stand at the sheet that they think offers the best way to deal with the situation. They discuss with others at that corner why they think that idea is best. They select a spokesperson to give their reasons to the class. Here are some scenarios to use:
- Bevan thinks that his stepmother gives his stepbrother Aidan fewer chores than him. He also thinks that Aidan gets off with just a lecture when he doesn't do his chores, whereas Bevan is often grounded. The more Bevan thinks about it, the angrier he gets.
- Ellie's parents won't let her go to the shopping centre with her friends after school during the week because her last school report was very poor and not as good as she normally gets. They want her to get stuck into her homework after school rather than wander around with her friends, but Ellie feels that she will lose her connection with the group if she doesn't spend time with them after school. The more she thinks about it, the angrier Ellie gets.

Ten thinking tracks

(See BLM 1.3 in Unit 1, 'Core values', page 21.) Students use this strategy to discuss the idea of a biofeedback watch that gives feedback about how angry the wearer is getting.

Media activities

- Ask students to view five sitcoms, movies or cartoons over a week and record how the characters deal with any angry feelings. Are these ways realistic?
- Give students newspapers and ask them to find articles about people who end up with serious negative outcomes as a result of being emotionally hijacked by anger.

ENGLISH ACTIVITY
Choose your own adventure

Students write stories in which there are two different ways (a positive way and a negative way) in which the central character can deal with his/her angry feelings and two different follow-up endings.

INTERVIEW
Managing anger

Students ask two adults (e.g. parent or adult relatives) to think about a time when they felt very angry but were reasonably satisfied with the way in which they had stayed calm and handled their angry feelings. They can use these questions as a starting point:
- What did you say or do to calm yourself down?
- Did you talk about your angry feelings with anyone?
- Did you tell the person why you felt angry? If so, did you do it at the time, or did you do it later after thinking about the best way to do it?
- What was the main goal you had in mind when you were deciding how to deal with your angry feelings?

Students then write up their interviews and work in groups of four to look for common themes about effective ways to handle angry feelings. Then debrief as a class. What are the most successful and the least successful strategies?

DRAMA ACTIVITIES
Turning things around

Give groups of students the story beginnings and endings below and ask them to add the middle section and then act it all out. Use 'asides' in which the characters describe their feelings and thoughts, as well as the 'freeze frame' strategy (see Chapter 11 of the *Teacher's Handbook*) to allow interaction with the audience. Also consider having an 'anger coach' for each character who works with the actor to prepare and then debrief with the audience afterwards.
- A boy is feeling angry because he was given a hard time by two classmates over a girl he spent some time talking to at lunchtime. The story ends with him giving a cool response (such as 'Haven't you got anything better to do than spend lunchtime watching me?') and calmly walking away.
- A girl is angry because her mother will not let her go to stay at a friend's house for the weekend because the girl's family are expecting visitors for the weekend themselves. The story ends with the girl doing a deal with her mother to go to her friend's house after dinner with the visitors on Saturday night and come back early on Sunday morning.
- A boy is angry because someone has borrowed his basketball without asking. The story ends with him firmly asking the kid not to do it again.
- A girl is angry because two classmates tell her that they don't want to sit with her at lunchtime any more. The story ends with her calmly tackling them later about why they are upset with her.

Was it an accident?

People often get angry when they incorrectly assume that something that happened to them was deliberately done to them. Use drama to identify the verbal and nonverbal behaviours that indicate 'deliberateness' as opposed to 'accidental' or 'without malicious intention' (e.g. when someone knocks your books off your desk; when someone uses your towel or breaks something that belongs to you). Students can look for 'accidental' indicators such as genuine and speedy apologies, offers of assistance, no smirks or sarcasm etc. Again, consider using a coach for each character.

ACTIVITIES
Predictor cards

X See Chapter 10 of the Teacher's Handbook.

Predict which of the following four anger-management strategies will be seen by the respondents as the most effective in this situation: Sarah is very angry because she has found out that a co-worker (Garry) has told a supervisor that Sarah has been regularly coming late to work when in fact she has been late on only one occasion. Sarah should:
- Immediately go and tell Garry calmly why she feels angry.
- Go away and calm down first so that she can work out the best way to deal with the situation.
- Ring her best friend and tell her about what has happened to get a second opinion.
- Tell Garry off and tell him if he does it again she will try to get him sacked.
- Stew over it but say nothing in case she makes things worse.

CLASS DISCUSSION **UNPLEASANT FEELINGS**

This section relates to the negative feelings of boredom, disappointment, jealousy, guilt, shame, rejection, loneliness and embarrassment.
   Read to the class and discuss the picture book *The Visitors Who Came to Stay* (see p. 133), and/or use this 'circuit brainstorm' (see Chapter 10 of the *Teacher's Handbook*):
- Name a situation in which someone of your age might feel very bored.
- Name a situation in which someone of your age might feel disappointed.
- Name a situation in which someone of your age might feel jealous.
- Name a situation in which someone of your age might feel guilty or ashamed.
- Name a situation in which someone of your age might feel rejected or lonely.
- Name a situation in which someone of your age might feel embarrassed.
- Name a situation in which someone of your age might feel disgust.

Discussion questions

- What is . . .? (go through each feeling)
- What does . . . (go through each feeling) look like, sound like and feel like?
- In what situations is someone your age likely to feel . . .? (go through each feeling)
- Is there one best way to manage each of these feelings? (No, it depends a lot on the circumstances, but what you say to yourself about the feeling and the situation [your self-talk] is especially important. It is also important to try to stay calm and not become emotionally hijacked so you can think more clearly.)

- What is meant by 'feeling sorry for yourself'? What does it feel like, 'think' like, look like (expression, body language etc.) and sound like (words, voice tone)? When do people tend to feel sorry for themselves? (when they are personalising something that has happened that they don't like ['poor me'] rather than seeing it as something that happens in life; when they are not being positive; when they are not using problem-solving; when they are not taking charge and being assertive)

Follow-up activities

- Students plan and carry out a survey to see which of the following feelings (in order) people in the class find most unpleasant:
  - Boredom
  - Disappointment
  - Jealousy
  - Rejection
  - Guilt and shame
  - Embarrassment.
- Make a version of the chart in BLM 6.7, 'Managing difficult feelings', with the second column blank, and ask students to complete it. The BLM offers some suggestions.
- Students work with a partner to draw or make a green-eyed monster with thought balloons about envy and jealousy.
- Students participate in the game (below) 'Four leaders'.
- Students work with a partner to draw, enlarge, copy onto card and cut out two large cartoon figures, each with a thought balloon. Cartoon character one should have a facial expression that shows a feeling (e.g. disappointment) and unhelpful words and action ideas in the thought balloon. Cartoon character two has a happier expression, with a thought balloon about good ways to manage that feeling.

ACTIVITY
Four leaders

Choose four students to be leaders. Privately give each leader a card listing one characteristic to look for to include others in the group (e.g. wearing glasses, light hair colour, taller than the leader). Each leader goes to a corner. Students silently walk past each corner and extend their hands, as if to shake. Each leader nods and shakes hands (accepted) or shakes their head and crosses their arms (rejected). When a student is accepted into a group they stand behind the leader. Discuss:

- Did anyone work out what the ridiculous criteria for acceptance in each group were?
- Does everyone get rejected sometimes? (yes)
- How did it feel to be not chosen and have no idea why?
- How did this activity help you to understand how it feels to be left out and not know why?
- Why *do* some people reject others? (on a whim at the time; those rejecting may incorrectly feel superior; they don't understand how it feels to be left out; they are not kind-hearted and friendly people; they enjoy using social influence in a negative way)
- Is it friendlier to accept people even if they are not your preferred associates?
- Sometimes people just want to be with their friends for a while. Is there a kind way to communicate 'we don't want to be with anyone else but our friends right now'?

UNIT 6—EMOTIONS

BOOK
The Visitors Who Came to Stay (Picture book)

Katy and her dad live together in a companionable routine until Dad falls in love with Mary and invites Mary and her son Sean to live with them. Mary doesn't do things in the way that Katy is used to and Sean is a messy practical joker who invades her space. After Katy says she doesn't like the arrangement, Mary and Sean leave. Initially Katy is very pleased, but then she realises that not only is her father happier when Mary is living with them but she actually misses Sean!

CLASS DISCUSSION **AMBIVALENT FEELINGS**

Read to the class the book *Farewell to Old England* (summarised in Unit 3, 'People bouncing back').

Discussion questions

- What feelings were expressed in the words of the song as well as in the pictures? (both positive and negative)
- What does 'ambivalent' mean? (Feeling several conflicting emotions in response to the same situation. For example, if you feel ambivalent about a decision, you may be scared by it in some ways but hopeful about it as well.)
- How can you have both a pleasant and an unpleasant feeling in response to the same situation? (you focus on different aspects; you try to find the positives as well as the negatives; some situations are quite complex)

Follow-up activities

- Use 'Throw the dice' (see Chapter 10 of the *Teacher's Handbook*) with these questions:
  - Someone might feel excited but also a bit scared if/when . . .
  - Someone might feel happy but also a bit nervous if/when . . .
  - Someone might feel pleased but also a bit guilty if/when . . .
  - Someone might feel proud but also a bit disappointed if/when . . .
  - Someone might feel loving but also a bit worried if/when . . .
  - Someone might feel thrilled but also a bit shy if/when . . .
- Prepare a container of positive feelings and another of negative feelings. Students draw a feeling from each container and then write a story where a character feels both of those feelings in response to a situation. You could also use this as a group drama activity.

CLASS DISCUSSION **EMPATHY**

Start by asking students to work with a partner and tell them about what they did or something that happened during the last school holidays, using only non-verbal language (i.e. no words). See if the partner can write down the story as well as the feelings that go with the story. Alternatively or additionally, read to the class and discuss one or both of the picture books *The Pain and the Great One* (see Unit 1, 'Core values') and *Voices in the Park* (see below).

Discussion questions

- What is empathy? (taking the time to work out how somebody else might be feeling and trying to understand; trying to see the other person's way of seeing things)
- Is empathy the same as sympathy? (Empathy is not the same as pity or sympathy. Pity and sympathy are more about feeling sorry for someone, which can devalue the person or make them seem inferior. Empathy is understanding.)
- How could becoming more empathic make you a better person? (you judge other people less; you have better relationships; you can more easily understand and care for people who are less fortunate than you or who need help; you can manage arguments better because you can see both sides; you respect yourself more for taking the time to understand and care; it stops you from being a smug 'know-it-all' whom people won't like; it stops you from harming or bullying others)
- How could you use empathy to help someone 'maintain face' after an embarrassing incident?
- If a bad thing happens to someone, is it because they deserve it somehow? (occasionally they do, but usually they have been less fortunate; challenge any student-thinking that is simply about 'victim blaming')
- Is the world always 'just'? (No. Many students have a 'just world view', whereby they believe that people who have bad things happen to them or who are in distressing circumstances must have brought it upon themselves or deserve it. This simplistic view of the world makes them feel safer because of its neat logic, but often bad things happen to people who do not bring it upon themselves. They are the victims of bad luck, unfortunate timing, disadvantaged circumstances, genetics, or the unfair and cruel behaviour of others. This is a particularly important understanding when peers consider a classmate who is being bullied.)

Follow-up activities

- Students complete and discuss BLM 6.8, 'Try a little understanding'.
- Students work in pairs to find and cut out pictures from magazines that feature two people together and both showing feelings (preferably different ones). Mix the pictures up. Each pair selects a picture from the class collection. One student takes the perspective of one character and the other takes the second one. Then they alternate. This can also be done using newspaper stories. The strategy can also be used with drama.
- Set up dramatic situations that involve a person charged with a crime (e.g. theft, malicious damage, arson) or a civil offence (e.g. defamation, or a violation of an equal opportunity rule). Appoint one person to each of these four roles:
  - Judge
  - Prosecutor (or lawyer for the plaintiff [the complainant])
  - Defendant
  - Lawyer for the defence.

  After the students have prepared and enacted their scene, ask them to swap roles and do it again from the perspective of another role e.g. the prosecutor becomes the defendant etc.

BOOK

Voices in the Park (Picture book)

Four gorilla characters (one father and daughter and one mother and son) go to play in the local park. The book is an intriguing tapestry of several different perceptions of the same situation. Students could write a similar story entitled 'Voices at the School/the Beach/the Footy/a Family Function' etc.

ACTIVITIES
Media activity

Students cut out and bring to school a media article. They attach the article to a sheet of paper and then write about the kinds of feelings that they think the different people in the story might have had. Discuss whether the media should publish photos of people when they are distressed about a tragedy or sad situation. (Consider using the ten 'thinking tracks' here. See BLM 1.3 in Unit 1, 'Core values', page 21.)

How do you know when someone is feeling . . .?

Students use 'Think–Pair–Share' to discuss and make posters about how one can recognise when someone else is feeling a particular way. For example, how do you know when:
- Your friend is feeling sad?
- Your brother or sister is worried about something?
- A classmate is scared?
- A teacher is disappointed?
- A classmate is shy?
- A parent is getting angry with you?

Empathic card matching

Give each group of four a scenario. Allow thinking time, then each student writes on a card or piece of paper three key emotions and one sentence to describe what the person in the scenario might be thinking and feeling. They place their card down in front of them and compare their responses. They then discuss how they could show understanding towards someone in that situation. Here are some scenarios to use:
- A friend breaks up with their girlfriend or boyfriend.
- Someone in your group doesn't have very much money to spend on clothes or CDs compared with the rest of the group.
- A classmate is continually teased and put down in class discussions and the teacher seems to be unable to stop it.
- A classmate's parents separate on the weekend before the school camp.
- A friend who is a very good athlete breaks her leg and can't compete in the inter-school athletics competition.
- A new student arrives in your year at school and they seem shy.
- A classmate has a problem with stuttering.
- Your brother or sister hates public speaking but has to give a class presentation.

What's it like to be . . .?

Students to discuss, act out or write about what it would be like to be in the shoes of a specific person (see below). Ask them to justify their conclusions by asking:
- What makes you think they might feel or behave like that?
- What similar experience or feelings of your own are you drawing on here?
    Specific people you can use include:
- Someone who is living on an Antarctic base for 12 months
- Someone whose pet is run over
- Someone who volunteered to take a friend's dog for a walk and it ran away
- Someone whose father died when they were only six
- Someone who gives up a child for adoption

- Someone who is the child of a famous person (or of a teacher at the same school)
- Someone who can't swim but who goes to a pool party.

Students can brainstorm a class list of other specific situations for ongoing usage with this activity.

DRAMA ACTIVITY
Chair swapping

Two students sit out at the front of the classroom on two chairs. Specify a scenario in which there are two main characters. Then let each tell their story. The students then swap chairs and tell the same story but now from the perspective of the other character.

CLASSROOM ORGANISATION
Community service

Involve students in community service and compassion programs. For example:
- As a class, sponsor a World Vision child.
- Raise money for the homeless (with the message that most homeless people have suffered difficult circumstances or are physically or mentally ill).
- Visit and perform services for the elderly in nearby nursing homes or residential settings (e.g. gardening, singing, story reading).
- Invite students or adults with severe disabilities to visit and develop ongoing connections with your students.

CONSOLIDATION
Working with younger students

- Students can make a class picture dictionary of feelings illustrated with magazine pictures or their own drawings. Each pair is given several different letters to work on.
- Students can work with younger students in singing 'If You're Happy and You Know It'. They can write new verses such as 'If you're angry and you know it, take a walk'.

Feelings spinner

Each group of four makes two six-section spinners (one for positive emotions, one for negative emotions) with six feelings written on them. (See A to Z list of emotions, Chapter 11 of the *Teacher's Handbook* for ideas.) Each student spins one spinner using a pencil through the centre and tells of a time when they had the feeling that the spinner lands on. Repeat the round with the other spinner.

'Throw the dice' 'Inside–outside circles' or 'Musical stop and share'

X See Chapter 10 of the Teacher's Handbook.

- What would be the best way to manage your feelings if you liked someone and you asked a friend to see whether that person liked you and they said 'No, I don't like them'?
- Have you ever seen someone cry (no names rule)? How did you feel?
- What do you think would be one way to handle feeling embarrassed after you have tripped over?

- George Bernard Shaw once said, 'The only way to avoid being miserable is not to have enough leisure to wonder whether you are happy or not.' Do you agree and why?
- What would you think about a boy who, after getting a 'no' answer when he asked a girl out, then emailed her and said, 'You're ugly anyway'?
- Tell about a risk you took even though you felt nervous about it but the risk paid off because something good happened to you.
- What does it feel like when you see someone lose control of their angry feelings? Do you admire them or feel embarrassed for them?
- What happens to people in sporting teams or events who lose control of their angry feelings? Have you ever seen this happen?
- What's likely to happen if you send an email to someone when you're feeling angry with them?
- What do you recommend as a good way to relax when feeling stressed and worried?

English activities

- Make an 'emotions' family word chart i.e. nouns, adverbs and adjectives for each word.
- Students write a 'roller-coaster' story featuring one or more characters experiencing strong positive and negative feelings that they manage well.

Drama/music activities and games

- Make emotions cards using A to Z list of emotions from BLM 11.1 on p. 189 of the *Teacher's Handbook*. Each group then draws out three emotions and then develops a short play or skit that incorporates characters who express the three emotions. Classmates identify how and when each emotion was expressed. Alternatively, use the cards for story writing or feelings charades where different groups take turns at acting out the emotion depicted on cards they have drawn from a container.
- Play feelings statues. Half of the students work with a partner and both act out the same emotion, which they have selected from the card container, and 'freeze' it when they have got it right. The other half go round and work out the feelings.
- Students compose a rap about a specific feeling.
- Play a feelings drawing game. Form two teams. Members of the teams take it in turns to draw the feeling (written on the card) on the board or on a large sheet of paper at the front of the class. Time each team to see how long it takes them to guess their feeling word. You could also give each team a point if they guess the word within two minutes, but then the other team can have one guess after the two minutes are up and get an extra point.

Feelings visual display

Students create a photographic, art or magazine display of feelings.

Management tools

Students work with a partner to make and fill in a chart about using the four tools (see the last key points) to manage a selected uncomfortable feeling in a situation of their choosing. The four tools are:
- Body calming (e.g. relaxing, jogging)
- Helpful thinking (be specific)
- Effective non-damaging communication (e.g. calmly speaking up, listening)
- Strategic problem solving.

Feelings cartoons

Students read and analyse the cartoons in BLM 6.9, 'Emotions cartoons', and write on another sheet what each means and how it relates to managing feelings.

Balloon burst quotes

X See Chapter 11 of the Teacher's Handbook.

- Whatever is done in anger ends in shame. (Theodore Roosevelt)
- Happiness can sneak through a door we didn't know we'd left open. (Barrymore)
- Happiness is when what we think and say is in harmony with what we do. (Gandhi)
- Chinese proverb: If you can stay calm in a moment of anger, you will save yourself hours and days of sorrow.
- Chinese proverb: He who plants a garden plants happiness.
- To be happy you need something to do, something to love, and something to hope for.
- We enjoy warmth because we have been cold. We can only experience joy because we have also known sadness.
- Anyone can become angry. That is easy. But to be angry with the right person, to the right degree, at the right time, for the right purpose and in the right way—that is not easy. (Aristotle)
- If the only tool you have is a hammer, you tend to treat everything as if it were a nail.
- Happiness is a by-product of what you do, not a goal in itself. (Eleanor Roosevelt)
- Happiness is the sum of many small satisfactions.

TEAM coaching

X See Chapter 10 of the Teacher's Handbook.

Students use this strategy to learn the spelling, the meaning, the synonyms and antonyms of feelings words. (see BLM 11.1 on p. 189 of the *Teacher's Handbook*)

Quick quotes

X See Chapter 11 of the Teacher's Handbook.

'I felt (name emotion) when . . .'

Cross-offs

Have students complete BLM 6.10, 'Cross-offs'. The answer is: All feelings are useful to us, even the uncomfortable ones, but they need to be managed.

RESOURCES

Books

Aliki, 1991, *Feelings*, HarperCollins, London.
Judy Blume, 1985, *The Pain and the Great One*, Heinemann, London.
Anthony Browne, 1999, *Voices in the Park*, Picture Corgi Books, London.
Joy Cowley & Chris Mousdale, 2001, *Brodie*, Scholastic, Auckland, NZ.
Tomie DePaola, 1998, *Nana Upstairs and Nana Downstairs*, Scholastic Australia, Sydney.
Mike Dumbleton & Terry Denton, 2001, *Passing On*, Random House, Sydney.
Nan Gregory & Ron Lightburn, 1995, *How Smudge Came*, Red Deer College Press, Canada.
Ralph Helfer, 1997, *Modoc: The Story of the Greatest Elephant That Ever Lived*, HarperCollins, Sydney.
Annalena McAfee, 1984, *The Visitors Who Came to Stay*, Walker Books, London.
Fergus McKinnon & Kim Gamble, 2002, *A Bee In Ben's Bonnet*, Random House, Milsons Point, NSW.
Marcus Pfister, 2000, *The Happy Hedgehog*, North-South Books, London.
Dr Seuss, 1973, *My Many Coloured Days*, Red Fox, New York.
Shaun Tan, 2001, *The Red Tree*, Lothian, Melbourne.
Taro Yashima, 1976, *Crow Boy*, Penguin, Ringwood, Victoria.

HOW FEELINGS CAN ENERGISE YOU

BLM 6.1

Feelings	What the feeling might 'move' you to do that is useful and could make things better	What the feeling might 'move' you to do that is NOT useful and may cause problems for you or others if not managed
Guilt		
Anger		
Love		
Sadness		
Jealousy		
Pride		
Worry		
Fear		
Nervousness		
Boredom		
Loneliness		
Shame		
Embarrassment		
Sympathy		

© Helen McGrath and Toni Noble, 2003. This page from Bounce Back!® may be photocopied for classroom use.

FEELINGS QUIZ

BLM 6.2

Tick one box for each emotion.

In which situation would you feel more nervous:
- ☐ giving a speech at assembly *or*
- ☐ going scuba diving?

In which situation would you feel more excited:
- ☐ meeting your favourite singer *or*
- ☐ winning a two-week trip to Disneyland?

In which situation would you feel more disappointed:
- ☐ not receiving the present you hoped for at Christmas *or*
- ☐ having to cancel your birthday party because your father was sick?

In which situation would you feel more sad:
- ☐ your pet dying *or*
- ☐ having to move house and not see your friends as much?

In which situation would you feel more lonely:
- ☐ not being invited to a party that most people were going to *or*
- ☐ not knowing anyone at a party that you are invited to except the person having a birthday?

In which situation would you feel more jealous:
- ☐ your boyfriend or girlfriend dancing with someone else *or*
- ☐ your friend winning an award in a competition that you had both entered?

In which situation would you feel more ashamed:
- ☐ badmouthing a friend behind their back *or*
- ☐ shoplifting?

© Helen McGrath and Toni Noble, 2003. This page from Bounce Back!® may be photocopied for classroom use.

HOW WELL DO YOU DEAL WITH NERVOUSNESS?

BLM 6.3

1. If you were worried just before a test, even though you had worked hard for it, how easy would it be for you to calm yourself down a bit?

   Very difficult   Somewhat difficult   Very easy

   What is one helpful thing you would advise someone else to say to themselves or do in this situation?

   _____

2. If you were feeling nervous when you were about to ring someone up and ask them to go to a movie with you, how easy would it be for you to calm yourself down a bit so that you could make the call and handle it reasonably well?

   Very difficult   Somewhat difficult   Very easy

   What is one helpful thing you would advise someone else to say to themselves or do in this situation?

   _____

3. If you were worried about whether you looked 'cool' enough just before you were about to leave for a party, how easy would it be for you to calm yourself down a bit and feel relaxed enough to look forward to the party?

   Very difficult   Somewhat difficult   Very easy

   What is one helpful thing you would advise someone else to say to themselves or do in this situation?

© Helen McGrath and Toni Noble, 2003. This page from Bounce Back!® may be photocopied for classroom use.

IN WHAT SITUATIONS DO PEOPLE OFTEN FEEL ANGRY?

BLM 6.4

Key feature	Description	Given an example of a time when this has happened to you	What is one thing a person could do, think or say to stay in control in this situation?
Hurt	When someone hurts your body or feelings		
Interference	When someone interferes with what you are doing		
Opposition and coercion	When someone tells you that you can't do something, or makes you do what you don't want to do		
Goal blockage	When someone does something that gets in the way of what you want to do		
Loss of face	When someone has humiliated you or you have embarrassed yourself		
Lack of respect and concern	When someone treats you rudely or as if you are unimportant		
Injustice	When you don't get a fair deal or are falsely accused		
Powerlessness	When you feel like you have no say in decisions that affect you		

© Helen McGrath and Toni Noble, 2003. This page from Bounce Back!® may be photocopied for classroom use.

WHAT DO YOU DO WHEN YOU'RE ANGRY?

BLM 6.5

How often do you use each of these strategies to deal with your angry feelings? Sum up the totals and write a conclusion about what you already do quite well and what you need to change.

Lose control   Often   Sometimes   Not much

- I scream abuse at anyone nearby even if it is not them I feel angry with. ☐ ☐ ☐
- I yell at the person I feel angry with and say nasty things to them. ☐ ☐ ☐
- I throw or kick things nearby. ☐ ☐ ☐
- I try to damage the thing I am using that has frustrated me. ☐ ☐ ☐
- I hit or hurt the person I feel angry towards. ☐ ☐ ☐
- I start a fight with whomever I next see, even if they had nothing to do with my angry feelings. ☐ ☐ ☐

Write down anything else you do in the category of 'Losing control'.

Cool down   Often   Sometimes   Not much

- I breathe slowly and deeply till I feel more in control. ☐ ☐ ☐
- I count backwards from 100 by 3s till I can think straight. ☐ ☐ ☐
- I walk away from the angry situation so I can work things out and deal with it later. ☐ ☐ ☐
- I go for a swim, a walk or a run or ride my bike or skateboard. ☐ ☐ ☐
- I kick a football or throw a basketball. ☐ ☐ ☐
- I cuddle or play with my pet or a stuffed toy. ☐ ☐ ☐
- I listen to music.
- I keep myself busy with a task that doesn't involve feelings.
- I spend some time by myself so that I can think.

Write down anything else that you do in the category of 'Cooling down'.

Get a reality check   Often   Sometimes   Not much

- I talk to someone I trust about my angry feelings and get a 'reality check' about how I am seeing things. ☐ ☐ ☐
- I think about whether or not the person I am angry with has behaved like this before. ☐ ☐ ☐
- I think about what really happened to make sure I have double-checked my facts and got them right. ☐ ☐ ☐
- I try to think calmly about whether any of it was my fault. ☐ ☐ ☐

Write down anything else that you do in the category of 'Getting a reality check'.

Get strategic   Often   Sometimes   Not much

- If I am angry about something small, I tell myself to let it go and not sweat the small stuff. ☐ ☐ ☐
- I remind myself that relationships are an important priority.
- I think carefully about the best way to deal with my angry feelings. ☐ ☐ ☐
- I tell the person I am angry with why I feel that way but not in a nasty way or in a loud voice. ☐ ☐ ☐
- I try to solve the problem if there is one as part of why I feel angry. ☐ ☐ ☐

Write down anything else that you do in the category of 'Getting strategic'.

© Helen McGrath and Toni Noble, 2003. This page from Bounce Back!® may be photocopied for classroom use.

ANGER CAN BE DYNAMITE!

BLM 6.6

Think of a time when you were angry and write it at the bottom of the sheet. Write what triggered your anger (trigger), what you said to yourself which exaggerated it (exaggerator) and what you could have done to stop yourself from blowing things sky-high (extinguisher).

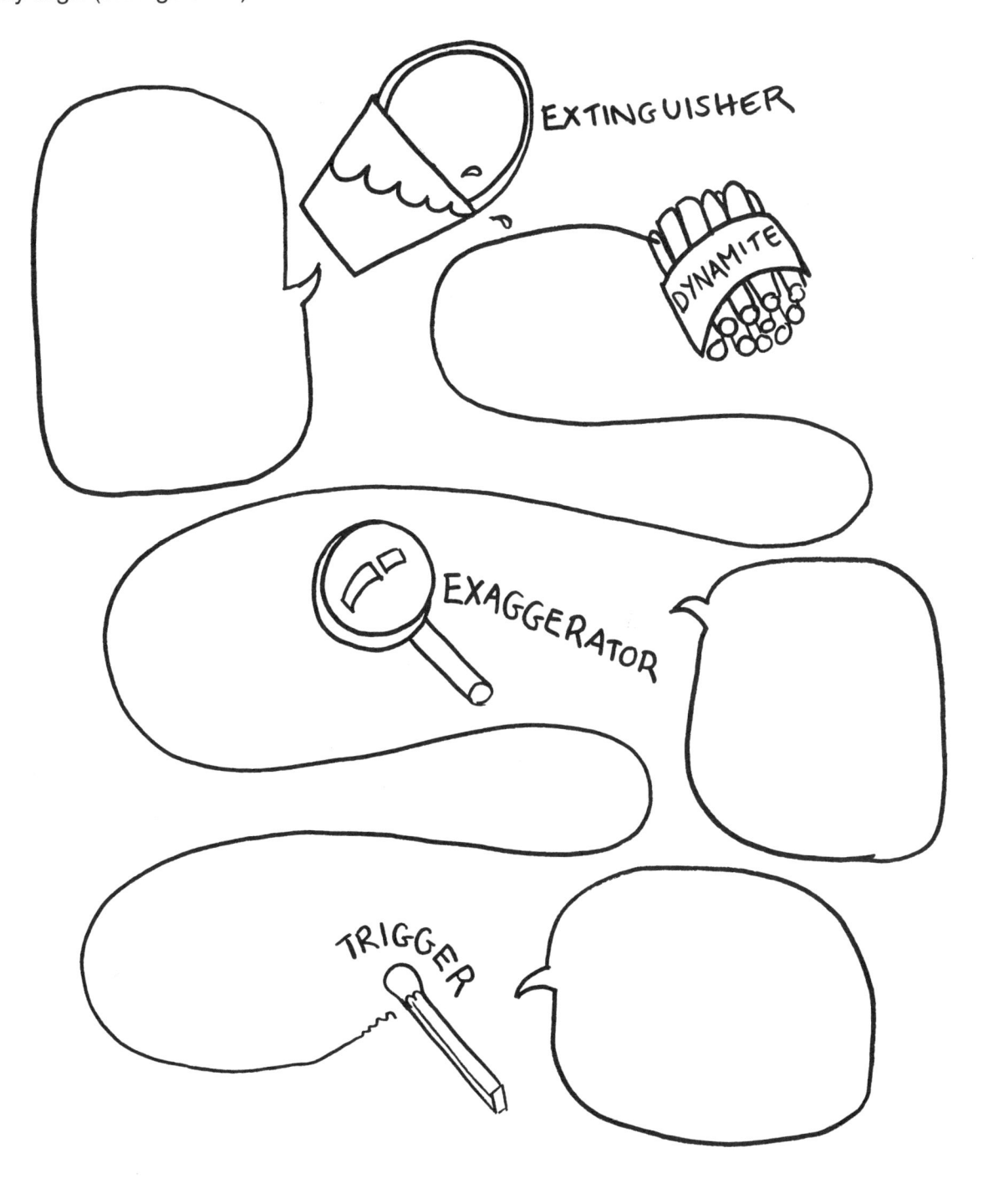

© Helen McGrath and Toni Noble, 2003. This page from Bounce Back!® may be photocopied for classroom use.

MANAGING DIFFICULT FEELINGS

BLM 6.7

Feeling	Good ways to manage the feeling
Disappointment: feeling down because your expectations have not been met and something you have wanted and been hoping for or looking forward to does not happen	Keep your mind on some of the positives in your life. Try to solve the problem if you can work out what has stopped you from getting what you expected. Try harder to see if you can make it happen. Keep busy and don't think too much about it. Change your expectations to make them more realistic. Accept that it won't happen and remind yourself that it is not a big deal and you will have other things to look forward to.
Boredom: feeling like there is nothing to keep your brain stimulated and there is no fun	Problem solve: what can you do that's constructive and won't get you into trouble? If you are 'trapped' and can't go anywhere, find a way to use your thoughts to keep your brain busy. Look around for people to spend time with in a non-harmful way. Make and keep a list of active things to do at home, such as board games, ball games etc. Use the time to get ahead in work that you have to do.
Guilt and shame: feeling bad and uncomfortable because you believe you have done something wrong, behaved badly or broken one of your own moral rules	Ask: 'What can I learn from the mistake I have made?' or 'How can I make amends?' Remember that feelings of guilt and shame can tell you about your values. Think about what they are. Remind yourself to behave in a better way next time.
Jealousy and envy: feeling upset because someone has something that you would like to have, or because someone important to you likes someone else and treats them as special, not just you	See the positive side of *not* having what you would like to have. Highlight your own positives and successes. Remind yourself that everyone feels jealous sometimes because no one is perfect. Stay calm and try to solve the problem of getting what you want in a moral way.
Embarrassment: feeling upset because you think others will think badly of you and not respect you because you have done something silly or looked like a fool	Remind yourself that others will probably forget pretty quickly. Try to see any funny side of it. Remind yourself that everyone gets embarrassed sometimes, not just you. Pretend that it never happened and don't keep thinking about it. Keep saying to yourself 'What is done is done. Don't dwell on it.'
Loneliness and rejection: feeling down because you don't have company or because others don't want to be with you	Remind yourself that everyone feels lonely occasionally. Remind yourself that most people get rejected sometimes. It may be that the other people who have rejected you are mean or not very nice people. Look for new people to get to know and don't be overly fussy. There are many nice people around but you may not have noticed them. Be proactive and organise ways to meet people. Take the risk of trying to get to know someone.

© Helen McGrath and Toni Noble, 2003. This page from Bounce Back!® may be photocopied for classroom use.

TRY A LITTLE UNDERSTANDING

BLM 6.8

What is empathy?

The word 'empathy' means trying to understand how someone else is feeling. If you can work out how they might be feeling, you can more easily show kindness and support and work out their intentions towards you.

Here are some things you can do that could help you to understand what it feels like to be in someone else's shoes:

- **You could try to remember your own similar experiences and feelings.**
  'What has happened to me where I have felt like they seem to be feeling?'
  Can I remember how I felt and what I thought at the time?'
- **Remember other people's experiences.**
  What have others close to me told me about how *they* felt in similar circumstances? (For example, if someone else seems to be shy, can I remember what another has told me about feeling shy?)
- **Remember what you have seen or read.**
  What have I read or seen on television or in the movies which tells me something about how this person might be feeling or thinking? (Be a bit careful here! Lots of television shows and movies give you the wrong ideas about people's feelings, because they make things seem too simple.)
- **Use your imagination.**
  If I haven't had a similar experience myself, can I use my imagination and try to predict how I would feel in the situation (e.g. If that was me, I think I would be thinking . . . and feeling . . .).

What can you say to someone who is feeling upset?

- The best thing to say is a simple statement of your understanding (e.g. 'That must have been so sad').
- Sometimes it can be helpful to share with them a similar experience (e.g. 'That happened to me when I started at my last school').
- Sometimes you could say what you imagine you would be feeling in their situation (e.g. 'I think I'd feel pretty angry too if that had happened to me').

© Helen McGrath and Toni Noble, 2003. This page from Bounce Back!® may be photocopied for classroom use.

EMOTIONS CARTOONS

BLM 6.9

On a separate page, write down how each cartoon makes a point about good or bad ways to manage feelings. Remember to name each feeling too.

1.
   - WE STUDIED FEELINGS IN CLASS TODAY.
   - WE FOUND OUT THAT TOO MUCH WORRY CAN BE BAD FOR YOUR HEALTH.
   - SO ENGLISH HAS TO GO.

2.
   - NICK I'M MAD AT YOU!
   - HUH, WHY?
   - BECAUSE OF YOU MY SOCCER BALL IS BUSTED!
   - I DIDN'T BUST YOUR SOCCER BALL.
   - I KNOW YOU DIDN'T, I DID!
   - SO HOW'S THAT MY FAULT?
   - CAUSE I WAS MAD AT YOU AND YOU WEREN'T THERE, SO I HAD TO TAKE IT OUT ON SOMETHING!
   - SORRY ... I THINK?

3.
   - TODAY I'M GOING TO ACTUALLY TALK TO JESS.
   - I HAD FOOTY TRAINING THEN WENT TO THE MOVIES AND THEN MUM SAID I WAS TOO LATE HOME AND THEN I....

4.
   - EAGLES 20 / HAWKS 20
   - I FEEL SICK.

5.
   - I'VE HAD ABOUT ENOUGH OF YOU, GO AND COOL OFF.
   - BOY, OF ALL THE THINGS I COULD HAVE DONE, KICKING THE CAT LITTER SHOULD HAVE BEEN LAST ON THE LIST.

© Helen McGrath and Toni Noble, 2003. This page from Bounce Back!® may be photocopied for classroom use.

CROSS-OFFS

BLM 6.10

mountains	All	parsnip	seconds	feelings	carrot	are
useful	furious	gymnastics	goggles	spinach	to	sour
elbow pad	us	hours	deserts	Holden	gnome	stomach
sheep	brain	sweet	Mercedes	heart	even	mouthguard
psychology	octopus	the	cross	knit	Saab	basketball
diving	uncomfortable	Ford	octagon	octet	ones	volcanoes
helmet	but	knowledge	spicy	they	potato	rabbit
need	annoyed	camel	liver	archery	minutes	to
gnu	be	days	oceans	kangaroo	managed	bitter

To find the message, cross off these words:

- 4 words that are body organs
- 4 words that are Olympic events
- 3 words that relate to the number 8
- 4 words that are geographical features
- 4 words that are measurements of time
- 4 words that are vegetables
- 4 words that are tastes
- 3 words that mean angry
- 4 words that are protective sports equipment or clothing
- 5 words that have silent first letters
- 4 words that are animals
- 4 words that are car brands

The secret message is _____

© Helen McGrath and Toni Noble, 2003. This page from Bounce Back!® may be photocopied for classroom use.

UNIT 7
RELATIONSHIPS

KEY POINTS

Having good relationships makes you feel happier and more confident.
If you can get along reasonably well with others, you feel a sense of belonging and satisfaction. Friends support each other and enjoy being together.

It isn't always easy to get along well with others and make friends.
'Social skills' is the term we use to describe behaviours that lead to good relationships. Nobody is born with good social skills. You have to learn and practise them. One of the most important skills relating to good relationships is thinking about the other person's rights and feelings, not just your own.

Most people have lonely times in their life when they are without close friends.
Everyone has periods in their life when they feel they aren't doing as well as they would like to in regards to friendships. Using good social skills and taking the risk of letting others get to know you helps you build better friendships.

Some social skills are especially important.
The most important social skills for getting along well with other people are: being positive, being a good listener, finding things in common, being a good winner and a good loser, being interesting, cooperating, negotiating, and being flexible. Other important social skills are being loyal, sharing information about yourself, and being understanding, and supportive.

Managing conflict well is an especially important relationship skill.
Conflict simply means disagreement. Conflict happens when people have different ideas, when they want different things, or both want the same thing, or when they feel that someone has done something unfair to them. Handling disagreements well is an important skill both for being a good friend and for getting along with others. The secret to handling conflict well is to keep quiet until you have made a plan to deal with it, and then think hard to find a solution that is fair, takes into account both points of view, and doesn't harm the relationship.

You can't deal well with conflict until you keep angry feelings under control.
People make a mess of trying to solve arguments and disagreements because they get angry and then find it very hard to control what they say and do. If you don't find a way to 'cool off', you can't remember good ways to deal with the conflict, and then you forget about finding a good way that lets you stay friends.

Keep your eye on the goal of 'good relationships'.
Sometimes you will be tempted to choose goals which are *not* about good relationships, e.g. getting revenge, winning at all costs, making someone feel guilty, or being by yourself because it feels safer. When you are tempted by these goals, remind yourself that the most important goal is usually the one of having a good relationship with the other person. This doesn't mean, however, that you should be prepared to do anything, no matter what, to be accepted. Also remember the need for self respect and ethical choices.

Learning to get along well with others now will help you to have a good romantic partnership later on.
The best way to have a good romantic partnership is to learn the skills for having good relationships with your classmates and friends now.

Good leadership skills are like good relationship skills.
Good leaders use many social skills, such as being positive, listening well, mediating, being flexible, respecting others and being supportive.

UNIT 7—RELATIONSHIPS

Class discussion—Getting along with others 152

Class discussion—Listening and conversation skills 152
- ACTIVITIES
- Practising listening and conversation skills 153

Class discussion—Popularity 154
- BOOK
- *Too Much to Ask For* 154

Class discussion—Shyness and feeling self-conscious 154
- ARTS ACTIVITY
- 'Terri/Terry terrified' 155

Class discussion—Friendship 155
- POEM
- *What Is a Friend?* 157
- BOOKS
- *Willy and Hugh* 157
- *Swashbuckler* 157
- MUSIC AND MEDIA ACTIVITY
- Friendship theme 157
- ACTIVITIES
- Making a book for younger students 157
- 'Musical stop and share' or 'Inside–outside circles' 157
- 'Throw the dice' 158
- Four corners 158
- ENGLISH ACTIVITY
- How to lose all your friends 158
- ENGLISH/ARTS ACTIVITY
- Metaphors for friendship 158

Class discussion—Friendship problems 159
- BOOK
- *Fox* 159
- STORY
- 'The Bear and the Two Travellers' 160
- ACTIVITY
- Think–Pair–Share 160

Class discussion—Managing disagreements 160
- DRAMA ACTIVITIES
- Dealing with conflicts 161
- BOOK
- *Voices in the Park* 162
- ACTIVITY
- Working with younger students 162
- TECHNOLOGY AND MATHS ACTIVITY
- The 'healthy conflict management' pyramid 162
- ARTS ACTIVITY
- Creating a poster about good apologising 162
- ENGLISH ACTIVITY
- Choose your own adventure 163
- CLASSROOM ORGANISATION
- Classroom meetings 163
- ACTIVITIES
- Choosing a group car 163
- Cooperative controversy 164
- Conflict research 164

Class discussion—Leadership and love! 164
- CLASSROOM ORGANISATION
- Leaders 165

Consolidation 165
- Balloon burst quotes 165
- Quick quotes 166
- Before or after? 166
- Cross-offs 166

Resources 166

BLM 7.1—The people skills quiz! 167

BLM 7.2—Getting along well with others 168

BLM 7.3—What turns people off? 169

BLM 7.4—What should they do? 170

BLM 7.5—What are the characteristics of a good friend? 171

BLM 7.6—Friendship similarities and differences 172

BLM 7.7—A quiz about friendship 173

BLM 7.8—Seven ways to deal with conflict? 175

BLM 7.9—BE CAREFUL! 176

BLM 7.10—What conflict strategy is this? 177

BLM 7.11—What's gone wrong here? 178

BLM 7.12—What's the best way? 179

BLM 7.13—How good a leader could you be? 180

BLM 7.14—Cross-offs 182

BOUNCE BACK!

CLASS DISCUSSION: GETTING ALONG WITH OTHERS

Give students a copy of the poem 'Wayne' from Judith Viorst's anthology *Sad Underwear*. Discuss the behaviours displayed by Wayne and ask students to help you compile a board list of behaviours that help/don't help in getting along with others. Follow up by asking students to write a verse to be added to the poem.

Discussion questions

- What are some of the skills of getting along well with other people (i.e. social skills or people skills)?
- Do these skills differ according to the age of the people and their relationship to you?
- Do we use fewer good people skills with our brothers and sisters? Why?
- What does it mean to have a 'good personality'? What does a person with a 'good personality' do? (it usually means that they have good skills for getting along with others, they manage their feelings well and they are positive, confident and fun)
- Can you teach someone to have a good personality? (yes)

Follow-up activities

- Students work with a partner to write their five most important pieces of advice to younger students about good ways to get along well with their classmates at school. They can use this as the basis of an activity with the younger children.
- Students complete BLM 7.1, 'The people skills quiz', and then use BLM 7.2, 'Getting along well with others', as the basis of follow-up drama. Students can create a skit around one or two skills (drawn from a container). Use a 'coach' for each character, who helps preparation and then explains or debriefs at the end. BLM 7.2 provides information about the skills assessed in the quiz.
- Use the cards in BLM 7.3, 'What turns people off?', and ask students to work in a group and rank the items. Use the cards for a follow-up drama activity in which students draw out a card and use that behaviour in a social setting.
- Ask students to write, act or put together an advertising campaign (all 'tongue-in-cheek') on 'how to turn people off'.
- Students work with a partner to draw 4-frame stick-figure cartoon stories using some of the skills (or their opposite) from BLM 7.2. They can use thought bubbles and dialogue balloons.

CLASS DISCUSSION: LISTENING AND CONVERSATION SKILLS

Start with a game of 'Chinese whispers'. Pass one of the balloon burst quotes on page 165.

Discussion questions

- What is meant when we say that someone is a good listener and conversationalist? (This skill involves:
  - Saying something to start the conversation
  - Paying attention
  - Talking about things that are based on what you know about the other person or what you know you have in common

- Taking turns to speak, doing your share, but not hogging the conversation
- Saying some things about yourself but also asking some questions of the other person
- Being a good listener, that is, giving a simple summary back of what you heard someone say, using a questioning tone and leaving out unnecessary detail (e.g. 'Oh, I see, your brother is actually your half-brother?')
- Making positive comments
- Leaving out unnecessary details
- Getting to the point quickly and not rambling or forgetting why you started to say it in the first place
- Using humour where appropriate to do so
- Checking every now and then to see if they have lost interest and then, if they have, changing the topic or asking them a question.

Follow-up activities

- Use some of the listening and conversation activities below.
- Students could write a brief story using dialogue that demonstrates good listening. In brackets, they can put self-talk. Alternatively, they could draw a (stick figure) cartoon story with thought balloons and dialogue balloons coloured in different colours.

ACTIVITIES
Practising listening and conversation skills

- Catalogue listening: you will need to have one copy of the same shop's advertising catalogue for each person in a group of three. Give each group several questions written on separate cards and placed in a pile, face down. Students take it in turns to pick a question card, look at their catalogue and then answer the question. One other person in the group then gives a simple summary of what they said, leaving out unnecessary detail. Here are some questions:
  - If you had ($200) to spend, which two things would you like to buy and why?
  - Which product looks good and how does the catalogue make it look good?
  - Which product would you buy if you had only ($10) to spend and why?
  - Which product would you *not* like to be given as a present and why?
- Students use the 'partner retell' strategy (see Chapter 10 of the *Teacher's Handbook*) using one or more of the questions below:
  - What was your best ever holiday?
  - What is your favourite rock band/movie/TV show/sport and why?
  - Tell about a time when you had to help someone.
  - Tell about something it took you a while to learn to do when you were little.
  - What takes too long?
  - What sound do you never want to hear again?
  - What is too complicated and you wish it was simpler?
  - What makes you really tired?
  - What do you wish there was more time for?
- Students form groups of three and discuss (for five minutes) their personal perceptions and experiences related to a given topic (e.g. 'holidays', 'pets', 'music'), and identify as many things as they can that they have in common. One person is the 'coach' who counts how often each person gives a 'simple summary' when they listen.
- There and back: this can be carried out on the oval or in a park. Review the steps before each 'trip'. Pair students up with someone they don't know very well. Give them a topic such as 'my perfect meal'. Nominate a finishing line. On the way to the finishing line

only one person talks and the other listens and gives a simple summary (without detail). On the way back, they reverse roles. Review the skill before they start.
- Conversations with another class: liaise with the teacher of another class in the same school or in another school, and select a topic for discussion. Each student is paired with a student from the other class and they have a ten-minute conversation on the selected topic. Before they start, renew the skill of listening and conversing. When they return, students complete a brief written reflection on how well they used the skill and recommendations for improvement.

CLASS DISCUSSION POPULARITY

Use the 'bundling' strategy (see Chapter 10 of the *Teacher's Handbook*) and ask students to write down five statements about school popularity. Alternatively, ask students to each write down one question they would like to ask anonymously about being popular. Read to the class and discuss the book *Too Much to Ask For* (see below).

Discussion questions

- Why do people want to be in some friendship groups more than others?
- Are there two types of popular people, that is:
  – Those that are positive and kind and can influence others in a good way
  – Those that are mean and like to control others and leave people out?
- How does each type influence other students?
- Should 'popular' people be encouraged to use their social influence responsibly rather than hurtfully? How could this be achieved?
- Do popular students automatically become popular adults or do the 'rules' change? (the rules change, but some popular people adapt and others fade)
- What does it mean to be 'cool'? How important is it to be 'cool'? Is it okay to choose not to try to be 'cool'?

BOOK
Too Much to Ask For (Chapter book)

Hannah desperately wants to be part of the 'cool' group in her Year 5 class. The price she ends up paying for her 'big chance' is very high. It costs her a longstanding friend, Izzy, and she is very disillusioned to discover that most (but not all) of the 'cool' girls are not very nice people.

CLASS DISCUSSION SHYNESS AND FEELING SELF-CONSCIOUS

Discussion questions

- What is shyness? What is self-consciousness? What do they sound like, look like, think like and feel like? (e.g. blushing, avoiding eye contact, worrying about embarrassing yourself or not being approved of; fearing rejection; expecting a bad outcome in a social setting; self-blaming)

- Does everyone feel shy at times? (Yes. Ask for personal examples of where and what it felt like.)
- Why do some people feel more anxious in social situations than others? (many people inherit this tendency genetically; some people lack social experience; some people use negative self-talk and this reduces their confidence e.g. 'They won't like me')
- What can people do when they feel shy to help them cope better? (Don't 'catastrophise' [see Unit 3] about bad outcomes in social situations; don't exaggerate what would happen if you did embarrass yourself or get rejected—it wouldn't be the end of the world; remind yourself that everyone feels embarrassed sometimes; practise using good social skills in smaller, safer social situations; use positive self-talk and remind yourself that you *can* do it)
- What does rejection feel like? (Stress that it happens to everyone and is a normal part of life. Stress the rational view that nobody is liked by everyone that they wish would like them. Discuss how hard it can be to reach out to somebody in friendship if you become too scared of being rejected.)
- What is the best way to handle your feelings of hurt, loneliness and sadness if someone who was your friend decides not to be your friend any more? (Use positive and helpful self-talk, such as 'So what! There'll be another one along soon. I'll try somewhere else'. Remind yourself that everyone gets rejected sometimes and that many friendships do not last. It's not necessarily a criticism of *you*.)

ARTS ACTIVITY
'Terry/Terri Terrified'

Students draw stories about a cartoon character ('Terry/Terri Terrified') with thought balloons who misses out on friendship until he/she realises that fear of rejection is stopping him/her from getting the friendship he/she really wants. This could also be a drama activity or puppet activity for younger students (see Chapter 11 of the *Teacher's Handbook* for puppet ideas.)

CLASS DISCUSSION — FRIENDSHIP

Introductory activities could include:
- Use the 'bundling' strategy (see Chapter 10 of the *Teacher's Handbook*) and ask students to write the three most important things to look for in a friend.
- Students complete BLM 7.4, 'What should they do?', and compare their answers with a partner's. Then debrief as a class: numbered answers must be written on a separate sheet.
- Make an overhead transparency of the poem 'What Is a Friend?' (see below) and discuss it.
- Read to the class and discuss *Willy and Hugh* (a simple picture book with some humorous sophistication) or *Swashbuckler* (see below).
- Using a compass, students draw three large concentric circles. In the inner circle they write the name of their best friend (someone you spend a lot of time with, just the two of you, and you know many private and personal things about each other). In the second circle they write the names of close friends (close friends might know quite a lot about each other and spend a bit of time together, but there are often other people around as well and you don't share as much of yourself as you do with a best friend). In the third circle they write the name of social friends (people you might hang around with a bit; sometimes they are in the same class or sports team as you, so you occasionally do things

with them, but you don't know them really well and you don't share a lot about yourselves with each other).

Discussion questions

- What is a friend?
- Why do we like having friends?
- What is a best friend? A close friend? A social friend? (see above)
- Everyone needs to express and receive signs of caring from the people in their life who matter to them. Do boys and girls have different kinds of friendships and show affection to their friends differently? Discuss the strengths of each gender's way of being friends and what changes would be advantageous for both genders to make.
- What are some of the skills needed to be a good friend? Some are mentioned in BLM 7.5, 'What are the characteristics of a good friend?'. The results of research give further clues (see below). Others are:
  - Using charitable interpretations, that is, positive and kind ways of looking at a friend's imperfections and annoying behaviours (e.g. 'Yes, she did say a mean thing to me yesterday, but she had been very upset over her cat being run over').
  - Being reasonably forgiving, that is, accepting that a friend may sometimes let you down.
  - Accepting friends as people who are not perfect. A good friend likes you for who you are, not who you could be if you tried harder.

Characteristics of a good friend

Research studies confirm that most people rank the top six characteristics (in order) as follows:
- Doesn't tell others what I have told them in private
- Is loyal
- Shows warmth and affection towards me
- Is supportive and caring when I need it
- Is honest and says what they think
- Has a sense of humour.

Follow-up activities

- Students write several versions of the sentence 'You know someone is your friend when she/he . . .'
- Students could:
  - Describe and label a tongue-in-cheek cartoon drawing of 'the perfect friend'
  - Make a list of music they and a friend both like
  - Complete BLM 7.6, 'Friendship similarities and differences' and, with a partner, or as a whole class, discuss whether friends can be different and still be friends.
- Students make up and complete a fact sheet about a friend and then check for accuracy. For example:
  - Liked/hated foods/music/sports/TV shows
  - Names and ages of brothers/sisters/pets
  - Birthday/last holiday/career aspirations/best and worst skills.
- Use the 'Musical stop and share' or 'Inside–outside' strategy (see Chapter 10 of the *Teacher's Handbook*) with BLM 7.4, 'What should they do?' Give each student a copy.
- Students complete BLM 7.7, 'A quiz about friendship', either individually or with a partner.

UNIT 7—RELATIONSHIPS

POEM
What Is a Friend?

A friend is one
to whom one may pour
out all the contents
of one's heart
chaff and grain together
knowing that the
gentlest of hands
will take and sift it
keep what is worth keeping
and with a breath of kindness
blow the rest away.
(Arabian proverb)

BOOKS
Willy and Hugh (Picture book)

Willy is walking through the park one day when he literally bumps into Hugh Jape (a 'huge ape'). Willy expects this giant gorilla to be nasty about the accident, but Hugh apologises and takes the full blame. Willy and Hugh become friends, sharing fun times together and standing up for each other in different ways.

Swashbuckler (Simple chapter book)

Peter, a new boy at Park Ridge school, is thankful to be rescued from the school bullies by Anton the Swashbuckler. The two boys then find a common interest and become firm friends. They find that they both have difficulties with their fathers, and help each other to deal with the challenges. Peter's father has gambled all his family's money, while Anton's father is dying of cancer.

MUSIC AND MEDIA ACTIVITY
Friendship theme

Students compile a reviewed list of recommended films, television shows, artworks, songs, poems and books that have a strong friendship theme. What 'rules' can be identified about being a good friend from these? Are they realistic?

ACTIVITIES
Making a book for younger students

Students prepare a book for younger students. It can either give direct advice about making and keeping friends or indirectly offer advice through a story about friendship, using the younger student as a character. They will need to interview the younger student first and try to incorporate their strengths.

'Musical stop and share' or 'Inside–outside circles'

X See Chapter 10 of the Teacher's Handbook.

- How do people make up with a friend after a fight?
- Why do friendships sometimes break up?

- Can a person still be your friend if they move a long way away from you?
- How many friends can a person have?
- Should you tell a friend something they need to be told but which might hurt them?
- What should you do if your friend is doing things that might be bad for them?
- How do you say 'no' to a friend?
- Do friends always agree on everything?
- How do most people feel if a friend breaks a promise that they made?
- Why do friends get upset if you don't return a favour?

'Throw the dice'

X See Chapter 10 of the Teacher's Handbook.

What would you say and do in the following situations?
- Your friend is unusually quiet but insists that there is nothing wrong.
- Your friend's dog is killed by a truck.
- Your friend's parents split up.
- Your friend's father loses his job.
- Your friend gets into trouble at school and is not allowed to go to anyone's place for a while.
- You notice that your friend has a mark on their T-shirt that might embarrass them.
- Your friend begins to give another student a hard time and call them nasty names, even though they have done nothing wrong.
- You heard your friend telling a small lie.

Four corners

X See Chapter 10 of the Teacher's Handbook.

Use the corners about who the students' first close friend was:
- A neighbour
- A relative
- At preschool or school
- A friend of the family.

They discuss one early memory of that friendship in their corners with one or two other people.

ENGLISH ACTIVITY
How to lose all your friends

Students write a story (and poster) in a group of three about a person who goes through a day doing and saying all the things that make sure they 'lose' all their friends.

ENGLISH/ARTS ACTIVITY
Metaphors for friendship

Ask students to write or draw their metaphor for friendship. An unfinished sentence such as 'A friend is like . . .' will be a helpful start. Give them these examples to get them started.
- Friendship cheers like a sunbeam, charms like a good story, inspires like a brave leader, binds like a golden chain, guides like a heavenly vision. (Newell D Hillis)
- May the hinges of our friendship never rust. (Traditional)
- Friendship is a sheltering tree. (Samuel Taylor Coleridge)

UNIT 7—RELATIONSHIPS

CLASS DISCUSSION **FRIENDSHIP PROBLEMS**

Talk about the issue of problems that arise in a friendship. Stress that all friendships have the occasional problem that needs to be sorted out. In advance, you could ask students to each interview two similar-aged students from another class to obtain some no-names class data to discuss. They could also prepare a written questionnaire, which each student gives to five other students from other classes. In groups of four they collate their results and then collate class results. Suitable questions might be:
- How do friends become friends?
- What is the greatest thing about friendship?
- How do friends help each other?
- How do friends sometimes hurt each other?
- What are the main problems that can happen in a friendship?
- Why do many friendships finish?
- What did you and a friend have a fight about when you were younger?
- How have you made up after a fight with a friend?
- How could someone embarrass their friend?

Alternatively, read to the class and discuss the picture book *Fox* and/or the fable of 'The Bear and the Two Travellers' (see below).

Discussion questions

- Why do friendships sometimes break up? (Some friendships break up after an argument that isn't handled well by one person or both people. Many friendships just start to 'fade away', but it doesn't mean that one of you has done something wrong or that one of you is a bad or unlikable person. Friendships can also change with new interests, being apart or not spending much time together, or a change in your life so that you no longer have as much in common.)
- How could a person cope if their group of friends says that they don't want that person in the group any more?
- What does 'being loyal' mean? (it means considering the other person to be special and important to you; seeing them as more important than the other people in your life, with the exception of family, and putting them ahead of others; protecting them)
- How do we show loyalty to a friend? (we stand up for them in an argument or if someone is being mean to them; we don't say bad things about them behind their back; we help them when they need it; we keep their secrets; we stay their friend even if they are not able to be with us or see us very much; we try to understand their problems and see their point of view; we say good things about them to other people; we stick with them even when they are a pain for a while)
- Does a good friend accept that you have the right to say 'no'? (yes)

BOOK
Fox (Picture book)

The two main characters, Magpie and Dog, have been friends for a long time and have always looked after each other. Magpie has a damaged wing and can't fly well and Dog only has one eye. A cold-blooded fox arrives in their midst and tries to cause trouble between them. Eventually he talks Magpie into leaving Dog and coming with him, by convincing her that he is more able to help her to fly. He then abandons her in the desert. The story has a slightly upbeat ending, as Magpie starts on the long journey back to Dog. The illustrations in and design of this book is also worth detailed analysis.

STORY
'The Bear and the Two Travellers'

(This story is often called 'The Whispering Bear' in collections of Aesop's Fables.) Two boys are travelling together when they are attacked by a bear. One boy is pinned down by the bear, while the other runs off. The bear whispers in the ear of the boy he has pinned, 'Never travel with a friend who runs off and leaves you at the first sniff of danger'. Then the bear leaves and the boy survives.

ACTIVITY
Think–Pair–Share

✘ See Chapter 10 of the Teacher's Handbook.

Students discuss their views on each example.
- Can a friendship be saved if one person feels that they always have to do what their friend wants to do?
- Can a friendship be saved if one person always seem to have excuses to not do things with the other person or to see them?
- Can a friendship be saved if one person feels used?
- Can a friendship be saved if one person is trying to persuade the other to do things they don't want to do, like bullying someone else or stealing?
- Can a friendship be saved if one person keeps hurting the other person's feelings and putting them down in public?

CLASS DISCUSSION MANAGING DISAGREEMENTS

Ask students to list all the words they associate with conflict. Write them on the board and ask students to categorise them as 'positive words', 'negative words', or 'neutral' ones. Discuss the idea that all people who coexist (live or work together) have conflict occasionally. This includes romantic partnerships, classmates, family, flatmates and workmates. Having a disagreement every now and then is normal and sometimes helpful.
- What are some of the things that students your age disagree about?
- Why are people usually worried about conflict or disagreements that happen? (They are fearful of social disapproval, of losing control and making a fool of themselves, of being disliked, of being hurt, or not treated fairly, of feeling bad about hurting others, or of the loss of a relationship. They don't focus on the advantages of sorting things out well. They may have seen a lot of destructive ways of handling conflict in their past. They are pessimistic about the outcome.)
- Why do some people become nasty and loud about a disagreement? (They think, incorrectly, that they have to *win* rather than sort it out. They think that the main goal is revenge when it should be sorting out the problems and staying friends. They may not have any other good skills to use in sorting it out.)
- Are there any good sides to having a disagreement? (If it is handled reasonably well, conflict can increase your confidence, because you become less scared about whether you can deal with disagreements if they happen again; it can make relationships stronger by showing that both people care enough to try and fix things up; it can make people feel happier that they are getting a fair deal.)
- 'An apology is the superglue of life. It can repair just about everything.' (Lynn Johnston) What does this mean? Do you agree or not? Why?
- What can stop people from apologising? (fear of having it used against them or of it not being accepted; fear of 'loss of face'; not looking at their own behaviour honestly)

- Can you say 'I'm sorry that you are upset' but not say that you are in the wrong?
- What do you lose by *not* apologising? (possibly a friendship; a chance to feel self-respect; a chance to be respected by the other person for your courage and honesty)
- Hand out BLM 7.8, 'Seven ways to deal with conflict', and go through each strategy. Differentiate between a 'response' (which is often a knee-jerk reaction) and a strategy (which is more planned and thoughtful).
- What are some of the things that people do that make it more likely that things *won't* be sorted out? (see BLM 7.9, 'BE CAREFUL!').

Follow-up activities

- Students draw a red-faced basketball referee blowing a whistle and raising their hand to indicate a 'foul.' They draw and write six dialogue balloons to show six ways people could be guilty of 'conflict fouls' using BLM 7.9, 'BE CAREFUL!' as the basis.
- Encourage students to use the 'BAD is good' thinking prompt when dealing with drama about conflict (see Unit 4, 'Courage', page 86).
- In pairs, students draw cartoon strips based on the seven strategies in BLM 7.8. Stick figures are okay. They use thought bubbles and dialogue balloons.
- After reading BLM 7.8 students complete BLM 7.10, 'What conflict strategy is this?'. The correct answers are:
  - Being a doormat
  - Asking for help in sorting it out
  - Forcing
  - Being assertive
  - Negotiating
  - Apologising
  - Agreeing to disagree.
- Students complete BLM 7.11, 'What's gone wrong here?'. The correct answers are:
  1. He didn't apologise when he was in the wrong.
  2. He jumped to conclusions and didn't do a fact check.
  3. She was insensitive and did not focus on being friendly.
  4. She let herself become emotionally hijacked.
  5. She wasn't prepared to listen to the other point of view.
- Use BLM 7.12, 'What's the best way?', in one or more of the following ways:
  - As a class discussion exercise or with the Think–Pair–Share strategy (see Chapter 10 of the *Teacher's Handbook*).
  - As a 'musical stop and share' (see Chapter 10 of the *Teacher's Handbook*)
  - As a cartoon drawing activity, where students complete the story with a last frame showing what they think is the best way to handle the conflict
  - As a drama activity. Prepare a container containing six of the seven strategies from BLM 7.8 ('agree to disagree' should not be included as a card, but tell students that it is always an option if appropriate. It is only useful in a few situations) written on cards and a second container containing the situations photocopied onto card and cut up. Each pair of students (or a group of three) draws a situation plus a strategy. They prepare an enactment based on the situation and card combination.

DRAMA ACTIVITIES
Dealing with conflict

- Have a box in the classroom where students can write and post stories about conflict situations they have seen or been involved in (using the 'no names' rule). These can be used as hypothetical examples to be acted out or discussed. In groups of three, students can prepare two enactments: a good way of dealing with the conflict and then a bad way. Use the 'freeze frame' strategy (see Chapter 11 of the *Teacher's Handbook*), also use the strategy of having a 'coach' for each actor who helps them to prepare the scene and then debriefs what happened with the class afterwards.

- Set up dramatic situations with each group drawing four cards.
  Card one: Who is involved or present?
  Card two: Where does it take place?
  Card three: What is the disagreement about?
  Card four: What response or strategy is used?
  Students can offer ideas for each of the card sets.

BOOK
Voices in the Park (Picture book)

Read to the class and discuss the book *Voices in the Park* (summarised in Unit 6, 'Emotions') to highlight the fact that there are many different views on the same situation.

ACTIVITIES
Working with younger students

Students can focus on the topic of handling disagreements and read picture books to younger classes (see *Teacher's Resource Book*, Level 1 for ideas), prepare and present plays, or puppet plays (see Chapter 11 of the *Teacher's Handbook* for puppet ideas), make booklets or posters and make pyramids as below (but the language will need to be adjusted—see *Teacher's Resource Book*, Level 1).

TECHNOLOGY AND MATHS ACTIVITY
The 'healthy conflict management' pyramid

Students draw or make a 3D model of a 'healthy conflict management' pyramid along the lines of the healthy diet pyramid. They use these categories:

Use hardly ever
Forcing
Being a doormat

Use sometimes
Apologising
Being assertive
Asking for support in sorting it out
Agreeing to disagree

Use all the time
Problem-solving negotiation

ARTS ACTIVITY
Creating a poster about good apologising

Students can discuss the skill of apologising well, and then, working with a partner, create a poster consisting of dialogue balloons about the Do's and Don'ts. For example:

Do's
- If you have been in the wrong, even a bit, have the courage to make the first move and apologise.
- Admit your mistake.
- Let the other person know that you feel badly about what happened. For example, say:
  - 'I'm sorry. I didn't mean to upset you.'
  - 'I made a bit of a mistake.'
  - 'I wish I hadn't said/done that.'
  - 'I didn't really mean what I said. I was just upset.' (Everyone says things they don't mean sometimes.)
  - Even if the other person was mostly in the wrong, you can still say, 'I'm sorry we had a fight' or 'I'm sorry you are upset'.
- Use a genuine tone of voice.
- Once you or the other person has said sorry, don't refer to it again. It is in the past.

Don'ts
- Don't be stubborn or too proud to apologise.
- Don't say 'Sorry . . . but' and then say that it was really the other person's fault.
- Don't say 'sorry' when you don't think you did anything wrong, and are just trying to make the other person like you.
- Don't use a tone of voice that says that you are not *really* sorry.

ENGLISH ACTIVITY
Choose your own adventure

Students write a story around a conflict situation and give it two different endings according to the character's choice of conflict management strategy. (Refer to BLM 7.8, 'Seven ways to deal with conflict'.)

CLASSROOM ORGANISATION
Classroom meetings

- Use classroom or year-level meetings or committees (see Chapter 5 of the *Teacher's Handbook* for suggestions) so that students can practise listening, respecting other points of view, and negotiation.
- Use small-group discussions or games where a negotiated decision has to be made. Make one student the observer and ask them to write down one disagreement that occurred and which of the seven strategies was used to deal with it. Examples are:
  - Flood (see *Friendly Kids, Friendly Classrooms*)
  - Boggle (see *Dirty Tricks*)
  - Shape makers (see *Dirty Tricks*)
  - Group paper-plate quizzes (see Chapter 10 of the *Teacher's Handbook*)
  - Predictor cards (see Chapter 10 of the *Teacher's Handbook*).

ACTIVITIES
Choosing a group car

The group has been kind to an elderly lady living next to the school. They have helped her with gardening, shopping, company etc. When she dies, she unexpectedly leaves them $40 000 to buy a 'group car' (assume that all the group will soon be able to drive). But she imposes the following conditions: they must make a negotiated decision within 15 minutes about the type of car, the colour, and one additional accessory for it. The car usage must be shared and the group must have a workable written-down plan for it.

Cooperative controversy

This strategy gives students practice in taking more than one perspective. (See Chapter 10 of the *Teacher's Handbook*.)
- People who get speeding fines can pay them off by donating blood.
- All police to have a device in their car that can disable the electronics of a fleeing or speeding car.
- A formal communication system for drivers, taught when you get your licence. For example, one hand turned palm-up means 'I'm sorry', a wave at shoulder height means 'Can I enter the traffic, please' and so on.
- If you are caught putting graffiti onto any surface, you can't get a driving licence for another twelve months after your eighteenth birthday.

Conflict research

Whenever you are looking at or engaging in literature, movies or music, or discussing them incidentally, ask students to comment on the ways in which conflict is dealt with. Ask them to use the language of the seven strategies as outlined on BLM 7.8, 'Seven ways to deal with conflict'. They create a grid with a partner, and watch TV and movies or read books using the following questions:
- What did you watch/read/listen to?
- What conflict occurred, what was the disagreement about, and who was involved?
- How was the conflict handled?

CLASS DISCUSSION LEADERSHIP AND LOVE!

Start by asking students to complete BLM 7.13, How good a leader could you be?'.

Discussion questions

- What does a leader do?
- What kinds of leadership roles are there in society/business/sport/schools/your age-group?
- What are the skills and attitudes of a good leader? (see BLM 7.13; leading by example; having respect for and faith in the people they lead; being optimistic to keep spirits high)
- What does a poor leader do?
- Can anyone be a leader if they learn good leadership skills? (Research suggests that once you have been given the job of leader, other people respond differently to you and you feel more confident and behave more like a leader. Skills training also makes a huge difference.)
- What social skills (getting along and friendship skills) make it more likely that a person will have a good romantic relationship with someone? (all of them, but research has identified the importance of conflict-management skills, avoiding put-downs, being positive, listening, and seeing the other's point of veiw, apologising and negotiating)

- Why do romantic relationships break up? (lots of reasons! lack of social skills; being young and unclear about what they want; incompatibility, even though at first they seemed compatible; different values; stressful circumstances [but skills can offset these])
- Who makes the best partner for someone? (Research suggests that you look for a long-term partner who is reasonably similar to you in terms of values, background, personality and interests. But this is not universally true!)

Follow-up activity

Students each interview two couples who have a long-term and happy relationship and ask them for the three skills they think are the most important in having a satisfying romantic partnership. Stress that they need to go past 'love, trust and mutual respect' and focus on *skills*. Collate the data and make a class poster or mobile using hearts.

CLASSROOM ORGANISATION
Leaders

Organise opportunities for all students to be in a leadership role. For example:
- Have rotating captains and vice-captains.
- Consider having students rotate in the role of class coach for different class teams.
- For each committee (see Chapter 5 of the *Teacher's Handbook* for ideas) have a chairperson.

CONSOLIDATION

Balloon burst quotes

X See Chapter 11 of the Teacher's Handbook.

Give students access to a dictionary. Ask them to link the meaning of the quote to the topic of relationships each time.
- A real friend is one who walks in when the rest of the world walks out. (Walter Winchell)
- Except in cases of necessity, which are rare, leave your friend to learn unpleasant things from his enemies; they are ready enough to tell him. (Oliver Wendell Holmes)
- If I mayn't tell you what I really feel, what is the use of a friend? (William Makepeace Thackeray)
- In order to have friends you must first be one. (Elbert Hubbard)
- Life is what happens when you're making other plans. (John Lennon)
- Misfortune shows those who are not really friends. (Aristotle)
- People will forget what you said. People will forget what you did. But people will never forget how you made them feel.
- You can always tell a real friend; when you've made a fool of yourself he doesn't feel you've done a permanent job. (Laurence J Peter)
- Your friend is the person who knows all about you and still likes you. (Elbert Hubbard)
- Do not spit in the well because you may have to drink out of it.
- My long experience has taught me to resolve conflict by raising the issues before I or others burn their boats. (Alistair Grant)
- Pick battles big enough to matter and small enough to win. (Jonathan Kozol)
- Friendship improves happiness and reduces misery by doubling our joy and dividing our grief. (Cicero BC 126)
- You have no right to an opinion for which you do not fully understand the opposing argument. (John Stuart Mill)

- We have been given two ears and one mouth so we can hear more and talk less.
- Just because you *have* a pain doesn't mean you should *be* a pain.

Quick quotes

X See Chapter 11 of the Teacher's Handbook.

'What I find hardest about dealing with disagreement is . . .' *or* 'one way I like other people to behave towards me is . . .'

Before or after?

X See Chapter 10 of the Teacher's Handbook.

Apologise	Flexible	Popularity
Argument	Force	Quarrel
Assertive	Friend	Quiet
Boring	Friendship	Relationships
Bossy	Generous	Romantic
Check	Goal	Skill
Conflict	Help	Social
Consequences	Leadership	Solutions
Disagree	Love	Support
Facts	Loyalty	Thoughtful
Fight	Negotiate	

Cross-offs

Complete BLM 7.14. The answer is: When you have a disagreement, find a solution that allows you to stay friends.

RESOURCES

Books

Anthony Browne, 1991, *Willy and Hugh*, Julia MacRae Books, London.
Anthony Browne, 1999, *Voices in the Park*, Picture Corgi Books, London.
'The Bear and the Two Travellers', in Sally Grindley & John Bendall-Brunello, 1999, *The Hare and the Tortoise and other Animal Stories*, Bloomsbury Publishing, London.
Helen McGrath & Shona Francey, 1991, *Friendly Kids, Friendly Classrooms*, Longman Cheshire, Melbourne.
Helen McGrath, 1997, *Dirty Tricks: Classroom Games Which Teach Students Social Skills*, Pearson Education, Melbourne.
James Moloney, 1995, *Swashbuckler*, University of Queensland Press, St Lucia.
Katherine & Mary K Pershall, 1998, *Too Much to Ask For*, Penguin, Melbourne.
Judith Viorst, 1995, *Sad Underwear and Other Complications: More Poems for Children and Their Parents*, Scholastic, Sydney.
Margaret Wild & Ron Brooks, 2001, *Fox*, Allen and Unwin, Sydney.

THE PEOPLE SKILLS QUIZ!

BLM 7.1

How good are you at doing these things?

	A bit better than most people my age	About the same as others my age	I need more practice
1. Starting a conversation with someone I don't know			
2. Staying cool in an argument and not losing my temper and making things worse			
3. Being positive (i.e. talking about the good things about people and situations more than the bad)			
4. Telling a story in an interesting way so people don't get bored			
5. Having the courage to give my own opinion even if others don't agree with me			
6. Getting along well with other people when working in a group or team			
7. Being a good listener			
8. Being a good loser when someone beats me			
9. Having good ways to draw attention to myself without being an idiot or showing off			
10. Being flexible enough to cope with changes in plans that others suggest without getting upset			
11. Giving compliments to others that are genuine			
12. Laughing at other people's jokes when the jokes are only slightly funny so they feel okay			
13. Offering to help people with work that has to be done			
14. Organising something interesting for myself and my friends to do together			
15. Being generous (e.g. willing to share my things)			
16. Not being bossy by always telling others what to do			
17. Speaking in front of the class with reasonable confidence even though I might be feeling a bit nervous			
18. Not talking about others behind their backs			
19. Not telling people off when they make a mistake			
20. Making sure I don't talk about myself all the time			

Scoring
Give yourself 3 points for 'A bit better', 2 points for 'About the same' and 1 point for 'I need practice'. Place a cross on the line below to show where your score places you.

30	40	50	60
I need lots of practice	I need a fair bit of practice	I'm pretty skilled	I'm very skilled

© Helen McGrath and Toni Noble, 2003. This page from Bounce Back!® may be photocopied for classroom use.

GETTING ALONG WELL WITH OTHERS

BLM 7.2

1.	Starting a conversation	Practise some good starting comments (e.g. 'Hi, my name is . . .'). Find something you have in common to talk about.
2.	Staying cool in an argument	Keep quiet until you have decided on the best way to deal with it. Think of the other person's point of view too. Don't insult or yell. Keep your eye on the goal of staying friends. Negotiate so that you *both* get a fairly good outcome.
3.	Being positive	Think of something positive to say. Be enthusiastic.
4.	Telling a story in an interesting way	Don't use too much detail. Get to the point quickly. Make sure that the story is relevant to the listener in some way. Check for interest.
5.	Giving an honest opinion	Say what you think with confidence. Firstly agree with what you can before you say how you differ. Don't try too hard to please others.
6.	Cooperating well	Do your share and take your turn. Respect others' opinions and share ideas. Be fair and think of others. Negotiate if disagreements occur.
7.	Being a good listener	Pay attention. Don't interrupt. Give a simple summary of what you have heard or ask a follow-up question. Ask 'Tell me more' questions a lot more than questions that only require a yes/no answer. Take your turn at talking too.
8.	Being a good loser	If you lose in a game or if others don't agree with you, just accept it. It doesn't make you a 'loser'.
9.	Using good ways to get others to notice me	Be interesting. Be a good listener. Suggest good ideas. Use good humour.
10.	Being flexible	Fit in with new plans unless there is a good reason not to.
11.	Giving genuine compliments	Look for and say the things in others that you appreciate/admire.
12.	Laughing at other people's jokes	Try and laugh when others make a joke or a funny throwaway remark even if it is only a little bit funny. But don't overdo it.
13.	Offering to help people	Look for ways to be helpful but don't overdo it.
14.	Organising something interesting to do	Think of good ideas. Remember what different people like to do.
15.	Being willing to share	Don't be too possessive with your food or with your things. If you do share, don't be critical of how they use it.
16.	Resisting the urge to be bossy	Let people do things their own way. If you have a suggestion for doing things better, say 'What about . . .' rather than 'You should . . .'
17.	Speaking in front of the class	Make a plan and prepare. Get the class to *do* something. Use humour. Remember: *No one* does it perfectly.
18.	Not talking about others behind their backs	Let people know directly if you are unhappy about something they have said or done. People often find out what you have said about them.
19.	Not telling people off when they make a mistake	Remember that everyone makes mistakes sometimes. You are not so perfect that you can freely criticise others. No one likes it.
20.	Making sure I don't just talk about myself all the time	Take turns in a conversation. Ask the other person about themselves.

© Helen McGrath and Toni Noble, 2003. This page from Bounce Back!® may be photocopied for classroom use.

WHAT TURNS PEOPLE OFF?

BLM 7.3

Cut out the ten cards. As a group, negotiate to decide how much each of the ten behaviours 'turns you off' and makes it harder to respond in a positive way to the person doing them, even if you know they are probably a nice person. Decide on a final group ranking from the biggest turn-off to the mildest turn-off.

Being negative
- Bad-mouthing others
- Complaining or moaning all the time
- Being in a bad mood a lot

Ego-tripping
- Talking constantly about themselves and how good they are
- Showing off or boasting
- Exaggerating or telling lies about themselves to look good

Being boring or inflexible
- Always wanting to do the same things the same way
- Going on and on and not getting to the point quickly enough
- Talking about things that no one is interested in much of the time
- Not being flexible when circumstances change

Staying too private
- Not telling others much about themselves and being 'reserved'
- Not saying what they think about something so you never know how they feel

Being selfish
- Trying to have things their own way all the time
- Not being prepared to do their share of the work or to help
- Being greedy (e.g. taking more than their share)

Being mean and nasty
- Criticising just about everyone and everything
- Talking about people behind their backs
- Saying mean or sarcastic things or using sly put-downs so you feel bad

Being argumentative and difficult
- Arguing about everything
- Starting fights and arguments over little things

Being bossy
- Trying to tell you what to do or how to do something even though they are not the boss
- Telling people that they've done something incorrectly

Being too serious all the time
- Having a scowl on their face and not smiling much
- Not having a sense of 'fun'

Being 'insecure' and under-confident
- Being too clingy and not being independent
- Not acting in a confident way

© Helen McGrath and Toni Noble, 2003. This page from Bounce Back!® may be photocopied for classroom use.

WHAT SHOULD THEY DO?

BLM 7.4

What is the best way for each of these people to deal with their situations?

1. Briony was running a bit late and her friend didn't save her a seat on the bus when they went on a school excursion. Briony feels hurt by her friend's lack of thoughtfulness.

2. George's friend forgot his birthday.

3. Brogan's friend complained that Brogan boasted and showed off a lot and that others felt embarrassed by her behaviour.

4. Brad's friend had a fight with a classmate. Deep down, Brad thinks that it may have been his friend's fault. But his friend wants him to be on his side.

5. A girl at school hangs around Rachael all the time and wants to be her friend. She is an okay person, but Rachael's friends don't want her to be part of their group.

6. A popular boy at school said to Liam, 'Your friend is a real loser. Don't hang around with him. Be in our group instead.'

7. Chen hangs out with three other boys. Two of them are always fighting and Chen keeps getting caught in the middle. They both expect Chen to take their side.

8. Harriet's friend never does his homework, and he keeps asking to copy hers.

9. Daria's friend told her that she and another girl had been shoplifting.

10. One of the people in Yasmin's group of school friends told Yasmin that she wasn't really good enough to be in the group, and that she was 'one step down from the cool group'.

11. Julian's friend asks to see his report card, but Julian feels uncomfortable about it.

12. Matthew often feels very shy and worries that if he says something it will be the wrong thing.

13. Rowan wants to get to know some kids who live near him, but he feels a bit nervous and fears that they will laugh at him if he tries.

14. Sivana wants to ask Jessica for a sleepover at her house, but she doesn't know if Jessica likes her enough to come.

15. Amelia's group of friends doesn't seem to want her to be in their group any more. She feels really upset.

© Helen McGrath and Toni Noble, 2003. This page from Bounce Back!® may be photocopied for classroom use.

WHAT ARE THE CHARACTERISTICS OF A GOOD FRIEND?

BLM 7.5

Decide for each characteristic or behaviour whether you think it is 'very important', 'pretty important' or 'desirable, but not so important'.

Characteristics	Very important	Pretty important	Desirable, but not so important
Is good looking			
Is loyal and stands up for me			
Is honest and says what they think when I ask them			
Is about the same age as me			
Has a sense of humour			
Doesn't tell others what I have told them in private			
Shows warmth and affection towards me			
Is supportive and caring when I need it			
Is a good listener			
Is good at sport			
Likes the same things that I do			
Is 'cool' and wears clothes that are in fashion			
Is popular			
Comes from a similar kind of family to mine			
Is fun to be with			
Is thoughtful and considerate			
Lets me be myself			

© Helen McGrath and Toni Noble, 2003. This page from Bounce Back!® may be photocopied for classroom use.

FRIENDSHIP SIMILARITIES AND DIFFERENCES

BLM 7.6

Pick one colour for yourself and one colour for a friend. Then place one coloured cross on each line to describe you and another to describe your friend.

Likes team sports _____Hates team sports

Organised _____Disorganised

Tidy _____Messy

Cheerful _____Gloomy

Likes reading _____Hates reading

Likes playing board games _____Hates playing board games

Likes water sports _____Hates water sports

Cautious _____Impulsive

Shy _____Socially confident

Likes school work _____Doesn't like school work

Is a saver _____Is a spender

Likes scary movies _____Hates scary movies

Likes being with lots of people all the time _____Hates being with lots of people all the time

© Helen McGrath and Toni Noble, 2003. This page from Bounce Back!® may be photocopied for classroom use.

A QUIZ ABOUT FRIENDSHIP

BLM 7.7

Decide whether the following statements are TRUE or FALSE.

1. Friendships just happen naturally.

    True   False

2. A true friend never lets you down and is always there for you.

    True   False

3. If you don't always have a close friend, you're not a well-liked person.

    True   False

4. A good friend is a friend for life.

    True   False

5. People who have some good friends are usually very popular too.

    True   False

6. Most broken friendships are a result of fights between the people.

    True   False

7. People who don't have a lot of close friends when they are young are still able to have good friends when they are adults.

    True   False

8. Boys and girls can't be good friends with each other.

    True   False

© Helen McGrath and Toni Noble, 2003. This page from Bounce Back!® may be photocopied for classroom use.

ANSWERS TO BLM 7.7

1. False: making friends doesn't come naturally for most people. It hardly ever just 'happens'. Someone is usually using good friendship skills and making an effort to get the friendship started.

2. False: friends are there for us a lot of the time but no friend is so perfect that they are there for us all the time and never let us down. It's inevitable that at some point you will think that a friend is not there for you when you need them.

3. False: sometimes circumstances mean that you don't have friends for a particular time in your life. This doesn't mean that you *can't* have a close friend, just that you don't have one at a particular time in your life.

4. True: a few good friends are for life, but many friendships do not last for a lifetime. Friendships end for lots of reasons. One person might be disloyal to another more than once, or be mean in a terrible or uncaring way; your lives might go in different directions and you drift apart; one or both of you may change and start having different values and ideas about what is important. Mostly friendships fade away rather than 'break up'.

5. False: popularity and having friends are not the same thing. Being popular involves admiration, acceptance and status from a lot of people. If you are popular, many people want to spend time with you and be part of a group with you. On the other hand, friendship is a close relationship with another person that is based on affection, loyalty and knowing each other well. Some people who don't impress others in the big picture are excellent at close friendships. Friendship is more important than popularity.

6. False: although friends *can* break up after they have had a fight, the *main* reason why friendships finish is because they just 'fade away' as either one or both people involved no longer feel as close or connected. Sometimes their lives change and that friendship is no longer as important to them as it was. It always hurts when that happens, but it happens to everyone at some point in their life.

7. True: sometimes when you are young you are among people who are not very friendly or are people that you don't have much in common with. But that can change when you become an adult and choose your own places to be. Sometimes when you are young you are not very experienced at good social skills, but you can get better at them as you get older.

8. False: boys and girls can be excellent friends with each other. Unlike previous generations, today's young people are much more likely to have good friendships with the opposite gender. It can be helpful to hear how a friend of the opposite gender sees things.

© Helen McGrath and Toni Noble, 2003. This page from Bounce Back!® may be photocopied for classroom use.

SEVEN WAYS TO DEAL WITH CONFLICT?

BLM 7.8

What is conflict?
Conflict is another word for disagreement. There are three main kinds of disagreement:
- Two people both want something but there isn't enough to go round.
- Two people have different views about what *should* happen or what *did* happen.
- One person believes that another person has behaved badly towards them.

There are some good and bad ways to handle disagreements.

Forcing doesn't work.
Forcing isn't a good way. Forcing means trying to make the other person do what you want by hurting them, insulting them or threatening them. If you force someone, then you usually make things worse. You damage your friendship and you may feel bad about what you said or did.

Being a 'doormat' doesn't work either.
Only walk away from a disagreement if it is unimportant. If it is important, then you need to stand up for yourself and deal with the problem. Some people are too scared to do this because they fear being disliked or yelled at. But if you don't stand up for yourself, you won't solve the problem and other people may lose respect for you.

Agreeing to disagree can be helpful.
Sometimes you just have different ideas about something and both people can be right. When this happens, and if you don't need to make any decisions or sort things out, you can just 'agree to disagree'.

Asking someone else to help you sort things out is sometimes necessary.
If you have tried to sort out a disagreement by yourself but it hasn't worked, you might need to ask someone else to help you sort it out. Do this only as a last resort. Try to deal with a disagreement by yourself first.

Being assertive is a good strategy.
Being assertive is a good strategy for dealing with a disagreement. Being assertive means speaking up about what you think isn't fair or correct without being angry or nasty. Start what you say with the words 'I feel' or 'I think'.

Apologising is also a good strategy.
If you have been unfair or done something wrong to someone, it is helpful to apologise, even if only some of the disagreement was your fault.

Negotiating to solve the problem is the very best strategy.
Negotiating means that you try to work out a solution that is fair to both people and that you can both live with. You should both feel that you have got some of what you wanted. By negotiating, you ensure that there is a much greater chance of staying friends and sorting things out.

© Helen McGrath and Toni Noble, 2003. This page from Bounce Back!® may be photocopied for classroom use.

BE CAREFUL!

BLM 7.9

No matter how serious or silly, most disagreements can be sorted out if you are prepared to try. But you need to BE CAREFUL about how you deal with it.

Be prepared to make the first move to try and sort out the problem and fix things. It takes courage to do this, but it's worth it.

Emotions can hijack you! Cool down first. Take time to think, plan and be strategic. Don't just act on angry and outraged feelings.

Check your facts first. Do a reality check with someone else if you can. You may be jumping to conclusions. You could look really stupid.

Assure the other person that you want to solve the disagreement between you and stay friends. Don't just give them the silent treatment.

Respect the other person by speaking and acting in a polite, calm and friendly manner if you want to stay friends. Avoid name-calling and insults and blaming them for everything.

Eye on the goal! Keep things in perspective. Your goal should be to fix the problem between you, show self respect and stay friends, not to WIN or pay them back.

Focus on the right things. For example:
- Focus on the problem not the person.
- Focus on the present not the past.
- Focus first on where you agree before you look at where you disagree.

Upbeat positive thinking creates goodwill. You can find a solution if you believe you can. Take a positive approach.

Listen to their view of things and don't interrupt. There are always two sides to any story. Sometimes both views can be right even though they're different because things are not always clear.

© Helen McGrath and Toni Noble, 2003. This page from Bounce Back!® may be photocopied for classroom use.

WHAT CONFLICT STRATEGY IS THIS?

BLM 7.10

- David was playing basketball at lunchtime with four others and Jack kept hogging the ball. David sulked and just walked away, saying that he had something he had to do. He spent the rest of the afternoon thinking angry thoughts about Jack, but saying nothing about it. _____

- Sally, Vince, Gino and Kim are on the school newspaper committee. Gino keeps missing meetings and then not doing his share of the work. The others tried to talk to him after he had missed four meetings, but he just got angry and walked away. Because they can't do Gino's workload as well as their own, they talk to the Year 7 coordinator to get help in sorting out the situation. _____

- Sarah's uncle has offered to pay for two tickets so that she and her cousin Mardi can see a movie of their choice. When Sarah says that she doesn't want to see the movie that Mardi suggests, Mardi says, 'You always want to get things your way. You are so selfish. I'm not going if we can't see my movie.' _____

- Two of Harry's friends wanted to graffiti the wall of an old house. Harry thought that it was a dumb idea and he didn't want to do it. He figured that they would probably get caught and he really didn't find the idea very exciting anyway. He said to them, 'I don't want to risk getting into trouble. I'm having a good year and I want to keep it that way.' They replied, 'You're such a wuss, Harry. There's no way we'll get caught.' Harry replied, 'Maybe, but I still don't want to do it.' _____

- Natasha's younger sister Kellie wanted to watch a TV show that was on at the same time as Natasha's favourite show. They have only one TV set in the house. Natasha did a deal with Kellie and offered to tape the show that Kellie wanted to see. She let Kellie watch the video at the time that Kellie chose, even though it wasn't all that convenient. _____

- Simon is sure that it's his turn to bowl in the lunchtime cricket game, but the other kids don't agree with him. He gets really upset and stubborn about it. One kid gives him two good reasons why it isn't his turn to bowl, and Simon realises that he has made a mistake. He feels very embarrassed, but says 'Sorry guys, I got it wrong' and the game continues. _____

- Five students are talking about different bands and Callum says to Jason, 'That band you listen to is absolutely hopeless. They're just technicians. They have no musical soul.' Jason feels a bit miffed, but he decides that there is no way that anyone can win this one. He says, 'Well, everyone has different ideas and your view is no better than mine.' _____

© Helen McGrath and Toni Noble, 2003. This page from Bounce Back!® may be photocopied for classroom use.

WHAT'S GONE WRONG HERE?

BLM 7.11

What did the person do in each cartoon that results in a bad outcome to the conflict? What could they have done to make a good outcome more likely?

1.
- WHY DID YOU TELL MR RULE I WAGGED CLASS!
- I DIDN'T.
- HE CALLED THE ROLL AND YOU WEREN'T THERE!
- I SHOULD SAY SORRY BUT I'LL LOOK LIKE AN IDIOT!
- GEE YOU'D THINK HE'D SAY SORRY!

2.
- GIVE ME BACK MY CALCULATOR.
- I DIDN'T TAKE IT.
- DON'T PULL THAT ONE I KNOW YOU TOOK IT YOU *#%#*
- GET LOST, LOSER.

3.
- I'M SENDING AN EMAIL TO SIMON TO APOLOGISE CAUSE I SAID HE WAS A MESSY EATER.
- SO WHAT DID YOU SAY?
- I SAID, 'DEAR SIMON I'M SORRY I NOTICED WHAT A MESSY EATER YOU WERE.'
- SO MUCH FOR THAT FRIENDSHIP.

4.
- HOW LONG HAS YOUR DAD BEEN OUT OF WORK?
- ?
- YOU ARE SUCH A BITCH!

5.
- ERIN, YOU SAID YOU WOULD GET THE BOOK ON PYRAMIDS!
- I TRIED TO BUT...
- DO I HAVE TO DO EVERYTHING MYSELF!
- BUT...
- I KEPT TRYING TO TELL HER THAT THE LIBRARIAN SAID THAT THE BOOK WAS LOST 2 MONTHS AGO!

© Helen McGrath and Toni Noble, 2003. This page from Bounce Back!® may be photocopied for classroom use.

WHAT'S THE BEST WAY?

BLM 7.12

Sharni finds out that a classmate, Josh, has been telling people that Sharni's younger sister has nits and it isn't true.	Brad sits behind Anthony in class and keeps kicking his chair. Brad can't concentrate on his work.	Four students are working together on a group project for school. Three people are doing their fair share of the work, but the fourth person isn't.
While Marnie is out, her younger brother goes into her room without permission and looks through some of her things as he tries to find his missing textas.	Vinh and Marcus have sent out invitations to a party they are having together. They can't agree on what kind of music to play at the party.	Ella shares an apartment with Jason and they share the cleaning equally. Jason is a bit of a 'neat freak' and Ella is a bit of a slob. Jason wants the kitchen and bathroom cleaned weekly, but Ella thinks monthly is enough.
A friend has borrowed one of Tom's CDs but hasn't returned it, despite assuring him that it would be given back the next day. It is now a week later.	Your mother insists on picking out your clothes when you go shopping. She thinks that if she's paying she gets to have some say in what you wear.	Samantha's parents have separated and they have negotiated that she will spend every second weekend with her dad. She loves her dad, and wants to spend time with him, but the arrangement doesn't really suit her. She wants more flexibility so that she can be available if something good is happening with her friends.
Troy's older sister plays loud music in her next-door bedroom and he can't sleep.	Craig wants to finish the project he is writing on the computer. His booked time is finished but he has a little bit to do to finish it. The student who has it booked after Craig wants to get started.	Jodie and a friend had arranged to go to the movies. One hour before they were to meet, the friend rings and says, 'Sorry, I can't go. My aunt and uncle just rang to say that they and my cousin are coming over to our place for the afternoon.'
Four students are having a heated argument over who is the best player in the league. It starts to become unpleasant.	Harry and Melinda plan to order a takeaway pizza. Harry likes ham and pineapple and Melinda is a vegetarian.	Iain is invited to a friend's house to swim in their pool and he is looking forward to it because it has been so hot. When he gets there, his friend says he'd rather play computer games.
Liam and Daniel go on a picnic together and each takes some of the stuff. When they arrive at the picnic spot, Liam realises that he has forgotten to bring the soft drink.	Soula told a classmate a secret about her aunt and uncle's import business. Although she didn't say 'Don't tell anyone', she expected that the classmate would keep the secret. The classmate didn't and now two other people know.	You are the driver on a one-hour car trip. Your passenger says, 'I'm too hot. Could you please turn the air-conditioner to high?' You're freezing!

© Helen McGrath and Toni Noble, 2003. This page from Bounce Back!® may be photocopied for classroom use.

HOW GOOD A LEADER COULD YOU BE?

BLM 7.13

Circle the number that best shows how well you use each skill. Pick four of the skills and write about a time when you used each well.

1. **Listening**
   A good leader is a good listener who makes sure that everybody has a chance to be heard and who listens to everyone's ideas. How good a listener are you?
   My rating is   1   2   3   4   5
                  (I need practice)   (I do this very well)

2. **Bringing out the best in others**
   A good leader brings out the best in people by finding out what they are best at, by giving them a chance to use those talents, and by giving them positive feedback about what they do well. How good are you at bringing out the best in others?
   My rating is   1   2   3   4   5
                  (I need practice)   (I do this very well)

3. **Creating a safe and friendly environment**
   A good leader makes people feel safe by thinking about the feelings of other people, helping people to sort out disagreements, and avoiding put-downs. How good would you be at creating a safe and friendly environment?
   My rating is   1   2   3   4   5
                  (I need practice)   (I do this very well)

4. **Good communication**
   A good leader gives people the information they need, and communicates clearly about what shared goal they are trying to achieve. How good are you at communicating well with others?
   My rating is   1   2   3   4   5
                  (I need practice)   (I do this very well)

5. **Good problem-solving**
   A good leader solves problems that affect his or her people by creatively thinking about different possible solutions and the possible consequences of each. How good are you at solving problems creatively?
   My rating is   1   2   3   4   5
                  (I need practice)   (I do this very well)

6. **Responsibility and organisational ability**
   A good leader does what he or she promises and is good at organising things. How good are you at being responsible and organising things well?
   My rating is   1   2   3   4   5
                  (I need practice)   (I do this very well)

7. **Enthusiasm and initiative**
   A good leader is enthusiastic and initiates things (i.e. gets things started and completes them). How good are you at being enthusiastic and initiating things?
   My rating is   1   2   3   4   5
                  (I need practice)   (I do this very well)

© Helen McGrath and Toni Noble, 2003. This page from Bounce Back!® may be photocopied for classroom use.

HOW GOOD A LEADER COULD YOU BE? (CONTINUED)

BLM 7.13

If you have been honest and accurate, this is what your score means:

7–15   You will need to practise the skills of leadership a lot more if you want to become a good leader.

16–25   You have a reasonable amount of leadership potential, but you will need to practise the skills of leadership as much as you can in order to improve.

26–35   You have a great deal of leadership potential because of your skills and attitudes. You will be a good leader if you use those skills.

© Helen McGrath and Toni Noble, 2003. This page from Bounce Back!® may be photocopied for classroom use.

CROSS-OFFS

BLM 7.14

rapid	gym	hammer	pillow	When	platypus	Florida
deed	you	summer	whale	small	shark	pool
koala	Alabama	decibel	Perth	bed	have	Hobart
a	ice-cream	snow skiing	California	snow-boarding	decade	speedy
dimmer	noon	disagreement	gag	mousse	find	tiny
quick	a	cheesecake	ice-skating	solution	decagon	stadium
that	snore	allows	decimal	seahorse	you	wombat
Brisbane	to	Adelaide	a	stay	court	apple pie
miniature	dummy	kangaroo	dreams	Texas	pup	friends

To find the message, cross off these words:

3 words that are creatures that swim in the ocean
3 words that mean fast
4 words that are sporting venues
4 words that are palindromes (i.e. 3 or more letters that read the same both ways)
4 words that are desserts
4 words that are American states
4 words that contain double 'm'
4 words that are Australian capital cities
3 words that mean 'little'
4 words that are about sleeping
4 words that are winter sports
4 words that are Australian native animals
4 words that relate to the number 10

The secret message is _____

© Helen McGrath and Toni Noble, 2003. This page from Bounce Back!® may be photocopied for classroom use.

UNIT 8
HUMOUR

KEY POINTS

Positive humour has many advantages.
Laughter and engaging in humour is enjoyable and fun. It makes you feel relaxed and more able to cope when you feel unhappy. Laughing can make your immune system more effective so that you can fight disease more effectively.

Positive healthy humour can make you feel more hopeful (optimistic).
Having a laugh can make you feel a bit better when you are feeling down or worried. It can take your mind off what is troubling you. It can help you to see that everything isn't sad or difficult, and then you can get things into perspective. Sometimes you can even find a small funny side to a sad, worrying or difficult situation. This doesn't mean that the problem goes away, but it can help you to feel better and more hopeful about things.

You can use positive humour to help someone else feel a little bit better.
Being funny can cheer someone up when they are feeling down or worried, but you need to be careful about how you do it. Don't continue to try to be funny if the other person lets you know that they are not enjoying it.

It is nasty and antisocial to laugh at other people's misfortune.
It is okay to see the funny side in your own bad luck and bad times, but let others laugh at their own misfortunes if they choose to.

Positive humour is an aspect of friendship.
One way in which friends get closer to each other is by sharing laughter. But if that shared laughter is at someone else's expense, it is a misuse of humour.

Humour can also be harmful to yourself if you misuse it.
Being funny is not helpful if it causes you to pretend that you don't have problems or that you don't feel sad or worried. This is called 'denial'. Laughter also isn't helpful if it is used to make a real and important problem seem unimportant. This is called 'trivialising'. You still have to face any problems you have.

Differentiate between a funny 'stir' and a put-down that attacks or humiliates.
It is not kind to laugh at or make fun of the way another person looks, thinks, speaks or acts. Humour should not be used to attack or to deliberately embarrass someone. This way of using humour hurts people's feelings and shows you up as having a lack of empathy and integrity. Funny 'stirring' is friendly but put-downs are not. Sometimes, if challenged, a person says 'we were just having fun', but its only funny if the person on the receiving end genuinely laughs too.

UNIT 8—HUMOUR

Class discussion—Why do people laugh and what do they laugh at? *185*

MATHS/ENGLISH ACTIVITY
Predictor cards: tabloid joke rating *185*

INVESTIGATIONS
When do we laugh? *186*

ACTIVITIES
Researching humour *186*
Collective classroom research *186*
Working with younger students *187*
Research projects *187*
Classroom recommendations *187*
Put-down humour *187*
Funny magazine advertisements *187*
Ten thinking tracks *187*
Self-reflections *188*
Quick quotes *188*

Class discussion—The social skill of telling a joke well *188*

ACTIVITIES
Telling jokes *188*
Multiply and merge *189*

Class discussion—Positive humour is healthy and enjoyable *189*

Class discussion—Positive humour helps us to cope better *189*

SONG
'Hullo Muddah, Hello Faddah' *190*

CLASSROOM ORGANISATION
Humour *191*

GAMES
Humorous games *191*

SONGS
'Beep Beep' *191*
'Pushbike Song' *192*
'(Flying) Purple People Eater' *192*

Class discussion—Negative put-down humour *192*

Consolidation *193*
Reviewing *193*
Limericks *193*
Compiling a glossary *193*
Funny poems *193*

Tongue-twister *193*
Parody *193*
TEAM coaching *193*
Graphical story *194*
Information scavenger hunt *194*
Balloon burst quotes *194*
'Throw the dice', 'Inside–outside circles' or 'Musical stop and share' *194*
Before or after? *195*
Cross-offs *195*

Resources *195*

BLM 8.1—Which one is funniest? *196*

BLM 8.2—Jokes *197*

BLM 8.3—Charles Schultz *198*

BLM 8.4—Cross-offs *199*

Many activities based around humour can be found in *Seven Ways At Once*, Book 2. For details, see the 'Resources' section on page 195.

CLASS DISCUSSION: WHY DO PEOPLE LAUGH AND WHAT DO THEY LAUGH AT?

Start by reading a funny picture book or poem to the class or by playing one of the funny games on page 191. Students then work with a partner to discuss why human brains seem to be 'pre-wired' by evolution to laugh, and why no other species has this characteristic. The most common theories are:

- Only humans suffer emotional pain and unbearable circumstances and laughter helps people to cope better at such times.
- Only humans need to live together in such large groups, and humour helps to build relationships and offset the hostility that can develop, so that we can all live in relative peace with each other.

Discussion questions

- What do we mean by a 'sense of humour'? What do you look for?
- Is a good sense of humour a sign of intelligence? (Research suggests that it is, depending on the type of humour.)
- Why do people laugh at different things?
- What makes you laugh? What are the typical things that students of your age find funny?
- What are the typical things that younger children such as toddlers and preschoolers find funny?
- Why does our sense of humour change as we get older?
- Is sarcasm (or putting others down) really the 'lowest form of wit'?
- What is a book, a television show or a movie that you find funny? What makes you laugh in this book or show?

MATHS/ENGLISH ACTIVITY
Predictor cards: tabloid joke ratings

X See Chapter 10 of the Teacher's Handbook.

Set up five tables. Place a numbered joke (see jokes on BLM 8.1) with squares of paper with that joke's number on each table. Students individually move from table to table rating each joke and recording their rating on the paper. They rate each joke as:

1. Very funny
2. Quite funny
3. Okay
4. A little bit funny
5. Not funny

Then in groups they use the 'predictor cards' strategy (see Chapter 10 of the *Teacher's Handbook*) to predict the order in which the jokes will be chosen as funniest. They also work out averages. Follow up with statistics and report writing. This survey could be extended to the rest of the school. The Watson and Holmes joke was considered to be the funniest in the LaughLab online experiment in the United Kingdom in 2001, with 47 per cent of the world-wide raters rating it as 'very funny' (www.laughlab.co.uk/home).

INVESTIGATIONS
When do we laugh?

- In groups students devise and carry out a survey to find whether or not humour in an advertisement creates a positive perception and a recall of the product. Can students match the product to the funny newspaper or TV ad? Use with procedural writing.
- Students can count how many times a day they (or someone else) laugh(s). (Note: the average for an adult is 15 times a day.)
- What makes little kids laugh? Students can devise an experiment (and make a video) to see what makes preschool students laugh most and then carry it out. They can look at:
  – Surprise
  – Incongruity (things that don't really go together, such as a cat saying 'quack, quack')
  – Silly voices or expressions
  – Silly slapstick (falling over).
- Students plan and implement an investigation to answer the question 'Do people laugh more when they are alone or when they are with other people?'(Research suggests that someone is thirty times more likely to laugh when in a group). Use with procedural writing.

ACTIVITIES
Researching humour

- Students can categorise jokes, cartoons and riddles in terms of some of the main theories of humour styles:
  – *Superiority humour*: the joke makes the teller and the audience feel superior to another group of people.
  – *Surprise humour*: the joke relies entirely on 'hijacking' the audience. That is, you end up where you didn't expect to go.
  – *Incongruity humour*: the joke combines aspects that do not fit together.
  – *Normalisation humour*: the joke contains a 'common reality' that many people in the audience will share.
  – *Attack humour*: the joke expresses hostility towards a group of people.
- Students work in groups of four to develop a classification system for humour.
- Students work in groups of four to research and identify all the different genres of jokes and riddles (e.g. 'Knock, knock' jokes, 'blonde' jokes, 'There was an Englishman, an Australian and . . .). They then write up a booklet with examples.
- Students use a Venn diagram to compare two humorous writers, illustrators, cartoonists, cartoon series, comedians, comic actors etc.
- Students categorise all of the comic performers they can think of as either 'They say funny things' or 'They say things funny' (i.e. in a funny way).

Collective classroom research

X   See Chapter 10 of the Teacher's Handbook.

Choose a specific category of humour for students to collect information about and (acceptable) examples of :
- You know it is going to be a bad day when . . .
- Knock, knock jokes
- Elephant jokes
- Light-bulb jokes
- Great comedy partnerships.

Working with younger students

- Students make a simple, illustrated, large-print riddle book for younger students and then present it to them. A good site for riddles is www.niehs.nih.gov/kids.
- Students work in groups of four to make an electronic riddle quiz (see Chapter 11 of the *Teacher's Handbook*) for younger students.

Research projects

- Students work with a partner to complete a project on a professional humourist of their choice and then create their own small sample of that style of humour. They could use the topic of 'moving to high school' or 'playing in your first grand final'.
- What kind of humour might the following groups have used? Can you find any evidence of humour being used in these periods of history?
  - The Egyptians
  - The Greeks
  - The Romans
  - People during the Gold Rush
  - People during wartime
  - People in medieval times (e.g. fools and court jesters).
- Students work with a partner to prepare and present a ten-minute class talk on a chosen humorist (e.g. actor, writer, illustrator, comedian, cartoonist).

Classroom recommendations

Compile a class book of different students' recommendations for:
- Funniest song/illustrator/poem/book/picture book
- Funniest joke/riddle/website
- Funniest TVshow/movie/cartoon/comedian.

Put-down humour

Students watch, analyse and discuss a funny TV show or video that relies on put-downs. Is the humour offensive?

Funny magazine advertisements

Students collect and make a room display of humorous advertisements from magazines. After a classroom stroll (see Chapter 11 of the *Teacher's Handbook*) they list all the things that make them funny.

Ten thinking tracks

X See BLM 1.3 at p. 21 in Unit 1, 'Core values'.

Use the 'ten thinking tracks' for this situation: the city council of Stockholm decided to encourage people to put their litter into the public litter bins. They wired all the bins so that when you stepped on the pedal that lifted the lid of the bin, you heard a quick joke or riddle.

Self-reflections

- Students make a personal timeline to show how their sense of humour has changed over time in terms of the kinds of TV shows, books etc. that make them laugh.
- Can they recall a time when a humorous show or book helped them to feel better in a difficult time?
- Students can keep a humour diary for a week. They make a note of every time something makes them laugh. Do any patterns emerge in regard to coping or relaxing? What did the students learn about themselves?

Quick quotes

X See Chapter 11 of the Teacher's Handbook.

What makes me laugh is . . .

CLASS DISCUSSION THE SOCIAL SKILL OF TELLING A JOKE WELL

Being funny in an appropriate and successful way is a social skill.

Discussion questions

- Why is 'being funny' a good people skill if it is done well?
- What are the worst 'sins' of telling a joke poorly?
- What do people who tell jokes well do? From this, develop a list of Do's and Don'ts for telling a joke well. For example:
  - Make sure you *know* the punchline before you tell the joke.
  - Try to make the joke relevant to something that has been said or that has happened.
  - Make sure you tell the right joke to the right person. Ask yourself, 'Will the joke I want to tell be offensive to or uncomfortable for them?'
  - Say it confidently.
  - Try to use different voices and acting to make the joke more interesting.
  - Look at people when you are telling your joke.
  - Don't spend too much time on the lead-up to the punchline.
  - Don't get too bogged down in detail.
  - Don't read your joke.
  - Don't laugh while telling your joke.
  - Don't laugh at your own joke when the punchline comes.

ACTIVITIES
Telling jokes

Use the 'jigsaw' strategy (see Chapter 10 of the *Teacher's Handbook*) with the jokes on BLM 8.2 to help students to improve their social skill of telling a joke well. Cut the sheet into three and enlarge each joke onto coloured paper.

Multiply and merge

X See Chapter 10 of the Teacher's Handbook.

Give students a sheet of twenty riddles or ask them to each collect 10 of their own that they think are both funny and acceptable. The class votes on the five funniest riddles.

CLASS DISCUSSION: POSITIVE HUMOUR IS HEALTHY AND ENJOYABLE

Discussion questions

- What positive effects does laughter have on our bodies? (it helps our bodies to relax; makes the brain release pleasure or 'feel good' chemicals; helps us to resist infection; activates natural 'killer' cells so we can fight disease more successfully; lowers the rate at which the heart beats so that we feel fitter; helps to produce stronger bones, especially if we have been stressed for a while; helps our body to grow and repair itself when it is damaged)
- Why do we like laughing with our friends? (it feels good; we share something special; we feel more relaxed with each other; friends help us to laugh more than we would if we were alone)
- Do you think people who laugh a lot are more popular? If so, why? (They seem more friendly; they are more fun; they seem more positive and confident. People who laugh and smile a lot are more appealing as friends and more attractive to the opposite sex.)

Follow-up activities

- Students trace around or draw bodies and label the illustration with the different effects of laughter on the body and brain.
- Twenty seconds of laughing equals three minutes of hard rowing. Ten minutes of laughter a day is equal to half an hour of an exercise workout. Students can make a plan for how they will attempt to laugh in a healthy way for ten minutes each day.

CLASS DISCUSSION: POSITIVE HUMOUR HELPS US TO COPE BETTER

Use the 'bundling' strategy (see Chapter 10 of the *Teacher's Handbook*) and ask students to write five statements about how humour is important to coping with life. Briefly talk about how kings and queens in history have had official clowns in the court to cheer them up (i.e. court jesters or 'fools'). Tell the students about a time in your own life when there was a funny side to a serious situation. Ask students to use the 'Think–Pair–Share' strategy (see Chapter 10 of the *Teacher's Handbook*) and talk about a similar time in their life.

Discussion questions

- Four days after the terrorist attack on the World Trade Center on 11 September 2001, the mayor of New York, Rudy Giuliani, appeared on the TV show 'Saturday Night Live'. He said 'we need laughter to help us heal'. Do you agree with this comment?

- How does laughter help someone 'maintain face' and cope better when they feel embarrassed? (it distracts attention; they seem more able to cope)
- Ask students for examples of times when they have seen someone fall over or trip and some people laughed. Talk about why people sometimes laugh when they see someone have a fall.
- Is it mean to laugh when someone feels embarrassed or is it helpful? There are some nasty reasons (e.g. they don't stop and think about how the other person feels; they want to make them feel even more humiliated) and some kind reasons (they want the other person to feel better and see the funny side).
- Can you think of a time when you coped better with something unpleasant when you found the funny side to it, either at the time or afterwards, even if it was a small funny side?
- Can anyone think of positive humorous activities or pastimes that can cheer people up if they feel unhappy and make people feel more hopeful that things will get better?

Follow-up activities

- Ask students to bring used humorous birthday (non-offensive) and get-well cards to class. Make a classroom display. Discuss and analyse the cards with the class and draw conclusions about why people send them, why we like to receive them, and what the purpose of the humour is. (it's usually about cheering others up)
- Imagine that the school council has asked the principal to find ways to make students laugh more at school. Students work in groups of four to advise him or her on the best way to do this.
- As a class, make up an interview sheet with some questions to use when interviewing a family member about a time when they felt very sad or worried but having a bit of a laugh helped them to feel a bit better, or they found a small funny side to a negative situation in their life. Each student should interview one family member.
- Ask students to read BLM 8.3, 'Charles Schultz'. Then use the 'collective classroom research' strategy (see Chapter 10 of the *Teacher's Handbook*) and encourage students to collect the work of Charles Schultz. They could each select one 'Peanuts' character and write the character's biography. Consider staging the musical production based on 'Peanuts' called *You're a Good Man, Charlie Brown*.

SONG
'Hello Muddah, Hello Faddah'

This very funny, classic song is the story of a boy who goes to camp and initially hates it because it rains all the time. He writes home to his parents with outrageous tales of the awful things that are happening at camp. Eventually things improve, and his final words in his letter home are 'kindly disregard this letter'. The song was written by poet Shel Silverstein and originally sung by Alan Sherman to the tune of the classical piece 'Dance of the Hours'. It's a great song to sing and discuss just before the students go to camp. Students can sing the song and then either act out or illustrate the story.

Lyrics and music can be found at www.kididdles.com/dcforum/DCForumID8/52.html.

Lyrics only are at www.humorcentral.com/humor/hcjoke157.htm or www.bbhq.com/lyrics.htm.

Original music from 'Dance of the Hours' by Ponchinelli is at www.classicalarchives.com/midi-n-s.html.

CLASSROOM ORGANISATION
Humour

- With the help of a rotating class committee, create and maintain a 'Humour zone' in the classroom or school. Include comic strips, funny books and poems, riddles and jokes and cartoons.
- Students can decorate the corridor outside their room with their favourite cartoon strips or their own humorous artworks.
- Have a section of the bulletin board set aside for the joke of the week. Students can write out jokes and give them to the teacher or the Humour Committee to evaluate before posting.
- Check that students' comments, throw-away-lines, jokes and riddles are not sexist, racist or offensive.
- Have a full-day 'humour fest'.
- Give students a five-minute humour break each day (or in a double period where appropriate). You could:
  - Ask students to draw something in the room with their non-preferred hand.
  - Ask them to make funny faces or adopt a funny walk.
  - Read the class a funny picture story book.
  - Allow them to tell jokes or riddles (previewed for acceptability).
  - Have them present a review of a funny show they have seen or a book they have read.

GAMES
Humorous games

There are more ideas in the Level 2 *Teacher's Resource Book*.
- Play 20 questions as a class where students try to guess the name of professional humorists/films/books etc.
- Play 'Where, Oh Where, is the Wonderwart?'. Students sit in a circle. One at a time they turn to the person on their left and say, 'Friend, this is serious. Where, oh where, is the wonderwart?' All the students then place their right hand over their eyebrows, turn their heads right, left, and right again, saying once, 'Where, oh where, is the wonderwart?' The person who has just been spoken to now turns to the person on his or her left and so on. You are out if you laugh or smile. The winner is the person who can keep a straight face the longest.
- Play humour charades using the titles of humorous TV shows, films, books, comic strips and songs for the whole class to guess. Alternatively, play in two teams.
- In groups of three, each student takes a turn at drawing the word they select from a container (e.g. teeth, fairy, castle, ring, cat, monkey, umbrella, clown, witch, handstand, horse, tambourine, shark, bridge, surfer, emu, magnet, queen, kiss, golf stick). They must draw the item blindfolded and the other two members of the group try to guess what they are drawing. What makes the drawings so funny? Make links to humour in art (e.g. the work of the surrealist artists such as Salvador Dali).

SONGS

Some of these songs can be fun to sing or listen to but they're not particularly 'cool'. Students can be asked to suggest others.

'Beep Beep'

Lyrics and sheet music in *The 1993 Sing Book* produced by the ABC.

'Pushbike Song'

Lyrics and sheet music are in *The Best of Sing* (1982–1990) and *Sing On* (1985), both produced by the ABC.

'(Flying) Purple People Eater'

Lyrics only are at www.bbhq.com/lyrics.htm. Lyrics and sheet music are in *The 1993 Sing Book* and *Let's All Sing* (1981), both produced by the ABC.

CLASS DISCUSSION: NEGATIVE PUT-DOWN HUMOUR

Talk about how humour can be a weapon of attack, not just a helpful tool. Link with the section on put-downs in Unit 9, 'Bullying'.

Discussion questions

- Why do students sometimes use 'mean' humour? (To make others think that they are tough; to show off or get noticed; to make someone look 'smaller' so others won't like them and thus to protect their own peer acceptance; sometimes they don't realise that they are hurting someone else's feelings.)
- What examples have you seen where humour is:
  - Designed to attack someone else
  - Intended to make someone look stupid/smaller
  - Aimed at maintaining a stereotype (e.g. jokes about blondes).

Follow-up activities

- In groups of four, students write answers to each of the following questions:
  - What kind of jokes might offend other people?
  - What could you say if you accidentally offend in this way?
  - List all the ways in which people show that they don't think that something said or done was funny. Don't forget to consider body language.
- Students can collect and analyse cartoon strips, jokes etc. as a starting point for the idea of stereotypes. For example:
  - Students and parents
  - Men and women; wives and husbands
  - Older people and younger people
  - Cats and dogs
  - Very bright people and not-so-bright people
  - People who wear glasses
  - Blondes.

  Discuss how students would feel if they belonged to the group that was being made fun of or stereotyped.

CONSOLIDATION

Reviewing

Students review a humorous performance, show, video, song, poem or book.

Limericks

Students read limericks, analyse the 'form' and then write their own.

Compiling a glossary

Students work in groups of four to prepare an A–Z glossary of terms related to humour (e.g. slapstick, parody, irony, deadpan, stand-up comic).

Funny poems

Students prepare and present (with a partner) a review of one of the following books of funny poems:
- *Sister Madge's Book of Nuns*
- *Selected Cautionary Verses*
- *Revolting Rhymes*
- *In the Garden of Bad Things*
- *Far Out, Brussel Sprout!* or *All Right, Vegemite.*

Details of these publications can be found in the 'Resources' section on page 195.

Tongue-twister

The 'sixth sick sheik's sixth sheep's sick' is said to be the toughest tongue twister in the English language. Can anyone get it right three times in a row without laughing?

Parody

Talk about the concept of 'parody' (a send-up of a recognisable genre or plot). Read to the class:
- The picture book by Tony Ross entitled *The Three Pigs*, a modern parody of the classic tale, set in a 40-storey apartment building and with a twist at the end
- *The True Story of the Three Little Pigs*, in which the wolf claims to have been framed
- Some of the stories in Roald Dahl's *Revolting Rhymes* or *Dirty Beasts*
- The picture book *The Paperbag Princess.*

Ask students to write their own send-ups of famous stories or fairytales.

In groups, students could write a parody by adapting *The Man From Snowy River* (e.g. There was movement in the classroom (or playground, assembly, staffroom) because the word has passed around . . .).

TEAM coaching

X **See Chapter 10 of the Teacher's Handbook.**

Use this strategy to assist students to learn vocabulary, concepts and spelling related to humour.

Graphical story

Students work in a group of three to create their own measure of laughter. They then make up a graph that features a time on the horizontal axis and four differing amounts of laughter on the vertical axis. They swap graphs with another group and create a story to explain the graph.

Information scavenger hunt

X See Chapter 10 of the Teacher's Handbook.

- Why can't you tickle yourself or tell yourself a joke?
- Do any other animal species really laugh?
- What was a court jester? What is the modern equivalent? Give reasons for your idea.
- What is a 'funny bone'?
- What is 'Murphy's law'?
- What comic actors have won acting awards?

Balloon burst quotes

X See Chapter 11 of the Teacher's Handbook.

Ask students to relate these quotes to using humour well and in a healthy way:
- Brevity is the soul of wit.
- Comedy and music come into their own at times of stress and strain. (Billy Connolly)
- Comedy is tragedy . . . plus time. (Carol Burnett)
- Everything is funny as long as it is happening to someone else. (Will Rogers)
- He who laughs, lasts. (Mary Pettibone Poole)
- Humour is a healthy way of finding 'distance' between one's self and the problem, a way of standing off and looking at one's problem with perspective.
- Humour is optimism in action. (Robin Williams)
- Laugh and the world laughs with you. Cry and you cry alone.
- The world is a comedy to those who think, a tragedy to those who feel. (Horace Walpole)
- You can turn painful situations around through laughter. If you can find humour in anything, you can survive it. (Bill Cosby)
- You grow up the day you have your first real laugh . . . at yourself. (Ethel Barrymore)

'Throw the dice', 'Inside–outside circles', or 'Musical stop and share'

X See Chapter 10 of the Teacher's Handbook.

- Name a cartoon series that makes you laugh (or has in the past) and say why.
- Who makes you laugh the most in your family and how?
- What does 'having a good sense of humour' mean?
- What is a funny movie or video you have seen and why was it funny?
- Has your pet or an animal ever done something that made you laugh?
- Describe a funny commercial that you like and tell why you think it's funny.
- How could you tell that someone is laughing *with* someone rather than *at* someone?
- What is a good way to remember jokes?
- Is it helpful to say 'We'll laugh about this next week' as a way of dealing with stress?

- Who is the teacher who has made you laugh the most? How did they do this?
- Tell about something that happened to you or someone you know (no names rule) that still makes you laugh when you think about it?

Before or after?

X See Chapter 10 of the Teacher's Handbook.

Amusement	Giggle	Pun
Banter	Hopeful	Punchline
Caricature	Humorous	Quip
Cartoon	Humour	Riddle
Chortle	Hysterical	Routine
Chuckle	Incongruity	Sarcasm
Circus	Jest	Satire
Clown	Jester	Skit
Comedian	Joke	Slapstick
Comedy	Joker	Smile
Comic	Laugh	Stereotypes
Cope	Laughter	Stir
Deadpan	Limerick	Surprise
Exaggeration	Mirth	Tickle
Facetious	Mock	Uproarious
Farce	Optimistic	Wit
Funny	Parody	
Gag	Prank	

Cross-offs

Students complete BLM 8.4, 'Cross-offs'. The answer is: A little humour can help in difficult times.

RESOURCES

Books

Hilaire Belloc, 1981, *Selected Cautionary Verses*, Puffin Books, Melbourne.
Roald Dahl & Quentin Blake, 1982, *Revolting Rhymes*, Jonathan Cape, London.
Roald Dahl & Quentin Blake, 1984, *Dirty Beasts*, Jonathan Cape, London.
June Factor & Peter Viska, 1985, *All Right, Vegemite*, Oxford University Press, Melbourne.
June Factor & Peter Viska, 1987, *Far Out, Brussel Sprout!*, Oxford University Press, Melbourne.
H McGrath & T Noble, 1996, *Seven Ways At Once*, Book 2, Longman, Australia.
Doug McLeod, 1981, *In the Garden of Bad Things*, Puffin Books, Melbourne.
Doug McLeod, 1986, *Sister Madge's Book of Nuns*, Omnibus Books, Adelaide.
Robert Munsch, 1980, *Paperbag Princess*, Ashton Scholastic, Sydney.
Tony Ross, 1983, *The Three Pigs*, Andersen, London.
Jon Scleszka, 1989, *The True Story of the Three Little Pigs*, Viking, New York.

WHICH ONE IS FUNNIEST?

BLM 8.1

The Duck
A duck went to the post office and asked, 'Do you have any corn?' The post office worker politely replied, 'No, sorry, we don't have any corn.' The next day the duck turned up again at the post office and said, 'Do you have any corn?' The post office worker replied, rather crossly, 'No, I told you, we don't have any corn.' The next day the duck came to the post office again and asked, 'Do you have any corn?' The post office worker was very angry and said, 'No, for the last time, we don't have any corn. If you come back here again asking for corn I'm going to nail your beak to the counter!' The next day the duck went to the post office again and asked, 'Do you have any nails?' The post office worker replied, 'No, we don't have any nails.' 'Well,' said the duck, 'do you have any corn?'

The vampire bat
A young vampire bat flew into his cave one night, covered in fresh blood. He perched himself on the roof of the cave to get some sleep. Before long, all the other bats smelled the blood and began hassling him about where he had got it. He was tired and needed a rest, so he asked them to leave him alone. However, it was clear that he wasn't going to get any sleep until he satisfied their curiosity. 'Okay,' he said with exasperation, 'follow me.' Then he flew out of the cave with hundreds of bats following him. He took them across the valley, across the river and into the deep forest. Finally he slowed down and all the other bats excitedly gathered around him. 'Do you see that tree over there?' he asked. 'Yes, yes, yes!' the bats all screamed in a frenzy. 'Good,' said the first bat. 'Because I DIDN'T!'

The pirate
A pirate was talking to a stranger in a bar. The stranger noticed that the pirate had a wooden leg, a hook in place of one of his hands, and a patch over one eye. The stranger wanted to know what had happened to him. First he asked the pirate, 'How did you lose your leg?' The pirate responded, 'I lost my leg in a battle.' Then the stranger asked, 'What about your hand?' 'I lost it to a shark in the South Seas,' the pirate replied. Finally, the stranger asked, 'I notice you also have an eye patch. How did you lose your eye?' The pirate answered, 'I was sleeping on a beach when a seagull flew over and pooped right in my eye.' The stranger asked, 'How could a little seagull poo make you lose your eye?' The pirate snapped angrily, 'Because it was the day after I got my hook and I wasn't used to it!'

The bilingual dog
A local business was looking for someone to work in their office. Their ad said, 'Position available. Must be able to type. Must be good with a computer and speak two languages.' A dog applied for the job. The surprised office manager led the dog into the office. The manager said, 'I can't hire you. The sign says you have to be able to write a letter.' The dog went to the computer and typed a perfect letter. The manager was stunned, but then told the dog, 'You have to be good at using other computer programs.' The dog showed that he could do all the things needed. By this time the manager was totally stunned. He looked at the dog and said, 'I realise that you are a very intelligent dog, and you have some interesting abilities. However, I still can't give you the job because the sign says you have to speak two languages.' The dog looked at him and said, 'Meow.'

Watson and Holmes
Sherlock Holmes, the famous detective, and his assistant, Watson, went camping. They pitched their tent underneath the stars and went to sleep. In the middle of the night, Holmes woke Watson up and said, 'Watson, look up and tell me what you see.' Watson replied, 'I see millions of stars and even if only a few of those stars have planets, it is quite likely that there are some planets like our earth, and that means there may be some which have life on them.' Holmes replied, 'Watson, you idiot, somebody has stolen our tent!'

© Helen McGrath and Toni Noble, 2003. This page from Bounce Back!® may be photocopied for classroom use.

JOKES

BLM 8.2

The clever prisoner
Three men are captured and put in jail. They are found guilty and ordered to be executed by a firing squad. When the first man faces the firing squad, he has a brilliant idea. He decides to confuse them and create a panic. Just as the soldiers raise their rifles and the officer says 'Ready, aim . . .', the prisoner yells out 'earthquake'. The soldiers panic and run off and the prisoner escapes. The second prisoner thinks that this is a good idea, and when he faces the firing squad and the soldiers raise their guns and say 'Ready, aim . . .', he calls out 'tornado'. The soldiers panic and run off and the second prisoner escapes. The third man is not as clever as the other two, but he thinks he will try to do the same thing and confuse them. When the soldiers raise their guns and the officer says 'Ready, aim . . .', he calls out 'Fire!'

What is intelligence?
Two men, Tom and Bob, were digging holes on a very hot day. Tom said to Bob, 'How come we're digging holes on this sort of day when our boss is standing in the shade having a cold drink?' Bob said, 'I don't know. I'll go and ask him.' So he did, and the boss said, 'I don't have to dig holes in the ground on a hot day like you do because of intelligence.' 'What do you mean?' said Bob. 'Well, I'll show you,' replied the boss. 'I'll put my hand in front of this tree and I want you to hit my hand with your fist as hard as you can.' Bob took a mighty swing and tried to punch the boss's hand, but at the last minute the boss moved his hand and Bob punched the tree instead. The boss said, 'That's intelligence.' Bob went back to Tom and said, 'I'm going to be a boss because now I know how to be more intelligent.' Tom asked, 'What do you mean?' Bob said, 'Here, I'll show you.' He put his hand in front of his face and said, 'Go on, hit my hand with your shovel.'

Who did you say was the stupid one?
Sam, a young boy, often hung out at the local milk bar. The shopkeeper often noticed boys teasing Sam. The boys said Sam wasn't very smart. To prove it, sometimes the boys offered Sam a choice between a one-dollar coin and a two-dollar coin. Sam always took the one-dollar coin. The boys told the shopkeeper that Sam took the coin that was worth less money because it was bigger! One day, after Sam had again been offered the two coins, and again had chosen the one-dollar coin over the two-dollar coin, the shopkeeper took Sam aside and said, 'Sam, those boys are making fun of you. They think you don't know that the two-dollar coin is worth more money than the one-dollar coin. Are you grabbing the one-dollar coin because it's bigger, or what?' Sam replied, 'No sir, but if I took the two-dollar coin, they'd quit doing it, and then I wouldn't get any more money!'

© Helen McGrath and Toni Noble, 2003. This page from Bounce Back!® may be photocopied for classroom use.

CHARLES SCHULTZ

BLM 8.3

Charles Schultz has been described as the greatest cartoonist the world has ever seen. Schultz was the creator and illustrator of a very famous comic strip called 'Peanuts'. For over fifty years his cast of characters entertained people with their predictable personalities and foibles. By the time Schultz died in 2000, his comic strip and characters had appeared in newspapers and magazines all over the world, as well as on mugs, greeting cards and clothing.

The main character in 'Peanuts' is an insecure boy names Charlie Brown. Charlie Brown is kind and caring, but he is also vulnerable and desperate for people to like and respect him. He has lost 10 000 games of checkers in a row and always strikes out at baseball, but he manages to handle his failures by 'bouncing back' each time and surviving. Another character in 'Peanuts' is Snoopy, Charlie Brown's faithful dog. Snoopy is always there for Charlie but also has a wild fantasy life of his own. Other characters include Lucy, who is overly confident but with little reason, and constantly criticises Charlie Brown and tries to make his life miserable. Lucy has a little brother called Linus, who has given the world the term 'security blanket', as he always has to have one with him.

The stories in 'Peanuts' are always gentle. The punchlines are funny but not cruel. Readers are able to laugh at the characters and their funny adventures and feel empathy for them at the same time.

As a child, Charles Schultz loved to draw and quickly became very good at it. He read other comic strips passionately and soon copied other well-known characters such as Mickey Mouse and Popeye. He then began to create his own characters and eventually submitted them to his school magazine. However, nobody seemed too impressed and his comic strips went unpublished.

At high school, Schultz wasn't particularly popular and the other students paid him little attention. He lacked confidence. He found it hard to generate enough confidence to ask girls out. He worked hard to become captain of the school's golf team but lost his only important match.

When Charles Schultz created comic strips as an adult, he drew on some of his more difficult experiences when growing up. He made fun of some of his failures in a gentle way. He once commented: 'I know what it's like to feel inferior and these are common feelings deep down for most people. My sense of humour has helped me survive and the strip reflects the basic fears and setbacks which are part of our human condition.'

Charles Schultz never let his setbacks and failures get the better of him. He learned from them, always looked on the funny side of life, and eventually became a success.

1. What is a security blanket?

2. What were some of the setbacks in Schultz's life that helped him to understand other people?

CROSS-OFFS

BLM 8.4

telescope	bark	basketball	netball	leaf	hill	A
French	hammer	slippers	apple	raspberry	tonne	Queensland
little	giggle	knife	seaweed	wall	German	socks
pear	floor	milligram	football	screwdriver	glasses	humour
magnifying glass	Pacific	branch	shells	chuckle	can	twig
English	pliers	valley	belly laugh	Chinese	fork	drill
gold	garage	steel	Atlantic	copper	lake	help
Tasmania	in	waves	water polo	chortle	apricot	boots
roof	sand	spanner	Greek	sandals	soccer	microscope
difficult	river	kilogram	plum	gram	aluminium	times

To find the message, cross off these words:

5 words that are languages
5 words that are fruits
5 words that are sports with 'goals'
5 words that are handyman tools
4 words that are geographical features
4 words that are kinds of laughter
4 words that are measurements of weight
4 words that are parts of a tree
4 words that are things worn on your feet
4 words that are names for parts of a house
4 words that are things to help you see more clearly
4 words that are things to do with the beach
4 words that are metals
2 words that are Australian states
2 words that are oceans
2 words that are types of cutlery

The secret message is _____

© Helen McGrath and Toni Noble, 2003. This page from Bounce Back!® may be photocopied for classroom use.

UNIT 9
BULLYING

KEY POINTS

There are many forms of bullying.
Bullying means repeatedly and deliberately trying to harm, humiliate or distress another person. It can be hurting someone, spreading rumours about them, playing nasty jokes, name-calling or deliberate social exclusion.

Bullying is a form of persecution.
'Persecution' means seeking out a person in order to harm them. The history of our world is full of examples of persecution of people because of their beliefs or race or just because they were different in some way. It is one of the worst aspects of our history.

Bullying and put-downs are totally unacceptable in this school and won't be tolerated.
Bullying is a serious antisocial behaviour and you will get into serious trouble if you are involved in it, even in a small way. The school and all teachers in it will swiftly act to stop it. Your parents will be involved. A put-down is a deliberately nasty, sarcastic or critical remark, expression or gesture made to try to damage the reputation or the self-esteem of another student. Using put-downs is also a serious antisocial act.

All animals have predators to deal with, including humans.
Predators are animals prepared to hurt or kill other animals in order to get what they want. Unfortunately, some people are predators among the rest of us. Research tells us that those students who bully others more than once and use put-downs a lot are more likely to become criminals at an early age and to beat up and abuse their partner and family later on. They are usually more cold-hearted than other people, and don't feel upset at the distress of others, as most people do.

Resist pressure from others to take part in harming other students.
If you make the choice to be involved in the bullying of another student, even in a small way, you are responsible for your actions and will suffer the consequences. It is not okay to say 'everyone else was doing it too'. If you do anything, however small, to take part in bullying, then you help to keep it happening.

Bad things such as bullying can happen to good, likeable people.
If someone is being given a hard time, it doesn't mean that they deserve it or that they are people you should dislike. People who get bullied are unlucky. Next time it could be you.

If you know that bullying is happening, act responsibly and tell someone.
Let a teacher know what is happening if you are aware that bullying is going on. This is not the same as dobbing, which is trying to get someone else into trouble. This is trying to help someone who is in trouble.

Don't make yourself an easy target for bullying, but if it does happen, get support quickly.
Students who want to bully look for people who seem easy to upset. It helps to look confident so that you don't attract their attention. But once a bullying pattern has developed, it is very hard to stop it happening by yourself. Let a teacher know what is happening and ask them to help you to handle the situation. The longer you carry a problem by yourself, the heavier and worse it gets.

Bad things keep happening because good people don't do anything.
Bullying is everyone's problem. Our history has shown that good people can stop bad things from happening to others when they decide to. You can refuse to support anyone who is bullying. Don't take part. Don't watch them or laugh at what they do. Bullying can be defeated if courageous and caring students, their parents and all teachers work together.

UNIT 9—BULLYING

Class discussion—What is bullying? *202*
- BOOKS
- *Capped* 202
- *Swashbuckler* 202
- *The Gift* 203
- *Birds of a Feather* 203

Class discussion—Why do some people bully others? *203*
- BOOKS
- *The Bully* 204
- *Blubber* 204

Class discussion—Put-downs *204*
- DRAMA ACTIVITY
- Put-downs 205
- CLASSROOM ORGANISATION
- No put-downs 206

Class discussion—Self-protection and self-defence: Dealing with being bullied *206*
- BOOKS
- *Mike* 207
- *Willy the Wimp* 207

Class discussion—Human predators *207*
- ACTIVITY
- Collective classroom research 208

Class discussion—How can we work together to stop bullying from happening? *208*
- BOOKS
- *Bruce the Goose* 209
- *The Present Takers* 210
- CLASSROOM ORGANISATION
- Circle of friends 210

Class discussion—Peer pressure *210*
- BOOKS
- *The Recess Queen* 211
- *Buzzard Breath and Brains* 211
- *Stargirl* 211

Class discussion—Rumours *211*

Class discussion—Mobbing *212*

Class discussion—Bullying, sport and the law *213*

Class discussion—Bullying in history *214*
- BOOKS
- *Let the Celebrations Begin* 215
- *Rose Blanche* 215
- POEM
- *First They Came for the Jews* 215

Consolidation *216*
- Websites about bullying 216
- English activities 216

Resources *216*

BLM 9.1—A quiz about bullying *218*

BLM 9.2—The bully movie: stars, support staff and crew *219*

BLM 9.3—The put-down pro in action *220*

BLM 9.4—How animals and plants protect and defend themselves *221*

BLM 9.5—Self-defence against bullying *222*

BLM 9.6—Having the courage to show compassion *223*

BLM 9.7—Memory test *224*

BLM 9.8—The Ku Klux Klan *225*

BLM 9.9—Bullying and the law *226*

BLM 9.10—The six steps of persecution *227*

BLM 9.11—The holocaust *228*

BLM 9.12—Good people can make a difference *229*

BOUNCE BACK!

CLASS DISCUSSION: WHAT IS BULLYING?

Use BLM 9.1, 'A quiz about Bullying', as a 'postbox' activity (see Chapter 10 of the *Teacher's Handbook*) to collect data to use during this initial discussion. The correct answers (where there *are* correct answers) are:

1. Yes.
2. Simon is right.
3. Research suggests that about three-quarters of all students feel distressed.

Alternatively, or additionally, read to the class and discuss one of the following books: *Capped*, *Swashbuckler*, *The Gift*, *Birds of a Feather* (see below).

The *Simpsons* episode called 'Bart the General' is also a useful introduction if you stop the video just after the second time that Bart gets bullied. The rest is pretty silly.

Discussion questions

- What kinds of things do some students do when they bully other students and try to hurt or humiliate them? (physical attacks, social exclusion, insulting and name-calling, nasty practical jokes, forcing people to steal or give them things, taking or hurting things that belong to them, spreading rumours)
- How might the person who is being cruelly treated feel? (scared, angry, lonely)
- What might be the long-term result of being bullied? (it is not easily forgotten; their spirit and self-esteem can be crushed; they might stop trusting people)
- How might the person doing the bullying feel? (superior, cold and uncaring, smug, confident about their power over others in a nasty arrogant way)
- How might the students who are seeing it feel? (scared, ashamed, worried; a few might be amused)
- How might teachers who find out about it feel? (shocked, ashamed if it is a member of their class, disapproving, worried)
- How might the parents of the student being bullied feel? (angry, worried)
- How might the parents of the student who gets into trouble for acting like a bully feel? (ashamed, angry, worried about what sort of adult they will become)

BOOKS

Capped (Simple chapter book)

At the end of Year 5, Jon is one of the most popular kids and in line to be selected as school captain. But he is feeling pretty down about his parents' separation. He gets bullied by Ben, the class bully, because of his friendship with a new boy at the school. There is a nice subplot about Jon helping his friend Kayla to deal with *her* parents separating which reflects 'bouncing back' ('It's never going to be the way it was, but it does get better'). The student who bullies in this story is portrayed in a stereotypical and unrealistic way as big, bulky and not too bright, but this can be discussed.

Swashbuckler (Simple chapter book)

This book is summarised in Unit 7, 'Relationships'. The two friends, Peter and Anton, are both bullied by Tony and his 'crew', and support each other.

UNIT 9—BULLYING

The Gift (Picture book)

This is a follow-on from the story of the Pied Piper of Hamelin. One young boy was not seduced into the cavern with the rest of the children because he was lame. He finds it lonely by himself but he doesn't miss the bullying he used to get at school because of his disability. A few years later, the piper returns and gives the boy the gift of a pipe, which he can use to bring the children back. But the first child he sees when the cavern starts to open is the boy who was the ringleader of the bullying he received. What will he do? Start with the original story of the Pied Piper.

Birds of a Feather (Chapter book)

Rosie is in Year 6 and life is pretty good until a new girl, Justine, arrives at the school. At first Rosie thinks that Justine is great, but soon she has managed to 'steal' Rosie's two best friends and shut Rosie out. Then she starts bullying Rosie. In this story, the bully is portrayed with great accuracy and not 'explained away' as a 'disadvantaged or abused' child, as happens in so many other books about bullying. (This book of 12 chapters could be read as a serial.)

CLASS DISCUSSION: WHY DO SOME PEOPLE BULLY OTHERS?

Start with students completing BLM 9.2, 'The bully movie: stars, support cast and crew'. Use this as part of the basis of the discussion. Also refer back to the 'postbox' quiz on BLM 9.1.

Alternatively or additionally, read to the class and discuss *The Bully* and/or *Blubber* (see below). As part of the discussion of each book, ask students to identify the 'ice-blocks' (relatively cold-hearted and unfeeling individuals). List them in order of how 'cold' they are.

Discussion questions

- Why do some students bully others? (to show off; to look tough; to look popular; because they are relatively cold-blooded [especially the ringleaders] and low in human compassion; they think it is okay to mistreat people to impress others; they haven't thought seriously about the harm they are doing)
- Do students who are the ringleaders in bullying have low self-esteem? Low school ability? Are they big and bulky? (The big brawny 'thick' student who has low self-esteem is an unrealistic stereotype. Students who bully are quite varied in terms of size and intellect, but all have an inflated sense of themselves, limited conscience, low empathy for others' feelings [they are ice-blocks], and a belief that it is okay to intimidate and humiliate another human being in order to gain social power.)
- We know that people who mistreat animals are more likely to bully other kids at school. Why might this be? (same as above)
- We know that students who bully others more than once are more likely to become people who are charged with criminal offences and/or who hurt, abuse and intimidate their wives/husbands and/or children. Why might this be? (same as above)
- Why do some kids watch and laugh when bullying is happening to someone else? (history is full of situations where this happened, for example the crowds enjoying

people being killed as entertainment in Ancient Rome and Greece; sometimes it relieves boredom; it is mostly a failure to think about how distressed the target is feeling, plus an incorrect belief that the people being bullied are lesser people)
- Why do good people sometimes not speak up when they see bad things such as bullying happen? (as above; they are worried about their own safety; they are concerned about being socially rejected by the bullies; they don't want to be seen to be dobbing)
- Why are most students kind to their classmates and *not* cruel? (they know bullying is wrong; they have good positive values, such as being kind, fair and compassionate; they would feel ashamed if they did it and if their parents knew; they realise that people who are bullied suffer; they have better ways to impress others)

Follow-up activities

- Stage a drama (or a sitcom series) that features the 'stars, support cast and crew' in bullying situations (see BLM 9.2). Allocate parts using the character names and perhaps labels around their necks. Discuss each enactment.
- Students analyse the style of the non-fiction picture book *Bully for You!*, which is a tongue-in-cheek book about how to be a bully. They could write a version for their own age group and situation.

BOOKS

The Bully (Chapter book)

Simon Mason is bullied unmercifully by Anna Royle and her friend Rebekhah. They enmesh Anna's younger brother David in their cruel schemes. But nobody at school believes that 'lovely' Anna could be doing this. It is only the support of a caring teacher that helps Simon survive. This is a harrowing book. The cold-bloodedness of Anna, the vengeful hatred of Simon and the frustration and confusion of Louise Shaw and the other teachers are all realistically presented. (The book has 16 chapters. Read it as a serial.)

Blubber (Chapter book)

Jill is one of many people in the Year 5 class who bully the slightly overweight Linda and call her 'Blubber'. Their tormenting of her is incredibly cruel and yet realistically presented. The ringleader is the cold-blooded Wendy who rules the class from a base of popularity and intimidation. The teachers are presented as unaware of what is happening. The turnaround comes at the end when Jill refuses to do one of the things to Linda that Wendy has planned and then Jill is on the receiving end of the same treatment as that dished out to Linda. (The book has 19 chapters and is suitable for Years 5 and 6.)

CLASS DISCUSSION PUT-DOWNS

Use the 'bundling' strategy to ask students to write four sentences about put-downs.

Discussion questions

- What do put-downs sound like? What do they look like? (See BLM 9.3, 'The put-down pro in action'.)

- What can put-downs feel like when you receive them? (you feel small, embarrassed, stupid and as though you are not a likeable or worthy person)
- Why are put-downs or nasty comments about our personal limitations more distressing?
- Why do some people use more put-downs than others? (to make others look bad so they look good; to make others think they are cool, popular or tough; they are cold, mean-spirited people; they want to try and stop others from being a person's friend so that they will like *them* more)
- What would happen if the school said it was okay to use put-downs? (no one would feel safe enough to say anything; we would always be arguing; we wouldn't like each other)
- What's the difference between having a joke and using a put-down? (a joke is between friends; if it is a joke, both people think it is funny, not just the person saying it)
- What are some good ways to let the other person know that you know that they are trying to put you down? (Make a 'thumbs down' and then a 'thumbs up' gesture and look straight at them and say, 'Good one, Andrew!' This means, 'I see what you're doing and I'm unimpressed'.)
- What is the difference between friendly stirring and put-downs? (stirring is exaggerated or deadpan; a genuine smile is added to 'cancel' the message; a known friendship exists and both people enjoy the joke)
- How are put-downs and bullying linked? (put-downs reflect the same cold-hearted and intimidatory state of mind as bullying; put-downs are a form of bullying if the same person is regularly on the receiving end)
- Why do some students pretend they don't mind when they are being put down in a funny way? (they're scared of being excluded or getting worse treatment)

Follow-up activities

- Students negotiate in small groups to decide on and then make the best slogan or poster to use to get the message across to students about the non-acceptability of put-downs. For example:
  - Our school is a 'no put-down zone'. (See BLM 9.3 in the *Teacher's Resource Book*, Level 2, for a poster example.)
  - Put-downs (or put-down pros) are poisonous (or pathetic/pathological).
- Students can watch a television sitcom and use BLM 9.3, 'The put-down pro in action', to analyse whether any of those put-downs occur.
- Use drama to identify the differences between friendly stirring and put-downs.
- Students can use the 'ten thinking tracks' (see BLM 1.3 in Unit 1) to discuss the following:
  - Geraldton's (WA) 'No put-down day' in February 2002 for the whole community.
  - Silent Sunday (no knocking; applaud only), organised by Queensland junior sporting bodies to discourage parental put-downs and abuse towards referees and players at their children's sporting matches.
  - Having a 'no whispering' rule across the school.

DRAMA ACTIVITY
Put-downs

Use drama where students act out situations in which a variety of different styles of put-downs are used towards others. This enables the students to dissect the nature of put-downs. Stress that most put-downs are non-verbal (75 per cent). Put-downs are cowardly, because the use of non-verbal attacks gives the person a degree of protection,

since it is harder to challenge them. The put-downs are more easily denied and harder to prove. Discuss how to dramatically represent terms such as:
- Sneering
- Contempt
- Derision
- Eye-rolling
- Smirking
- Mimicking
- Mocking
- Snorting.

On pieces of paper, write out a description of some scenes of people having discussions in which one person puts others down. Groups of four select a scene from a container and then prepare the enactment. Students use BLM 9.3, 'The put-down pro in action', as a guide. Ask the students in the audience to identify the put-down remarks and non-verbal behaviours that are used in the role-plays.

CLASSROOM ORGANISATION
No put-downs

- Set up classroom games and discussions to give students an opportunity to practise 'not using put-downs'. Draw ten circles on the board, each representing one or two minutes. Cross one off each time anyone in the class uses a put-down. At the end of the session the class has 'earned' however many circles (and time) are left. When a certain amount of time has accumulated, the class can have that many minutes of free time, games time, a preferred activity etc.
- If there are just one or two main offenders using put-downs in class, have a quiet talk with them and tell them that what they are doing is not acceptable. To help them stop using put-downs, you will give them a private 'daily count' of how often they do it for a week. In some classes, you can also use a 'daily class count' in the same way. After a week you should see reductions but if not, then apply consequences.
- Try responding with 'I can see that you are trying to make X look small in the eyes of others (show off/impress others) and I will not allow you to continue doing this at X's expense. It is unacceptable.'
- The book *Dirty Tricks* has more information on eliminating classroom put-downs. See the 'Resources' section (page 216) for publication details.

CLASS DISCUSSION SELF-PROTECTION AND SELF-DEFENCE: DEALING WITH BEING BULLIED

Read to the class and discuss *Mike* and/or *Willy the Wimp* (see below).

Discussion questions

- Is it a student's own fault if they get bullied? (No, the person bullying is always the person who is to blame. Most people who are bullied are just unlucky; even if someone is annoying or different they are entitled to be left alone.)
- Why do some students get picked on? (They were unlucky enough to be in the wrong place at the wrong time when a bully was looking for a target; they are new; they are

different in some way; they are temporarily without support; others may be jealous of them; they get more nervous about things and don't seem confident, so bullies think they will be easy to upset and intimidate them.)
- Why don't students always tell a teacher what is happening when they are being bullied? (they think that asking for support is the same as dobbing or narking; they are nervous about retaliation and rejection; they're not sure if the teacher will believe them or help them)
- What do we mean by 'acting confidently'? (Stand tall, smile, look into people's eyes, speak in a loud voice, give your own opinion instead of always agreeing no matter what, and don't use a babyish voice. Eliminate nervous mannerisms by asking a parent about any you might have.)
- How can acting confidently make it less likely that you will be bullied? (Any students who are looking for someone to bully will think that you could be hard to upset and that you might give them a hard time. They want someone they think they can push around.)

Follow-up activity

Students plan an activity for younger students around the picture book *Willy the Wimp*.

BOOK
Mike (Chapter book)

Mike, in Year 6, is very unhappy about three things. First, he hardly ever gets to see his father, who is in the navy. Second, his mother has made them move from Melbourne to Sydney and he is having trouble settling in to his new school. Third, Shane, the school bully, gives him a hard time. An elderly next-door neighbour, Riny, helps him to deal with the problem. Unfortunately the author stereotypically presents the bully as dominated and misused by a parent. The book has 24 chapters.

Willy the Wimp (Picture book)

In this delightful picture book, Willy the chimp feels unable to defend himself from the local bullies. So he undertakes a body-building course and develops muscles. This makes him feel more confident, and when the bullying happens again he is able to stand taller and frighten the bullies off. The main point of the story is that Willy never really gets nasty, mean or tough. He just bluffs when he warns them off. The last scene shows that Willy is still the same person, as he walks into a lamp-post and immediately apologises to it.

CLASS DISCUSSION **HUMAN PREDATORS**

Start by asking students to complete BLM 9.4, 'How animals and plants protect and defend themselves' (answers and other examples are in BLM 11.7 of the *Teacher's Handbook*). You will need to write in ten animals or insects or plants in the first column.

Discussion questions

- What is a predator? Can you think of any animals that are predators (i.e. hurt and use other animals for their own purposes)?

- Do some living things hurt and use living things that are from the same species as them? (yes)
- What species do humans prey on?
- Do humans have any predators? (Yes. Sharks, lions, crocodiles and tigers will hurt and use humans as food, but most humans avoid trouble by not going near these creatures.)
- Do humans sometimes hurt and use other humans? (Yes. Some people steal from other people, or hurt and use other people in many ways. Stress that most people do not do this, just some.)
- How are students who bully other students acting like predators? (they hurt and use another student for their own fun and to create a tough or popular image)
- Which plants, insects or animals give predators a warning to go away, and how? (emphasise that these insects, animals and plants are protecting and defending themselves, not attacking without reason)
- Discuss BLM 9.5, 'Self-defence against bullying'.

Follow-up activities

- Students play 20 questions using animals, plants and their self-protection and self-defence systems.
- Students make an electronic circuit quiz (see Chapter 11 of the *Teacher's Handbook*) about predators and prey or about animals/plants and their self-defence mechanisms.
- Students make a 'lift-up circles' interactive display (see Chapter 11 of the *Teacher's Handbook*). All answers are underneath the circles. The outside of the first circle should contain a picture or name and read 'How do I protect myself?'
- Students make up a true and false quiz about animal and plant self-defence.
- Students prepare a drama based around BLM 9.5, 'Self-defence against bullying'. Use a 'coach' with the character being attacked who helps with preparation and debriefs with the class afterwards.
- Refer to the chart in BLM 11.8 in the *Teacher's Handbook* entitled 'How humans protect and defend themselves'. Make it into a blank chart for students to complete.

ACTIVITY
Collective classroom research

X See Chapter 10 of the Teacher's Handbook.

- Medieval defences (e.g. armour; methods of fortifying castles because people couldn't easily escape once they stopped being nomadic)
- Protective sports equipment
- Camouflage in warfare
- Camouflage and illusions in art.

CLASS DISCUSSION **HOW CAN WE WORK TOGETHER TO STOP BULLYING FROM HAPPENING IN OUR SCHOOL?**

Read to the class and discuss *Bruce the Goose* and/or *The Present Takers* (see below). Also refer back to the 'postbox' quiz on BLM 9.1. Ask students to read BLM 9.6, 'Having the courage to show compassion'.

Discussion questions

- Why do people sometimes decide to stop being friends with someone who is being bullied? (to protect themselves)
- What makes it hard sometimes to be brave enough to be a friend to someone who is being bullied? (fear of rejection; fear of attracting the same mistreatment)
- How are these three actions different from each other even though they are all about involving a teacher?
  - Asking for support (this helps you to solve a serious problem that you haven't been able to solve by yourself)
  - Being responsible (this helps you to help someone else who is in trouble by accessing the power of authority)
  - Dobbing (also called 'narking') (this is trying to get someone into trouble rather than solve a problem).
- Whose problem is it if someone in the class or school is being bullied? (Bullying is everyone's problem, in the same way that it is everyone's problem if a dangerous animal was in our midst. We are all potential victims. The problem just won't 'go away' by itself. Bullying creates a culture of fear and intimidation that affects and distresses us all. We have a responsibility to try to stop students getting away with bullying behaviour, because that behaviour often leads to criminality. It's a good chance to develop our own moral courage.)

Follow-up activities

- Students read and discuss BLM 9.6, 'Having the courage to show compassion'. Drama can also be used here.
- Students make posters or fridge magnets (see Chapter 11 of the *Teacher's Handbook*) with a preferred slogan, such as:
  - Be a buddy, not a bully.
  - Bullying is everyone's problem.
  - Bullying spoils things for all of us.
  - Bullies are cowards who get their power from the pack.
  - Do whatever you can, no matter how small. If we all work together, we can make a big difference.
  - Bad things keep happening because of what good people don't do.
  - The best sign of a person's character is not what they do when things are okay, but what they do when things are difficult.
- Students display their 'quick quotes' (see Chapter 11 of the *Teacher's Handbook*) about what can be done about the problem of bullying. Use the stem, 'I'd like to see . . .'.

BOOKS

Bruce the Goose (Chapter book)

Bruce, aged eleven, has just changed schools. At his last school he wasn't considered 'cool' and was bullied because he was small and played the saxophone well enough to win prizes. His heart sinks when he starts to be bullied again by Barge. Barge manages to get almost the whole class calling him 'Bruce the Goose' and using a subtle finger-flapping movement (like wings) when they want to tease him without the teacher knowing. This depiction of whole-class harassment is very realistic. Two other students, Nut and Sponge, befriend him and help him occasionally score some points off Barge and find a solution. The portrayal of Barge as big-bodied and not very bright is unrealistically stereotypical.

Similarly, the conversion of Barge from bully to friendly classmate is also rather unrealistic, but it is a good starting point for discussion of how things really are. The book has 17 small chapters and is suitable for Years 5 and 6 (and perhaps Year 7).

The Present Takers (Chapter book)

Melanie, aged eleven, and her nasty gang of bullies intimidate other girls in their class and force them to give them 'presents' and shoplift for the items they want. Lucy is one of her newest victims. Eventually Lucy and her friend Angus make a plan in which the whole class cooperates to stop the gang of three, by writing and displaying stories about the gang and by standing around in groups as silent witnesses every time the gang tries to isolate and intimidate an individual student. The group pressure tactics that are used in the story are an excellent example for students. Melanie, the gang leader, is presented stereotypically, and the author gives the reader a 'too neat' reason for her cruel behaviour, but this issue can be discussed. The book has 15 chapters and is suitable for Years 5, 6 and 7. Read it as a serial.

CLASSROOM ORGANISATION
Circle of friends

Consider setting up several 'circles of friends' which can be rotated. These are groups of two or more students who are basically kind and caring and who are prepared to go and support a specific student when he or she is being mistreated.

CLASS DISCUSSION **PEER PRESSURE**

Read to the class and discuss *The Recess Queen, Buzzard Breath and Brains* or *Stargirl* (see next page).

Another good way to introduce the topic of peer pressure is to involve students in a time-estimate activity. Ask the students to sit on the floor. Tell them that you want them to mentally estimate when a minute has elapsed. Ensure that they are not able to use clocks or watches. They should return to their seat as quickly as they can so that they are sitting down when they think a minute is up. Repeat the activity for a two-minute estimate. Use the exercise to ask students how much they were influenced by other students' decisions to sit down and how difficult it is to resist peer pressure.

Discussion questions

- What is a peer group? (a group of people who are similar and roughly equal)
- Why do young people your age like to feel like they belong and are similar to others of their age?(it helps to have similar people to watch and learn from; you think they understand more because they are like you; you feel safer; you feel more likeable)
- What is the difference between peer pressure and peer influence ? (you can choose to be influenced but you feel coerced when it is peer pressure; the coercion is in the form of threats of put-downs or social rejection; everyone responds to some degree to peer influence; sometimes peer influence can be a good thing, such as when you see everyone else in your peer group behaving in good ways and decide to behave like that too)
- Why are some students more influential than others? (some appear to be more confident, and some are more socially skilled. But some are mean-spirited and make others scared of them, and some are good at 'conning 'people into being mean by offering them something such as status)

- Can someone insist on being themselves and still be 'acceptable' to the rest of the group? How?
- When should you trust your own judgment about how you behave? (when it negatively affects somebody else's wellbeing and feelings, such as in bullying and being nasty)
- What does this old chinese proverb mean? 'A stupid thing is still a stupid thing even if 1000 people say it.'

Follow-up activity

Students using the 'ten thinking tracks' (see BLM 1.3 in Unit 1, 'Core values') to consider the rule that P-plate (probationary) drivers are permitted to take only one passenger. How does this relate to peer pressure? (Research shows that the risk of accidents increases for P-plate drivers with the increase of number of peers in their car.)

BOOKS

The Recess Queen (Picture book)

This humorous tongue-in-cheek rhyming story is illustrated with cartoon-like drawings. Mean Jean, the Recess Queen, dominates all the students at recess ('nobody bounced until Mean Jean bounced, nobody kicked until Mean Jean kicked'). But a new girl, Katie Sue arrives and decides to do her own thing. The ending is a bit glib.

Buzzard Breath and Brains (Simple chapter book)

This is a complex story which has links to the book *Swashbuckler* (see earlier). 'Buzzard Breath' is Tony and 'Brains' is Rex. Tony manages to convince Rex to help him with his games of humiliation and intimidation of other kids in Year 6. Rex enjoys the sense of power he gets by being involved with Tony. Eventually, with the help of his cousin Natalie, Rex realises that he has been 'used' and that Tony just enjoys hurting people.

Stargirl (Chapter book)

This book is summarised in Unit 1, 'Core values'. It highlights how peer pressure can lead to social exclusion.

CLASS DISCUSSION **RUMOURS**

In advance, carry out the investigation using BLM 9.7, 'Memory test'. Enlarge the BLM to A3 size and make two copies. On one sheet write 'Group A' and then write these labels next to the drawings:
- Dumbbells
- Tennis racquet
- Plane
- Sun
- Ice-cream cone
- Duck
- Funnel
- Snake
- C-shape.

On the second sheet write 'Group B' and write these labels next to the same drawings:
- Reading glasses
- Magnifying glass
- Bird
- Ship's wheel
- Microphone
- Rabbit
- Torch
- (the letter) 'S'
- Moon.

Divide the class into half and call one half Group A and the other Group B. Ask them to write their name and their group letter on a blank sheet of paper. Tell them that you are going to show them a number of pictures and you want them to be able to remember them well enough to draw them in five minutes time. They cannot draw anything until then. Show the Group A pictures and labels to Group A while the other students have their eyes shut. Then repeat the process with the Group B sheet and the Group B students. In five minutes, ask them to draw the pictures they were shown. In all probability they will draw something that has detail which was not in the original drawing but which is consistent with the label they saw. They believe the label and make their perceptions and memory of it match by filling in more detail than they were originally given.

Just before the class discussion, you could also use the 'bundling' strategy (see Chapter 10 of the *Teacher's Handbook*) and ask students to write down four statements about rumours. Use the results of the memory test and the bundling activity as the basis of the discussion. (Another option is to use chinese whispers to 'pass' a detailed joke or to pass a drawing (e.g. a scene containing a boat, tree, shark, bridge, sun, clouds, beach towel and tree in context).

Discussion questions

- What is meant by the saying 'Don't judge a book by its cover'? Can anyone give an example of when they made the mistake of assuming that they knew about another person because of superficial qualities or perceptions?
- How is the process of spreading rumours connected to the memory test investigation we have just done? (We 'see' what we are led to believe. We 'change' what we see and remember to fit what we have already been told.)
- What are some other reasons why people believe rumours without doing a reality check? (they believe that the person telling them the rumour is truthful; they don't realise that ordinary people will somewhat dishonestly add 'credibility' to a story they are telling about someone else by saying something like 'A close friend told me' or 'I was there')
- How can rumours contribute to the process of bullying? (If someone is being bullied, you might think they deserve it, because you have heard these rumours about them. So you don't feel so concerned for them or try to help them.)

CLASS DISCUSSION MOBBING

If possible, find an old western film on video to show in which there is one of those classic scenes in the bar where two men get into a fight at the bar and then everyone else starts fighting each other too. This is an example of mobbing. When people sense that everyone else is behaving in an antisocial way, they assume that there is less chance of being caught and punished if they do it too. So 'mobbing' offers protection and allows people to feel less responsible for their actions and to feel less scared of having to face the consequences of what they have done. They argue that 'everyone else was doing it too' so it must have been okay. They say, 'I didn't start it', as though only the ringleader had any responsibility for an outbreak of antisocial and unpleasant behaviour.

Discussion questions

- What is a 'lynch mob'? (one or two people 'egg on' a crowd to execute someone they *believe* is guilty of a crime, but who usually hasn't been charged, tried or convicted)
- What do we mean by 'individual responsibility'? (accepting that you made your own choice and can't let yourself 'off the hook' because others did it too)
- What are the characteristics of sporting games where incidents of mob riots have occurred? What are your beliefs about why such mob outbreaks occur?
- What do you think happens when riots, violence and theft occur after a natural disaster such as an earthquake?
- How is mobbing related to bullying? (people will take part in bullying more readily in a mobbing situation because they think they won't get caught and it is OK)

Follow-up activity

Students research incidents of mobbing, such as football riots and hooliganism and the riots and looting that sometimes occur after natural disasters.

CLASS DISCUSSION BULLYING, SPORT AND THE LAW

Discussion questions

- What is sledging? (saying abusive things to your opponents during a sporting competition)
- What rules are in place to try and stop sledging?
- What racist behaviour has been observed in professional football in Australia?
- What is racial vilification?
- Why do you think the police are so involved with helping schools to get rid of bullying behaviour in schools? (Students who bully others and get away with it are very likely to become adult criminals or people who behave in other antisocial ways. Sixty per cent of students who bully more than once have a criminal conviction of some kind before they are 21 years old. Also, the justice system realises that bullying can often involve serious crime, such as assault or sometimes manslaughter.)
- At what age can a student be charged with a criminal offence? (It varies according to the country and state. In Victoria anyone 10 years or older *can* be charged.)
- What is an 'intervention order' or a 'restraining order'? (An order issued by the courts that instructs a person to stay away from another person who has stated that they are being harassed, threatened or harmed. Some have been taken out by students.)
- Who can be sued over bullying at a school? (schools are sometimes sued for failing to protect students from being bullied by other students)
- Can students who bully another student be criminally charged? (Yes. Students who bully other students can be charged with a range of offences, including assault, stalking and malicious damage.) (You may want to omit this question if you haven't yet used BLM 9.9, 'Bullying and the law'.)

Follow-up activities

- Students research and collect media articles on the issue of workplace bullying, which costs industry $13 billion a year in Australia. In some states companies can be charged with failing in their duty of care to keep workers physically and psychologically safe.
- Students work in groups of three to draw up a list of guest speakers who could be invited to visit the class, such as a lawyer, an equal opportunity officer, a police officer, and a representative of Amnesty International (to speak on persecution and human rights).
- Students use the 'ten thinking tracks' (see BLM 1.3 in Unit 1) to discuss the idea of having a law against bullying in schools, as they do in Scandinavia. Under this law, students can lay bullying charges with the police against another student.
- Students use the 'ten thinking tracks' to discuss the concept of 'restorative justice' (also called 'community conferencing') in bullying situations. This concept is outlined in Chapter 8, 'Bullying' in the *Teacher's Handbook*. It has recently been used successfully with teenage arsonists and bushfire victims.
- Students use the 'collective classroom research' strategy (see Chapter 10 of the *Teacher's Handbook*) to find newspaper reports of workplace bullying and harassment. (Harassment is similar to bullying, but it is not necessarily repeated and can be a one-off event.)
- Students research the rules and punishments regarding sledging and racial vilification in cricket and football.
- Students work in groups of three to complete a table titled 'Bullying and the law'. Use BLM 9.9, with columns 2 and 3 left blank. You may want to give students the charges and claims from the final column as a mixed-up list of options to use when they are filling in the sheet.

CLASS DISCUSSION BULLYING IN HISTORY

There are many different ways to introduce this aspect of bullying. Here are three:
- Read to the class and discuss *A Picture Book of Ann Frank*, a moving book in which the illustrations have been based on photographs. Another picture book you could use here is *The Children We Remember*, which uses photographs to depict the story of the Holocaust with very simple text. The photographs create the mood and the tone of the book. Two other picture books for older students which would be effective as an introduction are *Let the Celebrations Begin* (see below) and *Rose Blanche* (see Unit 4, p. 82).
- Students complete the BLM 9.10, 'The holocaust'.
- Use 'bundling' (see Chapter 10 of the *Teacher's Handbook*) and ask students to write down five sentences about Hitler, Nazi concentration camps and the persecution of the Jewish population.

Discussion questions

- Read the poem 'First They Came for the Jews' (see below) and ask: 'How is this like what happens in a bullying situation?'
- How could this appalling situation happen? (The answer is obviously a very complex one, but for this age-group you could concentrate on the idea of propaganda [like rumours], threats and evidence of what can happen leading to fear and self-protection [like not associating any more a bullying victim] and the failure of some good people to accurately see what was happening or to take any action.)

UNIT 9—BULLYING

Follow-up activities

- Students research other examples of persecution and atrocities (e.g. Rwanda, Serbia).
- Students complete BLM 9.10, 'The six steps of persecution', and then look at the concept of propaganda and rumour. Students can analyse text (e.g. articles, films, newspapers, brochures) with these questions in mind:
  - Has the text been written by someone with a specific purpose? How can you tell?
  - To what extent have any of the facts been altered or manipulated and why?
  - How do the headings, tone, phrases and specific words make a difference to what the reader might feel or think?
  - What emotive language has been used and what effect does it have?
  - Have any generalisations or simplifications been made?
  - Have any statistics that are cited been used accurately and fairly?
- Students complete BLM 9.11, 'Good people can make a difference'.
- Students can visit the nearest Jewish museum.
- Research other examples of historical and contemporary persecution. BLM 9.10, 'The six stages of persecution', can also be applied to these examples.

BOOKS
Let the Celebrations Begin (Picture book)

The story is set in the few days before the liberation of victims from a concentration camp. A group of women have been imprisoned there for four years and are aware that their freedom is imminent. They excitedly scrounge small scraps of material from their old clothes to make simple toys for the children in the camp to have at their celebration 'party', at which they have their first proper meal in four years.

Rose Blanche (Picture book)

This book is summarised in Unit 5, 'The bright side'. It is set in a Holocaust context.

POEM
'First They Came for the Jews'

First they came for the Jews
And I did not speak out—
Because I was not a Jew.

Then they came for the communists
And I did not speak out—
Because I was not a communist.

Then they came for the trade unionists
And I did not speak out—
Because I was not a trade unionist.

Then they came for me—
And there was no one left
To speak out for me.

Pastor Niemöller

CONSOLIDATION

Websites about bullying

Students can explore and write reviews about some of these websites about bullying and find others:
- www.copas.net.au/cah (Centre for Child and Adolescent Health)
- www.dotu.wa.gov.au/know/bully.html
- www.kidshelp.com.au
- www.nobully.org.nz
- www.antibully.org.uk/

English activities

- Students write a 'Choose your own adventure' story about someone who is bullied. The choices and endings can vary according to whether or not the student seeks teacher support or handles it well/poorly.
- Students compare two books with a bullying theme.
- The following poems are all about aspects of bullying and can be used as an introduction to the topic or a follow-up. They focus mainly on the feelings of the recipients or the observers:
  - 'Back in the Playground Blues' by Adrian Mitchell from his anthology entitled *Heart on the Left*. This poem is particularly recommended. At the time of publication, it could also be accessed at www.free-range-education.co.uk/poetry.html.
  - 'See the Jolly Fat Boy' by Judith Viorst in her anthology *Sad Underwear and Other Complications*.
  - There are also many poems about bullying in the book *A Literature-based Approach to Bullying*.

RESOURCES

Books

Chana Byers Abells, 1987, *The Children We Remember*, Julia MacRae Books, London.
David Adler & Karen Ritz, 1993, *A Picture Book of Anne Frank*, Holiday House, New York.
G W Allport, 1954, *The Nature of Prejudice*, Addison-Wesley, Cambridge, Mass.
Judy Blume, 1981, *Blubber*, Picolo Books, London.
Anthony Browne, 1984, *Willy the Wimp*, Julia MacRae Books, London.
Brian Caswell, 1993, *Mike*, University of Queensland Press, St Lucia.
Aden Chambers, 1987, *The Present Takers*, Macmillan, Basingstoke.
Toni Goffe, 1991, *Bully For You!*, Child's Play, Swindon, New York.
Libby Hathorn & Gregory Rogers, 2000, *The Gift*, Random House, Sydney.
Roberto Innocenti & Ian McEwan, 1985, *Rose Blanche*, Johnathan Cape, London.
Rowena Cory Lindquist, 1996, *Capped*, Scholastic, Sydney.
Lyn Linning, Margaret Phillips & Rayma Turton, 1997, *A Literature-based Approach to Bullying*, The Literature Base, Queensland.
Peter MacFarlane, 1996, *Bruce the Goose*, Angus and Robertson, Sydney.
Sophie Masson, 1996, *Birds of a Feather*, Reed for Kids, Melbourne.
H McGrath, 1997, *Dirty Tricks*, Longman Australia, Melbourne.
Adrian Mitchell, 1996, *Heart on the Left*, Bloodaxe, Newcastle, UK.
James Moloney, 1995, *Swashbuckler*, University of Queensland Press, St Lucia.

James Moloney, 1998, *Buzzard Breath and Brains*, Queensland University Press, St Lucia, Queensland.
Jan Needle, 1995, *The Bully*, Puffin, London.
Alexis O'Neill & Laura Huliska-Beith, 2002, *The Recess Queen*, Scholastic, Sydney.
Jerry Spinelli, 2001, *Stargirl*, Orchard Books, London.
Judith Viorst, 1995, *Sad Underwear and Other Complications: More Poems for Children and Their Parents*, Scholastic, Gosford, NSW.
Margaret Wild, 1991, *Let the Celebrations Begin*, Omnibus, South Australia.

Video

The Simpsons ('Bart the General' episode), 1990, Fox (G Rating).

A QUIZ ABOUT BULLYING

BLM 9.1

Circle the answer you agree with.

Question 1
Do you think that it is true that 60 per cent of the students who often bully other students become adults who have a criminal conviction by the time they are 21 years of age?

    YES   UNSURE, BUT PROBABLY NOT   NO

Question 2
Mary says that most kids who are bullied probably deserve it, but Simon says that they are just unlucky. Who is right?

    MARY   SIMON   NEITHER OF THEM   BOTH OF THEM

Question 3
How many students do you think feel upset and worried and wish it could be stopped when they see other kids being bullied?

    A QUARTER OF THEM   ABOUT HALF OF THEM   THREE-QUARTERS OF THEM   ALL OF THEM

Question 4
Would you call it dobbing if someone told a teacher that their classmate was being bullied and needed help?

    YES   UNSURE   NO

Question 5
Have you ever taken part in deliberately looking for and giving another student a hard time?

    YES, WHEN I WAS YOUNGER BUT NOT LATELY   YES, FAIRLY RECENTLY   NO, NEVER

Question 6
Jaimon says that if a kid is getting bullied that's their problem and we should mind our own business, but Trina says that bullying is everybody's problem because it affects us all. Who do you agree with?

    JAIMON   TRINA   NEITHER OF THEM

Question 7
Would you have the courage to stand up for someone who was being bullied by other students at the school?

    YES   UNSURE   IT DEPENDS   NO

Question 8
Vinh says that there's no point in trying to help someone who is being bullied because it makes no difference and just causes trouble for yourself. Chris disagrees. He says that you should say something to the kids doing it, because sometimes it makes a difference and, even if it doesn't, at least you have a bit of self-respect because you didn't just stand by and do nothing. Melanie agrees that you should do *something*, but she thinks that the best thing is to let a teacher that you can trust know what is happening and ask them to keep your name confidential. Who do you agree with?

    VINH   CHRIS   MELANIE

Question 9
What, in your opinion, is the main reason that some good kids who are not normally mean go along with bullying someone else when a ringleader starts it?

_____

_____

© Helen McGrath and Toni Noble, 2003. This page from Bounce Back!® may be photocopied for classroom use.

THE BULLY MOVIE: STARS, SUPPORT CAST AND CREW

BLM 9.2

The star: the tough guy
The tough guy is cowardly, cold-blooded and unkind. He is cunning enough to know that he needs the 'power of the pack' and so he cons them. He is a self-inflator and thinks he is better than he really is. He wants to show others how tough, dominant and powerful he is. The tough guy thinks it is perfectly okay to pick someone and inflict humiliation and cruelty on them whenever he can.

The star: the queen bee
The queen bee is another cold-blooded and unkind star. She really wants to show all the other girls how popular she is! What better way could there be than to pick another girl and 'sting' her to make her life truly miserable. Name-calling is part of her strategy, but she is a master at social exclusion and saying who can and who can't be 'in'. She gets other girls to be nasty too by being 'sweet' to them and allowing them to be 'in' her group. If she finds that there is another girl who is liked by other people, especially one who is cleverer, prettier, smarter or nicer than she is, she makes sure that *that* girl gets 'stung'.

The stars: the cool group
These kids want to try to convince everyone that *they* are the cool group, so they choose a student who they think is not as good as them and torment and arrogantly and cold-bloodedly exclude or attack him or her. 'See how good we are! We wouldn't have *this* person in *our* group.' They are *not* superior, but they certainly *think* they are.

The reluctant star: the bully targets
Bully targets are the people who are selected by tough guys and queen bees for cruelty and humiliation. They do not do anything to deserve this mistreatment. They are just unlucky. They were in the wrong place at the wrong time or they are different in some small way. They are denied their right to be themselves. You could be the next person to star in this role. There are always vacancies.

The support cast: the wannabes
The wannabes would just *love* to be more powerful and popular, so they do a lot of the dirty work for the so-called stars, hoping that some of the star's seeming social power rubs off.

The support cast: the hangers-on
Hangers-on are scared of what could happen to *them*, so they crawl to the tough guy or the queen bee to protect themselves from being bullied.

The crew: the urgers and believers
The urgers laugh at the pain and discomfort of the bully target and urge on the stars. Great stuff! Keep it up! It's entertaining when they're bored. They never stop to think how bad it must feel to be on the receiving end of bullying. The believers take part in the mistreatment of another person in small ways because they don't think for themselves. They incorrectly believe what has been said about the bully target without ever checking to see if it is true so they think they deserve it, and it's okay.

The crew: the fearful bystanders
The fearful bystanders don't like to see bullying happen and feel bad about it, but don't have the courage to do anything because they fear they will become the next victim or be rejected.

The *real* stars: the compassionate supporters with courage
Compassionate, courageous supporters try to help bully targets, either by standing up for them or by getting a teacher to help. They refuse to take part in helping in bullying another student, no matter how much pressure is put on them. They communicate their disgust at the mistreatment they witness.

© Helen McGrath and Toni Noble, 2003. This page from Bounce Back!® may be photocopied for classroom use.

THE PUT-DOWN PRO IN ACTION

BLM 9.3

A put-down pro has turned sneering at and humiliating others into an art form. They really enjoy trying to make someone else feel small and damaging their reputation in the eyes of others. Boys who are put-down pros hope that attacking someone like this will make other boys think they are powerful and cool. Girls who are put-down pros want to show how popular they think they are. They want to make sure that the person they attack isn't liked by other girls in order to protect their own social position.

A put-down pro uses two types of attack weapons. One is the verbal put-down and the other is the non-verbal put-down. About 75 per cent of all put-downs are non-verbal.

Verbal put-downs are comments that are said to another person (or said about them in their presence) that are designed to make that person feel small and humiliated. Examples might be:

- 'That's stupid (ridiculous, absurd, dumb, rubbish).'
- 'What would you know!'
- 'How can you say that? It's so stupid.'
- 'You're such an idiot.'
- 'Oh yes, *you'd* know.'

A put-down pro is a cowardly master of the hidden attack that they think won't be noticed by the teacher and commented on, so they rely mostly on non-verbal put-downs. The attack is hidden in a mocking, sneering or sarcastic tone of voice and/or a facial expression of contempt. Sometimes a put-down pro laughs, snorts or smirks at what someone says. Often they roll their eyes and then look at a friend as if to say 'Aren't they stupid!' They might 'pretend' to speak seriously but use an exaggerated and mocking tone of voice that says 'We are really sending you up'. They like to mimic another person's mannerisms to highlight the difference to others. They may make deliberate and exaggerated movements and sounds to communicate that they find what the person is saying very boring. For example, they may make extreme gestures of impatience (e.g. drumming their fingers or sighing), raise their eyes to the ceiling or lower them to the floor, or slump in their seat in an obvious way. Sometimes they choose to whisper to someone else while looking at the speaker (to make sure that the speaker is aware of what they are doing) and smirking at the same time.

- Choose two words to describe your feelings if you were put down.

- What do you think is the best way to react if someone puts you down?

- What is your response when you see or hear someone else being put down?

© Helen McGrath and Toni Noble, 2003. This page from Bounce Back!® may be photocopied for classroom use.

HOW ANIMALS AND PLANTS PROTECT AND DEFEND THEMSELVES

BLM 9.4

Living Things	Self-protection How does it stay safe, not draw attention to itself and keep out of trouble? e.g. • Avoids predators' territory • Uses camouflage • Safety in numbers • Has protective covering • Plays tricks • Has 'danger' colours or sounds	Warning the predator to go away How does it warn predators to back off and leave it alone? e.g. • Makes loud angry noises • Squirts unpleasant smells or fluids • Bluffs by making itself look larger and more dangerous than it really is	Escaping How does it get away fast from the predator and out of trouble?	Counterattacking If attacked, how does it act in self-defence to try to drive the predator away, get support or outsmart it?
1.				
2.				
3.				
4.				
5.				
6.				
7.				
8.				
9.				
10.				

© Helen McGrath and Toni Noble, 2003. This page from Bounce Back!® may be photocopied for classroom use.

SELF-DEFENCE AGAINST BULLYING

BLM 9.5

Use helpful thinking and reality checks.
- If you *are* bullied, remember that it is not your fault and it doesn't mean anything about who you are. The person doing the bullying is in the wrong and has the problem.
- Get a reality check. Ask others you trust about how they have dealt with similar situations in their lives. Access helpful information from websites and books.
- Keep your eye on the goals of maintaining your self-respect and solving the problem.
- Once bullying has developed, it is difficult to stop it by yourself, so ask for help.

Stay away from trouble, act confidently and don't draw attention to yourself.
- Avoid people and places that you know are currently dangerous or hostile.
- Act confidently. Stand tall, use good eye contact. Speak clearly and loudly. You may need to fake it till you make it!
- Don't be wishy-washy when giving your own opinion.
- Be a good loser. Don't 'lose it' when you are angry or annoyed. Don't be rigid and get overly upset about rules. This all signals that you can be easily upset.
- Ask people you trust about nervous mannerisms you have and try to get rid of them.
- Smile a lot and don't have a gloomy look on your face.

Use thoughts that help you stay cool.
- Smile without looking at them and say to yourself 'But I'm not the one with the problem. You are!'
- Think about a time when they looked silly or their faults.
- Remind yourself that nearly half of all students have this happen to them sometime during their school life.
- Think about something else if you start to feel upset.

Stay calm by acting cool when the bullies test you out.
When someone gives you a hard time, try to stay cool and act as if you think they are a joke. Don't let them think you can be easily upset. Try these while smiling and acting like they haven't upset you:
- Act like a chicken and make chicken noises. Don't look at them while you do it.
- Clap, wave or bow.
- Count their nasty comments out loud (e.g. 'One, two') and say, 'I'm keeping score because I can see how important it is to you.'
- Look, blink, raise your eyes, shake your head and turn away in disgust.
- Walk away smiling as though you have a secret.
- Respond with a comment such as:
  – 'Gee, that's original' or 'Good on you!' (and put your thumb up).
  – 'Thank you for sharing that' or 'Will that help you sleep better tonight?'
  – 'Tell my hand, my ears aren't working today' (and hold the palm of your hand up without looking).
  – 'Absolutely!' or 'No doubt about it' or 'Chill out. It's not that serious'.
  – 'Anything else you wanted to add to that before you slide/slither off?'
  – 'Could you repeat that?' or say 'What?' every time they speak to you.
  – 'Small things amuse small minds' or 'Whatever amuses you'.
  – 'I wouldn't dream of taking that honour from you' (if they have said something like 'You're an idiot!').
  – 'Oh, is it Pick on (Ben) Day again already! It comes around so quickly.'
  – 'That's what you said last time. Can't you use variety?' or 'Feel bigger now?'

Warn them off.
- Say 'Back off!' or 'Get lost' (with a snarl and firm eye contact).
- Yell 'Stop it. Go away' very loudly and very close to their face (no smiling).
- Take notes about their behaviour (i.e. date, time, place and witnesses) in an obvious way.
- Use a dictaphone and say 'Just a minute. I need to get the sound levels right.'

Escape as soon as things turn nasty or dangerous.
Find a safe place to go to, preferably where there is a teacher as a witness.

Find a way to get some support that doesn't cause you more trouble.
- Ask other students who you know are nice people to help you by just standing near you.
- Tell a trusted teacher or counsellor and ask them to help you to solve the problem. This is *not* dobbing.
- Let the teacher know of any plans you have to deal with it, so you can check they're OK.

© Helen McGrath and Toni Noble, 2003. This page from Bounce Back!® may be photocopied for classroom use.

HAVING THE COURAGE TO SHOW COMPASSION

BLM 9.6

The challenge for every human being is to keep a check on our own unkindness and to stand up for anyone who is unjustly and cruelly treated.

Think first
- *No one* is safe when bullying is happening. Next time it could be you. How would you want to be supported if it *did* happen to you?
- Bad things *can* happen to good people. Just because someone is being given a hard time doesn't mean that they deserve it or that they are people you should dislike.
- Bad things keep happening because good people don't do anything. What sort of person are you?

Level One actions
Decide never to take part in bullying, even in a small way. Don't laugh, use a nickname or stand by and watch, because bullies love an audience. Don't exclude someone just because everyone else is doing it.

Level Two actions
You can decide to take more direct but still low-key actions. Here are some suggestions:
- Just move a bit closer and stare at the person bullying and shake your head sadly, as if to say that you are ashamed for them and that what they are doing is being witnessed. This works especially well if several people do it at once.
- Look in a disgusted way at the people who are bullying and say something short and simple such as:
  - 'Don't be so nasty/vicious.'
  - 'Give it a rest. We're sick of what you are doing.'
  - 'Why are you doing that? It's not normal.'
  - 'We don't do that in *this* school.'
  - 'Haven't you got anything better to do?'
  - 'I'm not enjoying this much. Let's find something else to do.'
  - 'Let's not do this. It's not fun.'
  - 'Cut it out. We're embarrassed for you. You're embarrassing us.'
- If the bullying is by nasty words, subtly change the topic to a safer one.
- Say to the mistreated person, 'Let's go and . . .', and then go elsewhere with them.

Try to protect yourself when you are standing up for someone else. Don't lecture the people who are doing the bullying about what they are doing. This may draw their fire onto you. If they start to pick on you too, walk away immediately and say nothing.

Level Three actions
You can take more serious direct action to help someone. Don't keep the problem hidden. Act in a responsible and compassionate way. You can let your *parents* know about the mistreatment this person is receiving. You can let a *teacher* know what is happening and ask them to keep your name confidential. This is not the same as dobbing. When you dob, you are wanting to get someone into trouble. When you act in a responsible way, you are trying to help someone who is in trouble.

© Helen McGrath and Toni Noble, 2003. This page from Bounce Back!® may be photocopied for classroom use.

MEMORY TEST

BLM 9.7

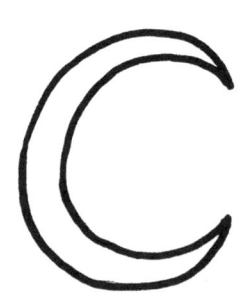

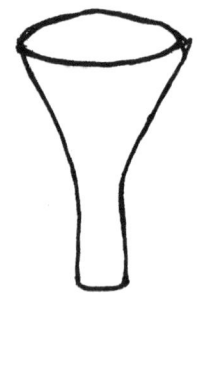

© Helen McGrath and Toni Noble, 2003. This page from Bounce Back!® may be photocopied for classroom use.

THE KU KLUX KLAN

Until the end of the American Civil War in 1865, black people didn't have the same rights as white people. In fact, any *negro* or black person living in the South of the United States was probably a slave. But when Abraham Lincoln and the 'North' defeated the 'South' in the American Civil War, they made slavery illegal. White people were no longer assumed to be superior to black people and many whites were unhappy about it.

The Ku Klux Klan (KKK) was founded by a man named Nathan Forrest in 1865. The group consisted of men from the Southern American states who still believed that Whites were superior to Blacks and that equality between the races was wrong. Rather than accepting the rights of black people, they decided to persecute, harass, hurt and sometimes kill them. Even though members of the KKK claimed to be proud of their belief that Whites were superior, they hid their identities by wearing white sheets and hoods with only eye holes. At night they gathered secretly in mobs to fly their confederate flag, burn crosses and organise their anti-black activities.

In the late 19th century, millions of people from all over the world travelled to the United States to live. People from Germany, Italy, Hungary, Russia and many other nations began to join the American population. The United States had developed into a nation of many different cultures. The KKK decided to turn its hatred to anyone who was not of an *Aryan* background—that is, 'fair skinned'. As well as persecuting and harming Blacks, they now added Asians, Jews and a host of other nationalities to their list. They also tormented homosexuals.

Over a century later, the KKK is still active in the United States. Although nowhere near as powerful as they were in the 19th century, members still meet in mobs and work together to bully minority groups, especially Blacks. Many have been jailed for their activities, but their secrecy and their mobbing tactics make it difficult to identify and prosecute them.

Some Australian members have been reported to be working with their American KKK associates to try and block native-title claims by the Muthi Muthi tribe on the Victorian–New South Wales border. KKK graffiti was painted on bus shelters and school buildings. The KKK also applied to the Australian government to be a respondent to the land claim. The application was rejected by the Australian Federal Court.

- How is bullying like what the KKK do?

- Why do the KKK act in mobs and cover their faces?

BULLYING AND THE LAW

BLM 9.9

Type of bullying	Example	Possible legal charge/civil claim/industrial claim or sporting rule violation as a result
Physical attacks	Punching; throwing stones; kicking; pushing; tripping	Physical assault; manslaughter; personal compensation claim; grievous bodily harm
Making others give you things	Threatening if money isn't given	Extortion; demanding money with menace
Deliberate isolation and exclusion	Encouraging others not to speak to someone	Harassment; bullying (workplace context)
Taking or damaging personal property	Defacing school bag; cutting a person's jumper; taking their pencil case	Theft; malicious property damage
Insulting and name-calling	Offensive remarks; calling someone a 'slut'; making racist remarks	Sledging; sexual harassment; racial vilification
Forcing another to behave in an antisocial way	Making someone take another student's property by threatening to tell the teacher a lie about them	Blackmail
Spreading rumours and telling lies about someone	Dishonestly saying that a student cheated on an exam; sending notes around containing lies or slurs	Defamation; slander; libel
Helping someone else to harass another student	Giving out someone else's locker password; letting them use your computer to send a malicious or prank email	Accessory before the fact; accessory after the fact
Following someone around and making their life unpleasant and uncomfortable	Leaving unpleasant things in their mailbox; calling and hanging up; constant emails	Stalking

© Helen McGrath and Toni Noble, 2003. This page from Bounce Back!® may be photocopied for classroom use.

THE SIX STEPS OF PERSECUTION

BLM 9.10

	How this happened in the holocaust	How this happens in bullying
Step 1: Antilocution The ringleaders spread rumours and speak badly about the victims, and damage their reputations. This makes other people feel less concern for them.		
Step 2: Stereotyping The victims are described as belonging to a 'category' (or stereotyping) rather than being seen as individuals. It is assumed that all people in that category are the same, in a negative way.		
Step 3: Avoidance The ringleaders refuse to have any positive association with the victims and encourage others to do the same.		
Step 4: Discrimination The ringleaders treat the victims in a way that denies them the rights that others have.		
Step 5: Dehumanisation People begin to accept the ringleaders' assertion that the victims deserve what has happened to them and hence are 'less than human' and not worthy of concern.		
Step 6: Attack The ringleaders directly harm the victim and encourage others to do it too.		

These six steps are based on the work of Gordon Allport.

© Helen McGrath and Toni Noble, 2003. This page from Bounce Back!® may be photocopied for classroom use.

THE HOLOCAUST

In the early 1930s, a man named Adolf Hitler decided that he would make Germany strong again after its defeat in World War I. He formed the *Nazi Party* whose policy was to rebuild Germany and restore its sense of pride. However, much of the Nazi philosophy was based on the idea of 'racial purity': anyone who was not 'pure' German was inferior. Hitler convinced the German people that pure Germans, or *Aryans*, were superior to people of other races such as gypsies, Blacks and, in particular, Jewish people.

He also convinced the German people that the Jews, who made up a large percentage of the population in Germany and Europe, were the cause of Germany's defeat in World War I and therefore enemies of the new, proud Germany. He established a group of thugs called the 'brownshirts' who devoted their time to bullying and threatening German Jews.

When the German President died in 1934, Hitler, who had been the Chancellor, declared himself the 'Führer' or leader of all Germany. Now his power was total. Anyone who opposed Hitler's ideas was arrested and placed in a concentration camp. He killed or jailed the teachers, university lecturers and journalists. He burned millions of books in schools, libraries and universities so that people wouldn't learn too much and criticise his actions. Soon people became too scared to criticise him and they decided to support his policies.

Hitler also used *propaganda* to encourage German school children to bully their Jewish teachers or classmates. He then made a law taking away the rights of Jewish citizens. He made hatred of the Jews, or *anti-Semitism*, legal. Jewish people were no longer allowed to be seen with non-Jewish people. They were forced to leave their homes and live with other Jews in areas called *ghettos*, which were surrounded by walls and patrolled by guards and had curfews. Jews were also forced to wear a yellow Star of David on their sleeve so that non-Jewish people could easily identify them.

Now that Germany was powerful again, Hitler decided to invade many of Germany's neighbouring countries. The Jews in countries such as Poland and Hungary were also seen as the enemy. Many tried to flee to the United States or safer parts of Europe, but only a small number were successful. The majority were captured and sent as slaves to concentration camps. In the camps, their heads were shaved and they were stripped of their clothing and made to wear uniforms. Instead of names, they were given numbers, which were tattooed on their wrists. They were given very little food, they were regularly beaten and they were made to work day and night. Those Jews who were unable to work, such as old people and children, were usually shot, and some were used as guinea pigs in terrible medical experiments. Even those who were able to work often died because of exhaustion or starvation.

The Nazis decided that it was taking too long to kill the Jewish population, so they used the slaves to build large gas chambers. The chambers were filled with poisonous gas and millions of Jews were taken into them in large groups and gassed.

Germany's invasion of other countries and its attempt to destroy an entire race resulted in World War II. As the Allied armies began to defeat the Germans, the rate at which the Jews were murdered increased. By the end of the war, Hitler and the Nazis had killed over six and a half million Jewish people, as well as 250 000 gypsies. One and a half million of those killed were children. History refers to this as *the holocaust*.

Eventually it became obvious that the Germans were losing the war. Rather than face the consequences of their actions, Hitler and many of the high-ranking Nazis killed themselves. Other Nazis escaped to South America and were never heard of again. Those who were captured were brought to trial in Nuremberg, where they were found guilty of crimes against humanity. Some were executed and some served long prison sentences.

© Helen McGrath and Toni Noble, 2003. This page from Bounce Back!® may be photocopied for classroom use.

GOOD PEOPLE CAN MAKE A DIFFERENCE

BLM 9.12

Many people have said that bad things keep happening because good people don't do anything to try to stop them. Two people who did try to stop some of the evil of the Holocaust were Oscar Schindler and Raoul Wallenberg. Even in the worst of circumstances, ordinary people can act courageously and help others who are being mistreated.

Oscar Schindler

During World War II, many Jewish people left Germany and went to Poland because of the terrible things that were being done to Jewish people in Germany. However, after Germany took over Poland, those terrible things began to happen to Jewish people in Poland too. They were beaten and killed, and their businesses and houses were stolen from them. An ordinary German businessman, Oscar Schindler, who was not Jewish, had a factory that made pots and pans, and, under instruction from the Nazis, ammunition. He saw that Jewish people were being murdered, and he decided to hire as many Jewish people as he could to work in his factory, so that he could keep them from being sent to the death camps. He persuaded the German soldiers that he couldn't run his ammunition factory without these Jewish workers. Sometimes he also had to bribe the soldiers. Schindler treated his Jewish workers with kindness and respect and made sure they were fed and looked after. In this way he kept 1300 Jewish people alive. Some of these people were small children. When the German soldiers tried to send the children of his Jewish workers to the death camps, Schindler convinced them that he needed the children as workers in his factory because their thin fingers meant that they could do jobs that adults could not do.

Raoul Wallenberg

Raoul Wallenberg was a Swedish diplomat in Hungary. He was a representative of Sweden, a country not at war with Germany. Wallenberg became aware that the Nazis had already killed over 20 000 Jewish people in Hungary, and that they planned to kill off everyone else in the Jewish community as well. Because he was a diplomat of a country that was not at war with Germany, Wallenberg could issue 'protection passes' to all Swedish people in Hungary. If you had a 'protection pass', it meant that you would be given safe passage out of Hungary, even if you were Jewish. Wallenberg arranged for more than 4000 Jews to receive forged passports saying they were Swedish. Then he was able to give them protection passes that allowed them to leave Hungary. He also set up 'safe houses' in Hungary. These were for Swedish citizens in Hungary to go to for safety, but he encouraged Jewish people to go there and hide until they could be helped to escape. Unfortunately, Wallenberg disappeared at the end of the war. It is assumed that he was executed by the Nazis.

© Helen McGrath and Toni Noble, 2003. This page from Bounce Back!® may be photocopied for classroom use.

UNIT 10
WINNERS

KEY POINTS

'WINNERS' is an acronym for behaviours that lead to successful goal achievement, self-respect and self-esteem.

Who am I and what am I best at?
Everyone has some things that they do well and other things that they don't do well or need to improve on. The things we do well are called our 'strengths'. You need some evidence for what strengths you think you have. When you know your strengths, you can use them to help you achieve your goals. When you understand your 'limitations' (things you don't do well), you can take steps to overcome them, or to find a way around them.

Interesting mistakes will happen (and don't be afraid to make them).
Mistakes and failures may feel like a kick in the stomach but they are necessary steps on the journey to success. All mistakes and failures teach you something.

No pain, no gain.
No one ever achieved anything important to them without hard work and self-discipline. You need to work hard, manage time well, be organised, get rid of distractions, and finish what you start. People who don't achieve their goals are poorly organised, let other things get in the way, or give up when some bits are boring or hard.

Never give up (well, hardly ever). Obstacles are just problems to be solved.
See obstacles as temporary setbacks and look for new ways to get around the problem. Be creative, persistent and resourceful until you find a way. Nobody ever achieves *everything* they set out to achieve. Sometimes, even with hard work, patience and persistence, you can't achieve a particular goal. But you can still tell yourself, 'I had a go and gave it my best shot.' Maybe it was not a good goal for you or maybe your goals changed.

Ethics and decency must be the rule (or it's not worth it).
A goal that is achieved through lying, cheating, conning or treating others badly is worth nothing. You won't like yourself and neither will other people.

Risk-taking is sometimes necessary (but think about it first, and be prepared).
There are always risks attached to trying to achieve something important to you. There is the risk that you will fail, or that others will disapprove. But the person who risks nothing achieves nothing. Move out of your comfort zone. Take the risks, but make sure you think them through first so that they are reasonable risks and you know what to expect. Be prepared.

Smart goal-setting helps you succeed.
Always 'keep your eye on your goal' and what you need to do to get there. There are many different kinds of goals that you can try to achieve. Some are short-term (e.g. doing homework, finishing a project on time, making new friends). Some are long-term (e.g. representing the school at sport, completing Year 12 with good results, achieving a certain career, or becoming a top performer in some area). You need patience, because sometimes the rewards for your hard work may be a long time coming. You have to make *plans* because they give you good directions for what to do to achieve your goal step by step. You often need to modify your plans along the way.

UNIT 10—WINNERS

Class discussion—Goal-seeking and being successful *232*
- BOOKS
  Five Times Dizzy 232
  Nips XI 232
  I Had a Lot of Wishes 232
  The Glorious Flight Across the Channel with Louis Blériot 233
- ACTIVITY
  Self-reflection 233

Class discussion—Who am I and what am I good at? *233*
- PICTURE BOOK
  Stephen's Useless Design 234

Class discussion—Interesting mistakes will happen *234*

Class discussion—No pain, no gain *235*
- BOOK
  Ollie Forgot 236

Class discussion—Being organised and managing yourself *237*
- ARTS ACTIVITY
  Technology 3D time-management poster 237

Class discussion—Removing distractions and temptations *237*
- ACTIVITY
  Making lists 238

Class discussion—Never give up *239*
- BOOKS
  Bored, Nothing to Do 240
  The Lighthouse Keeper's Catastrophe 240
  The Lighthouse Keeper's Lunch 240
  The Great Candle Scandal 240
  The Sparrow's Story at the King's Command 240
- VIDEOS
  Rabbit-Proof Fence 240
  Fly Away Home 240
- ACTIVITY
  Ten thinking tracks 241

Class discussion—Ethics and decency must be the rule *241*

Class discussion—Risk-taking may be necessary at some point *242*

Class discussion—Smart goal-setting helps you succeed *243*
- ACTIVITIES
  SMART Goal-setting 243
  Group goal-setting 243
  Goal success interview 243
  Organisational interviews 244

Consolidation *244*
- A smorgasbord of activities 244
- Curriculum integration 245
- WINNERS! probability race 245
- Cross-offs 245

Resources *246*

BLM 10.1—Think like WINNERS do *247*

BLM 10.2—My strengths *248*

BLM 10.3—The hare and the tortoise *249*

BLM 10.4—Tidy houses lead to success! *250*

BLM 10.5—Charles Kingsford Smith *251*

BLM 10.6—Goal contract *252*

BLM 10.7—WINNERS cartoons *253*

BLM 10.8—WINNERS probability race *254*

BLM 10.9—Cross-offs *255*

BOUNCE BACK!

CLASS DISCUSSION: GOAL-SEEKING AND BEING SUCCESSFUL

Introduce the topic of goal achievement with one of these activities:
- Show the video *Fly Away Home*.
- Read to the class and discuss one or more of these books (see below):
  - *Five Times Dizzy*
  - *Nips XI*
  - *I Had a lot of Wishes*
  - *The Glorious Flight Across the Channel with Louis Blériot.*
- Play the 2000 Olympics theme song 'Dare to Dream'.

Discussion questions

- What is a goal? (something specific you decide to try and do or get; an aim or purpose; a plan; can be short-term or long-term)
- What is a wish? (a vague dream of something you hope to achieve, with no specific plans to it)
- Why is it good to have goals? (they give direction and satisfaction to our lives, help us to see progress, make us happier; improve performance, increase motivation, give a sense of competence and confidence, give a feeling of pride when the goal is achieved, help us try to achieve more)
- What are examples of goals that students of your age often have in the following categories? (family, social, financial, study, career, leisure time, sport, performance)
- What is a short-term goal? (within four to six weeks)
- What is a long-term term goal? (won't be achieved for six months or more)
- What makes a goal achievable? (refer to BLM 10.1 'Think like WINNERS do')

BOOKS

Five Times Dizzy (Chapter book)

Mareka, a young Greek girl, is worried about her grandmother, who led a happy and busy life back in Crete but in Australia has nothing meaningful to do. Mareka hatches a plan to raise money to buy her a goat. The book has 13 chapters.

Nips XI (Chapter book)

Lan, in Year 6, wants to be a true-blue Aussie, so he makes a plan to put together a NIPS XI cricket team, composed of other students who have recently arrived from various Asian countries. They have to get players, equipment, permission, a coach and a sponsor. They manage all this and then issue a challenge to the local private school. The students involved gain in confidence and form new friendships, as do their parents.

I Had a Lot of Wishes (Picture book)

The illustrations are watercolour and the story features an adult looking back on the wishes he has had at various points in his life. It concludes with the line, 'A lot of the wishes I made a long time ago are coming true.'

The Glorious Flight Across the Channel with Louis Blériot (Picture book)

This is an illustrated narrative of Louis Blériot's determination to fly from France to England, across the English Channel, in 1901, eighteen years before Lindbergh's flight across the Atlantic ocean.

ACTIVITY
Self-reflection

Students talk to a partner about one goal they have in different areas of their lives (e.g. family, leisure time, sport, financial, relationships, career, study). These can be recorded in personal journals.

CLASS DISCUSSION **WHO AM I AND WHAT AM I GOOD AT? WHERE IS MY EVIDENCE?**

Read to the class and discuss the picture book *Stephen's Useless Design*.
   Ask students to complete the MICUPS questionnaire from *Seven Ways at Once* (Book 1) (see page 246 for publication details). In pairs, students discuss their profiles (not absolute scores). Make a class graph of how many times each of the intelligences occurs as one of the top three.
- Does everyone have the same strengths? The same things they are not so good at?
- What are some of the ways in which we can collect evidence for our strengths and limitations? (test scores, feedback from others, comparing self with others, self-recording achievements and personal bests, testing ourselves out in competitions)
- Why is evidence important? (knowing your strengths and limitations helps you achieve goals; it isn't helpful to think you are good at something without doing a reality check)
- What can you do to overcome or compensate for your limitations? (find a way around them, ask for help, practise more)
- We experience flow when the task is challenging and requires skill, there are clear goals, we get immediate feedback on our progress, we feel in control, time stops as we are deeply involved and we forget about ourselves. What are good examples of experiencing flow? (painting, playing a musical instrument, playing sport, writing [linked to your strengths]) What are bad examples? (listening to CDs, watching TV are passive activities)
- When are you most likely to be bored? (when doing something that is undemanding or not your choice or repetitive or requires skills you don't have)
- What are some ways to deal with feeling bored?
- Does knowing what we are good at help us to cope when times are unhappy for a while or we feel small? (Yes. Our strengths are our islands and we clamber up onto them.)

Follow-up activities

- Students share with a partner one of their relative strengths, one job they would like to have and one way their strength would help them succeed in that job.
- Students find and answer a job ad in a newspaper, highlighting and giving evidence for their strengths. For example, 'I am a capable organiser, as shown when I undertook the role of coordinator for the tabloid sports.' (This could also be a role-play of an interview.)

- Students complete BLM 10.2, 'My strengths'.
- Students draw a sea of sharks with several islands and palm trees. On each island they write one of their strengths. Call it 'My strength islands'. When you have a self-doubt or challenge to your self esteem, you can climb onto a 'strength island' as a way of coping.
- Students complete BLM 10.3, 'The hare and the tortoise'.
- Students each prepare a 'self showbag' (or shoebox) that reflects some of their strengths. Leave them on display.
- Students work with a partner to make a display poster with ideas of good ways to deal with being bored (e.g. organise something you've wanted to sort out for a while; keep books you might like to read at a later point when you have nothing to do; practise a skill; do something for someone else; find a problem that needs solving; make something; cook something).

BOOK
Stephen's Useless Design (Older picture book)

Stephen goes to industrial design school and wants to be an engineer. The teacher gives the students an assignment in which they have to make something from a fence post. The other students make functional things such as a tool box and a jewellery box. Stephen makes something interesting but 'useless'. He notices that everyone likes to play with what he has made, so he makes it again in plastic with a few refinements, and the result is 'Struts', the construction toy. He goes on to become a successful designer of building toys.

CLASS DISCUSSION — INTERESTING MISTAKES WILL HAPPEN

Interesting mistakes will happen, but don't be afraid to make them and learn from them.

Begin the discussion by showing (on an overhead transparency) the statement made by Ian Thorpe when he was preparing for the 2000 Olympic Games: 'If I put everything into it, I can't lose. I mightn't win in terms of gold medals, but I will win my own personal battle and that's what it's all about.' Then talk about how the Australian women's 4 × 100 swimming relay team was disqualified at the World Championships in 2000 for making the mistake of jumping into the water after they had won but before all the competitors had finished swimming. Then read this quote by Michael Jordan, renowned basketball player:

> I've missed more than 900 shots in my career. I've lost almost 300 games. On twenty-six occasions I have been trusted to take the game-winning shot and missed. I've failed over and over and over again in my life. I've never been afraid to fail and that is why I succeed.

Discussion questions

- Is Ian Thorpe a winner? Does he place more importance on doing his best or winning the race? What might happen if you were only concerned about winning?
- If your focus was only on winning, what might happen when you made a mistake or didn't win? (you would be very discouraged, might give up, might not persevere, or think you didn't have enough ability)

- Why are mistakes 'interesting'? (they often highlight problems or limitations you aren't aware of; they show new directions; they create character)
- In what ways can mistakes actually help our performance in sport, schoolwork, friendships etc? (they show us what we need to work on to improve our performance)
- Is there anyone who doesn't make mistakes? (Absolutely not! Mistakes are essential.)
- What did the swimming relay team learn from their mistake?
- What makes a good sports coach? Is it one who focuses on the athletes' winning or on athletes doing their best? (doing their best)
- What does a good sports coach do to communicate that message to their athletes or teams? (they give positive feedback and encouragement on progress, they reward effort, they focus on mastery of the sport so that the sportspeople work harder when they experience difficulties and set goals for their own personal skill development that are independent of just winning and losing)

Follow-up activities

- In groups, students use BLM 10.1, 'Think like WINNERS do' to analyse what successful coaches do.
- Students design and implement an interview with someone they think is a good sports coach, using BLM 10.1, 'Think like WINNERS do'.
- Use the 'Think–Pair–Share' strategy (see Chapter 10 of the *Teacher's Handbook*) and ask students to tell about a time when they learned something important from a mistake.
- Students conduct research into people who made mistakes and still achieved success. For example:
  - Michael Jordan
  - Winston Churchill
  - Abraham Lincoln
  - Thomas Edison
  - Albert Einstein.

CLASS DISCUSSION NO PAIN, NO GAIN

Hard work and self-discipline are needed whenever you really want something.

Introduce this key concept by using 'bundling' (see Chapter 10 of the *Teacher's Handbook*) on the topic of things that need willpower or self-discipline. You could also read to the class and discuss the book *Ollie Forgot* (see below).

Discussion questions

- What kind of willpower do you need to use when you are trying to:
  - Get fit
  - Get a good result on a test or project
  - Save money for a specific purpose
  - Perform well in a team?
- What kind of willpower do athletes, models, singers, actors and writers have to use?
- In what way is willpower like improving your muscles? (the more you use them, the stronger they get)

- How do people get 'willpower'? (they stress to themselves the benefits that will come from taking the action; they highlight the negative outcomes of *not* doing it; they make plans)
- What can you do to practise exercising willpower? (sustained effort and hard work, not being hijacked by more attractive alternatives, talking to yourself about what you hope to gain, highlighting the negative outcomes of not doing it, making visual prompts to remind yourself of your goal, rewarding yourself when you stick to your plan)
- What are New Year's resolutions? Why do people make them? What are some examples?
- Why do some people think that hard work isn't necessary to achieve a goal? (they've never achieved one; they don't see the amount of work that others put into achieving their goals)

Follow-up activities

- Each student makes two New Year's (or mid-year's) resolutions and implements them.
- Students write or draw about where they have been able to use willpower and how it helped them to achieve a goal.
- Students choose an activity that requires willpower and self-discipline and then practise it. They record in a logbook the details, date and time, plus what they did and said to themselves which helped them to use willpower.
- Students practise some of the following and keep self-reflections and data:
  - When you are tempted to say something, hold back and don't say it.
  - When you want to do something pleasurable immediately, don't. Postpone it instead to a definite specified time in the future.
  - When you want to put off something unpleasant till later, do it immediately instead.
  - Do something you don't want to do. For example, don't put sugar on your cereal for a week, or do an unpleasant chore that a parent has been asking you to do.
  - Think of a situation you would like to avoid doing and then do it.
  - Set a daily task and see how long you can do it for. For example, take a daily walk, do your homework immediately when you return home, exercise for fifteen minutes a day, drink eight glasses of water a day, have water instead of a soft drink, or tidy your school bag every Sunday.
  - Have a shorter shower.
  - Get up earlier or go to bed at a regular time.
  - Watch less TV at night or spend less time on the computer.
  - Read more books and newspapers.
  - Eat less chocolate or junk food.
  - Save money.

BOOK
Ollie Forgot (Picture book)

Set in medieval times, this story is about Ollie who never seems to be able to remember what he is supposed to do. His mother sends him to market to get several items and he decides to rehearse the items in his head. But things go hilariously wrong along the way as he gets things very mixed up.

UNIT 10—WINNERS

CLASS DISCUSSION: BEING ORGANISED AND MANAGING YOURSELF WELL TO ACHIEVE YOUR GOALS

Give this definition: Time management is organising your time to make sure that you do the things you *have* to do so you have enough time left to do the things you *want* to do.

Discussion questions

- Why do people have timetables and schedules?
- What are the dangers of not having one?
- What can make you waste time or be late?
- What are some good ways to deal with procrastination? (The salami analogy is a good one here. Eating a whole salami is unthinkable, but you can get through the whole thing if you tackle it one slice at a time, that is, break the task into small pieces.)

Follow-up activities

- Students make timetables/schedules for themselves for:
  - Homework
  - A Saturday at home
  - A school night at home
  - A half-day at school
  - A sporting match.
- Students create a homework timetable for themselves.
- Students make a poster about salami and procrastination or one about good time-management strategies.
- Students read and discuss BLM 10.4, 'Tidy houses lead to success!'.

ARTS ACTIVITY
Technology 3D time-management poster

Students make a poster with moveable parts to show good ways to manage time.

CLASS DISCUSSION: REMOVING DISTRACTIONS AND TEMPTATIONS

Another important aspect of organisation is resisting distractions and temptations, usually in the form of a 'better offer'. Begin the discussion by sharing one of your own examples. For instance, you decide to finish some marking but a friend rings and you talk to them for an hour instead. Then it is often too late to 'start', so you don't do *anything*. This process is usually followed by guilt.

Discussion question

Give one example of something that often distracts you from doing what has to be done. (One student records them on the board under the heading 'Time wasters and things that get in the way'.)

Follow-up activities

- Students write down three situations where they get distracted and sometimes don't do what they intend to do. They list what the distractions are. They then work with a partner and discuss ways to help each other with the situations. Debrief as a class.
- One aspect of time management and organisation is easy access to and storage for personal possessions and other things so we don't waste time looking for them.
- Use 'multiply and merge' (see Chapter 10 of the *Teacher's Handbook*) on the five best ways to store things so you can find them again!
- Students create illustrated class posters on:
  - The top ten ways to make sure you don't get your homework done properly
  - The ten best ways to miss a deadline
  - Ten terrific tips for losing things
  - Five fabulous ways to forget someone's birthday.
- Students observe and analyse one storage system in their household (e.g. pantry, laundry) and then make recommendations and plans (with costings) for improved access and storage. They can then do the same for their bedroom.

ACTIVITY
Making lists

Making lists is one important organisational strategy and is really an art form! As a class, brainstorm all the reasons why lists are useful. For example, lists:

- Give you the big picture of what has to be done.
- Help you to rehearse and remember.
- Help you to achieve your goals.
- Show what you have achieved (because you cross things off) and what you still need to do.
- Save time, because they are a short way of writing a lot of information.

Brainstorm as a class the good features of lists. For example:

- Dot points
- Headings
- Numbers
- Categories
- Information about time or place
- Abbreviations
- Colour highlighting, asterisks or different-sized print
- Looked at regularly
- Updated daily
- The more important items prioritised in an eye-catching way
- A sense of achievement as items completed are crossed off
- Big enough to catch the attention
- Placed in a prominent position where they can't be missed, such as:
  - On the fridge
  - As 'stickies' on the computer
  - On a brightly coloured piece of card in the diary or school bag.

The class together can then create the 'perfect list' that contains as many of the above elements as possible, or a poster or brochure about good list-making. Alternatively, each pair can make a list of the same week's tasks and the class votes on the best one.

UNIT 10 — WINNERS

CLASS DISCUSSION   NEVER GIVE UP

Never give up (well, hardly ever). See obstacles as problems to be solved
Start with students completing BLM 10.5, 'Charles Kingsford Smith'. You could also show the video *Rabbit-Proof Fence* or *Fly Away Home*. The following books are also suitable for reading to the class and discussing as an introduction:
- *Bored, Nothing to Do*
- *The Lighthouse Keeper's Catastrophe*
- *The Lighthouse Keeper's Lunch*
- *The Great Candle Scandal*
- *The Sparrow's Story at the King's Command*.

Discussion questions

- What is 'determination'? (being prepared to put up with discomfort and hard work and solve problems along the way; persisting no matter what)
- What does 'persistence' mean?
- Give an example of when you (the teacher) have needed to be persistent (e.g. getting a tertiary degree, learning a new skill, saving money for something special) and then ask students for their own examples.
- Does persistence usually pay off? (yes)
- How would we feel if we didn't persist at something that was important to us? (we may be disappointed with ourselves; giving up becomes a habit and we lose self-respect)
- Does persistence always pay off? (not always, but if you have not given up too quickly and given it your best shot you can be pleased with your effort)
- What does it mean to be resourceful? (it means to find different and creative ways to use available resources to solve a problem)

Follow-up activities

- In groups of three, students brainstorm what they would do if they:
  - Suddenly had no lights in their house
  - Locked themselves out of their house and did not have a key
  - Lost their fare home from town
  - Forgot their school lunch and had no money to buy any
  - Didn't understand what they had to do for homework.
- Students make posters about how to be resourceful when there is nothing interesting to do.
- Use this 'three wise monkeys' activity (below) to practise resourcefulness.

Three wise monkeys

This game requires resourcefulness as well as cooperation. It is best played in a gym or some open area. Split students into groups of three. Two of the students are blindfolded and the third is able to see.
- One of the blindfolded students is the 'body' and can walk but is not permitted to see or speak.
- The other blindfolded student is the 'voice' and can speak but is not permitted to see nor walk (they can move their arms, legs and head, but they must remain stationary).
- The third student is the 'eyes' and can see but is not permitted to speak nor walk.

Place one ball somewhere within the playing area for each team of students. Also place a basket or similar receptacle in which the ball must be placed. Each team's goal is to guide their 'body' to their team's ball, pick it up, and then place it in the basket. The 'voice' and the 'eyes' for each team will have to give the 'body' directions to find and place the ball. Give each group a ten minute planning period beforehand to work out the way they will communicate directions (e.g. hand signals for left, right, number of steps).

BOOKS

Bored, Nothing to Do

A simple picture book with two teenage characters who are bored and make their own plane. Unfortunately, they have to remove sections of the car, the pram, the TV etc. in order to do it! There is a design plan of the Piper Super Cub at the back of the book.

The Lighthouse Keeper's Catastrophe

The lighthouse keeper and his wife are in big trouble. A terrible storm is brewing and, after a series of small events, the keeper ends up losing the key to the locked lighthouse. He and his wife have to be very resourceful as they experiment with different ways to solve the problem of how to get into the lighthouse in order to warn the ships in the storm.

The Lighthouse Keeper's Lunch

The lighthouse keeper and his wife have to be resourceful in solving the problem of the seagulls eating the keeper's lunch.

The Great Candle Scandal

Set in medieval times, this story begins with the Bishop ordering a candle as tall as the cathedral for the coming Easter ceremony. Dan, the apprentice candle-maker, is determined that it can be done. Despite setbacks, obstacles and doubters, he finds resourceful strategies to make the candle, transport it to the cathedral and then light it.

The Sparrow's Story at the King's Command

The king commands the kingdom's storyteller to write a story to celebrate his son's birth. The storyteller entrusts the story to a sparrow. The sparrow sets off on his mission but endures many hardships along the way. When he nearly drowns, the ink on the manuscript washes away. The sparrow is devastated, but, with the help of an owl, he writes out the story of his mission and his hardships. The sparrow's story becomes the story the king uses to celebrate the birth of his son.

VIDEOS

Rabbit-Proof Fence

Three young aboriginal girls are taken from their family in 1931 to be trained as servants. They are resourceful in escaping and finding their way back home.

Fly Away Home

A fourteen year old girl who has had some very difficult times after her mother's death finds a creative way to help orphaned geese fly south for the winter. Her solution involves learning to fly an ultra-light plane.

ACTIVITY
Ten thinking tracks

See BLM 1.3. One British father was concerned with his children's lack of exercise and overuse of television instead of doing their homework. So he rigged up a system whereby the only way enough electricity could be generated to run the television was if they pedalled!

CLASS DISCUSSION: ETHICS AND DECENCY MUST BE THE RULE (OR IT'S NOT WORTH IT)

Introduce the discussion through the following story. In winter 2002 the National Rugby League team the Bulldogs (Canterbury/Bankstown in New South Wales) were at the top of the League ladder and were favourites to win the premiership. But someone found out that the Bulldogs management had paid their players a lot more than the ceiling cap on the players' salaries determined by the League. All the other teams and their supporters felt that the Bulldogs management had cheated, which meant that the competition was unfair. The club was fined $500,000 and the team lost all its competition points. Most people felt that the Bulldogs had not acted ethically or decently.

Similarly in 2002, the Carlton Football Club in Victoria was penalised for salary cap violations with a fine of over a million dollars and the loss of first 'draft' picks for two years.

Discussion questions

- What does acting ethically mean? (conforming to the moral standards of conduct of a profession or organisation)
- What are examples of unethical behaviour? (lying, cheating, breaking rules, conning or treating others badly)
- Did the Bulldogs and Carlton football clubs receive the logical consequence of their unethical behaviour?
- What are some of the ways that people can act unethically at school? At work?
- What are other examples of unethical behaviour reported in the media recently?

Follow-up activities

- Students carry out a media hunt for examples of unethical practices in sport, business or the community.
- Students research ethical codes of behaviour in different professions (e.g. law, medicine, psychology, politics) and organisations (e.g. scouts, guides, sporting teams).

CLASS DISCUSSION: RISK-TAKING MAY BE NECESSARY AT SOME POINT

At the beginning of the lesson choose a mystery item and ask each student to take a risk by estimating its size by tearing off a piece of toilet paper. The student who has torn off the piece that is closest in measurement will keep the Daily Measurement Trophy (a special ruler perhaps, or a treat).

Then read this poem to the students:

The Dilemma

To laugh is to risk appearing a fool.
To weep is to risk appearing sentimental.
To reach out for another is to risk involvement.
To expose feelings is to risk rejection.
To place your own dreams before the crowd is to risk ridicule.
To love is to risk not being loved in return.
To go forward in the face of overwhelming odds is to risk failure.

But risks must be taken because the greatest hazard in life is to risk nothing.
The person who risks nothing does nothing, has nothing, is nothing.
They may avoid suffering and sorrow, but they cannot learn, feel, change, grow or love.
Only a person who risks is free.
(Anonymous)

Discussion questions

- Was it easy or hard to take a risk in the measurement activity?
- What kinds of activities make risk taking more difficult?
- What are the risks referred to in the poem?
- Why is the greatest hazard in life to risk nothing?
- When are risks sensible? Stupid? (They are not sensible when your actions endanger you or others, when you are showing off, or when the consequences are not worth the risks. See the discussion on 'foolhardiness' in Unit 4, 'Courage'.)
- What does 'but think first and be prepared' mean?
- What does someone who always goes for self-protection do? (takes very few risks; stays in their comfort zone; won't put up with discomfort.)

Follow-up activity

- Students make posters around the ideas that 'too much self-protection leads to self-rejection', and 'if you self-direct you self-respect'.
- Students write out, illustrate and make posters based on the poem or parts of it.

UNIT 10—WINNERS

CLASS DISCUSSION **SMART GOAL-SETTING HELPS YOU SUCCEED**

Introduce with a 'bundling' activity, where students list five possible goals for students their age.

ACTIVITIES
SMART goal-setting

Each student thinks of a personal series of academic/sporting short-term goals and then fills in BLM 10.6 'Goal contract' using the SMART acronym.

Goal-setting

- Students draw their own goals as arrows and targets.
- Students keep records in their journal of their 'personal bests' in areas where they can measure goal progress, for example:
  – How many times they and a partner can hit a shuttlecock before one person misses
  – Results on tests
  – Number of specific exercises (e.g. push-ups) they can do in a set time
  – Number of goals accurately shot through a basketball ring
  – Number of acts of kindness done per day.

Group goal-setting

Here are some ideas for students (as a group or class) to practise goal-setting:
- Run a school-wide or class tournament or sporting activity (e.g. card games, Scrabble, table-tennis.)
- Make an age-appropriate big book for younger students on WINNERS principles.
- Put together a class concert.
- Make a wall mural on a current class theme.
- Make up a giant crossword, word search or cross-off on a current class theme.
- Learn a poem to recite.
- Make a mini-golf course or safe obstacle course.
- Organise a mini fête.
- Have a 'show and teach' session where students teach the class something they are good at.
- Make benches and playground equipment.
- Negotiate with the infants' teachers to make things they need (e.g. sandpit, indoor cubby, coat hooks etc.).
- Make a class garden or a 'leisure area' in the room, assemble a basketball ring, or paint the playground with hopscotches, tables or alphabet grids etc.).
- Devise a plan to rent deck chairs to people at outside events such as an airshow, open-air cinema or concert.
- Make up a simple treasure hunt for younger students.

Goal success interview

Students interview someone who has achieved a goal that was important and meaningful to them (e.g. an older sister who has bought her own car, or a parent, friend or sibling who has finished a training, diploma or degree course), using the BLM 10.1, 'Think like WINNERS do'.

Organisational interviews

Students devise and conduct surveys with adults to investigate the strategies they use to:
- Remember what they have to do
- Get up on time
- Manage their time well
- Remember the birthdays of people they care about
- Meet deadlines without a last-minute rush.

Students meet in a group to identify common themes from their surveys and follow up with posters.

CONSOLIDATION

A smorgasbord of activities

- Students research and analyse different school mottos in terms of WINNERS principles (BLM 10.1).
- Students make a wallet card, fridge magnet or poster (see Chapter 11 of the *Teacher's Handbook*) of the WINNERS acronym (BLM 10.1).
- In groups, students write the WINNERS acronym in their own words (BLM 10.1).
- Students make WINNERS class mobiles (BLM 10.1).
- Students draw a WINNERS life maze with obstacles (BLM 10.1).
- Students analyse a successful team using the WINNERS acronym (BLM 10.1).
- Students read and analyse the cartoons in BLM 10.7, 'WINNERS cartoons', and write in detail what each means and how it relates to the WINNERS acronym (BLM 10.1).
- Pairs can set the goal of trying to maintain an average score in either the game of 'Guess the square' or 'Word mastermind' (see Unit 1, 'Core values', for game details).
- Use 'quick quotes' (see Chapter 11 of the *Teacher's Handbook*) and ask students to write about their best tip for being organised.
- Students categorise the following quotes into the WINNERS statements (BLM 10.1), draw them, or use them as balloon burst quotes (see Chapter 11 of the *Teacher's Handbook*).
  - A dream is just a dream. A goal is a dream with a plan and a deadline. (Harvey Mackay)
  - A person is not finished when he is defeated. He is finished when he quits.
  - A setback is an opportunity to begin again more intelligently. (Henry Ford)
  - Aerodynamically the bumble bee shouldn't be able to fly, but the bumble bee doesn't know that.
  - Behold the turtle. He makes progress only when he sticks his neck out. (James B Conant)
  - Better to get a stiff neck from aiming too high than a hunch back from aiming too low. (Jacques Chancel)
  - Don't wait for your ship to come in—start swimming.
  - Failures are like skinned knees . . . painful but superficial. They heal quickly. (Robert Perot)
  - Fate deals the cards but you play the hand.
  - Genius is one per cent inspiration and ninety-nine per cent perspiration. (Thomas Edison)
  - He who risks and fails can be forgiven. He who never risks and never fails is a failure in his whole being. (Paul Tillich)
  - If you travel a path with no obstacles, it probably doesn't lead anywhere.

- Losers visualise the penalties of failure. Winners visualise the rewards of success. (Rob Gilbert)
- Neither you nor anyone else will know how high you can fly and soar until you fully spread your wings.
- Nothing in the world can take the place of persistence. Talent will not; nothing is more common than unsuccessful men with talent. (Calvin Coolidge)
- Opportunity is missed by most people because it is dressed in overalls and looks like work. (Thomas Edison)
- The person who has never done anything wrong has probably never done anything.
- When opportunity knocks, open the door, even if you are still in your pyjamas.
- You can stand tall without standing on someone. You can be a victor without victims. (Harriet Woods)
- You miss 100 per cent of the shots if you never take aim. (Wayne Gretzky)
- The ultimate reasons for setting and trying to achieve goals is to encourage ourselves to become the kind of person we need to be to achieve them.
- To be successful you need a backbone not a wishbone.

Curriculum integration

Use the WINNERS principles BLM 10.1 with topics such as:
- Explorers
- Antarctica
- Scientific breakthroughs
- Famous achievers.

WINNERS! probability race

This is a game for two people. Photocopy onto card and cut out the 13 cards in BLM 10.8, as below. You will also need two dice. One player is on the Obstacles (O) side. The second player is on the WINNERS (W) side. The aim is for the 'W' player to turn over all their cards (and hence achieve their goal) before the 'O' player turns over their 4 cards and blocks them from achieving their goal.

Each player places their cards in front of them with the numbers facing up. The 'W' player begins by throwing the dice and turning over the card that corresponds to the sum of the two dice. Then the 'O' player throws the dice but can only turn over one of their cards if they throw any double.

The game illustrates the laws of probability. The likelihood of throwing a double is 6 in 21. Students play the game several times and record the number of throws and the numbers thrown each time. Did the 6 in 21 law operate over a number of games? Should there be five or six Obstacle cards to make the game more equal? Should there only be three obstacle cards? Why?

Cross-offs

Students complete BLM 10.9. The message is: Keep your eye on the goal all the time and keep going.

RESOURCES

Books

Ronda Armitage & David Armitage, 1977, *The Lighthouse Keeper's Lunch*, Puffin, London.
Ronda Armitage & David Armitage, 1988, *The Lighthouse Keeper's Catastrophe*, Puffin, London.
Tedd Arnold 1989, *Ollie Forgot*, Heinemann, London.
Jean Chapman & Roland Harvey, 1982, *The Great Candle Scandal*, Hodder and Stoughton, Sydney.
Judith Crabtree, 1983, *The Sparrow's Story at the King's Command*, Oxford University Press, Melbourne.
Rodney Martin & John Draper, 1982, *Stephen's Useless Design*, Keystone Picture Books, Flinders Park SA.
MICUPS (Multiple Intelligences Checklist for Upper Primary and Secondary) in Helen McGrath & Toni Noble, 1995, *Seven Ways at Once: Classroom Strategies based on the Seven Intelligences*, Book One, Addison Wesley Longman, Melbourne.
Alice & Martin Provensen, 1983, *The Glorious Flight Across the Channel with Louis Blériot*, Viking, New York.
Peter Spier 1979, *Bored, Nothing to Do*, World's Work, Surrey.
Ruth Starke, 2000, *Nips XI*, Lothian, Port Melbourne.
James Stevenson, 1995, *I Had a Lot of Wishes*, Greenwillow Books, New York.
Nadia Wheatley & Neil Phillips, 1982, *Five Times Dizzy*, Oxford University Press, Melbourne.

Videos

Rabbit-Proof Fence (PG) 2002, Mirimax Films.
Fly Away Home (PG) 1996, Columbia Tristar Pictures.

THINK LIKE WINNERS DO

BLM 10.1

Winners are people who achieve what they set out to do, because they remember these rules for success:

What am I best at?
(And what is my evidence?)

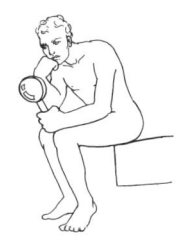

Interesting mistakes will happen.
(And don't be afraid to make them and learn from them.)

No pain, no gain.
(No one achieves anything important without hard work and self-discipline)

Never give up (well, hardly ever).
Obstacles are problems to be solved.

Ethics and decency must be the rule
(or it's not worth it).

Risk-taking is sometimes necessary.
(But think about it first and be prepared.)

Smart goal-setting helps you succeed.
Specific: State exactly what you want to achieve.
Meaningful: Make your goal something that you really want to achieve.
Action-based: What can you DO to start achieving your goal?
Realistic: Select a goal where there is a good chance you will be successful.
Time-linked: How long is each step likely to take?

© Helen McGrath and Toni Noble, 2003. This page from Bounce Back!® may be photocopied for classroom use.

MY STRENGTHS

BLM 10.2

Circle your strengths and add some of your own if you wish to. On a new sheet of paper make a list of ten of these strengths. Beside each quality write one example of what you have done to show that strength or a situation where you showed it.

Adventurous	Energetic	Patient
Affectionate	Enterprising	Persistent
Ambitious	Fair-minded	Polite
Artistic	Friendly	Practical
Assertive	Funny	Punctual
Calm	Generous	Reliable
Caring	Hard working	Resourceful
Cautious	Helpful	Responsible
Compassionate	Honest	Spontaneous
Confident	Independent	Strong
Considerate	Inventive	Tactful
Cooperative	Kind	Tolerant
Courageous	Neat	Trustworthy
Creative	Non-judgmental	Understanding
Curious	Open-minded	
Dependable	Optimistic	
Determined	Organised	
Easy-going	Outgoing	

© Helen McGrath and Toni Noble, 2003. This page from Bounce Back!® may be photocopied for classroom use.

THE HARE AND THE TORTOISE

BLM 10.3

Australian short-track speed skater Steven Bradbury won a Gold Medal at the 2002 Winter Olympics in Salt Lake City, at the age of 28. Stephen had been skating on the international circuit for ten years and had had two life-threatening accidents. He knew it was important to skate within his own limitations. The other skaters in the final, all of whom had faster times than he did, were younger and less experienced. He knew that younger skaters are more likely to make mistakes under pressure. He started the race by staying at the back, waiting to see if he would be able to use clever tactics to win this important race. He had successfully used such tactics to outmanoeuvre his opponents in the heats leading up to the final. Suddenly, on the final bend near the finishing line, the Chinese skater tried to muscle his way to the front and made an error that caused him to fall over. As he went down, he took the American, Canadian and Korean skaters with him, leaving Stephen, the only one left standing, to glide across the line, the winner.

- What were Steven's strengths? What were his limitations?

- How did his knowledge of his strengths help him to win the race?

- What risks did Steven take? Were they calculated risks or silly risks? In what ways did Steven's experience help him in his judgment of the risks?

- What do we learn about Steven's willpower?

- Why is this story titled 'The Hare and the Tortoise'? How does it relate to the fable of the same name?

© Helen McGrath and Toni Noble, 2003. This page from Bounce Back!® may be photocopied for classroom use.

TIDY HOUSES LEAD TO SUCCESS!

BLM 10.4

Next time your mum or dad tells you to clean up, you'd better listen. Researchers at a university in the United States wanted to know whether tidy students became more successful as adults. They discovered that students who lived in relatively clean and tidy houses when they were young went on to earn more money as adults than students who lived in messy, untidy houses.

The researchers found that parents who keep their homes reasonably clean and tidy were likely to be more organised than those who didn't. These characteristics were likely to be passed on to their children through 'modelling'.

The researchers also found that students raised in untidy and messy homes were more likely to leave school before they finished Year 12. Students raised in tidy homes were more likely to complete Year 12.

Being messy and disorganised often means:
- You can't find what you are looking for.
- There are too many different things in one container (such as a drawer or school bag) and you have to go through everything to see if what you need is in there.
- All the things you need are scattered over too many places, such as in a schoolbag, in a box, under the bed, left near the computer etc.

Good organisation means:
☐ Placing things in clearly labelled folders and sorting things into those folders fairly regularly.
☐ Going through collections of things in folders, drawers and containers every now and then and throwing out what is no longer useful.
☐ Using categorisation and putting several similar things into a plastic container (the see-through sort is best) and using good labelling.
☐ Using colour coding for different items (e.g. different-coloured folders for different school subjects).
☐ Keeping a separate drawer or container for a set of items such as pens and pencils, stationery, jewellery, cards etc.
☐ Recording in a small book where your important items or papers are stored.
☐ Having a container such as a shoebox, an ice-cream container or a folder where you put things 'temporarily' until you can sort them into their folders or correct drawer/container. But you have to remember to come back and do it later!

Put two ticks in the box for the organisation ideas you are already doing. Put one tick in the box for an idea you would like to try.

© Helen McGrath and Toni Noble, 2003. This page from Bounce Back!® may be photocopied for classroom use.

CHARLES KINGSFORD SMITH (1897–1935)

BLM 10.5

An Australian pilot called Charles Kingsford Smith ('Smithy') is one of the world's greatest pilots. In the 1920s, planes had not been flying for very long. People could not believe that a plane could fly all the way across the Pacific Ocean from Australia to America. Smithy's dream was to demonstrate that people could fly safely and cheaply between countries and across oceans and not take too long to do it.

In 1927, Smithy and another pilot, Charles Ulm, were the first people in the world to fly from Australia to America. They also flew from Australia to New Zealand.

In 1928, Smithy and Ulm formed an airline company called Australian National Airways.

In 1933, Smithy flew from England to Australia in seven days. This was a world record and showed that his dream was possible.

Today people can get good information about the weather before they fly. When Smithy flew, there was little information about the weather. Sometimes he flew in very bad weather. This greatly tested his courage and his flying ability.

Smithy set himself difficult goals. He made sure he planned every flight carefully. He checked all of his equipment before he flew. His success was due to his planning, his hard work and his willingness to keep trying and not give up.

- What was Kingsford Smith's dream?

- What did he do to help achieve his dream?

- What is one fact that makes flying today different from flying in the 1920s and 1930s?

- Why was Smithy so successful at achieving his goals?

- Use BLM 10.1 'Think like WINNERs do' to analyse what Kingsford Smith did that made him a WINNER.

© Helen McGrath and Toni Noble, 2003. This page from Bounce Back!® may be photocopied for classroom use.

GOAL CONTRACT

BLM 10.6

Name: _____ Date: _____

Specific Be specific. Say exactly what you want to achieve.
I want to _____

Meaningful Make your goal something that *you* really want to achieve. I want to achieve this goal because _____
_____

Actions Say three actions you will take to start to achieve your goal
1. _____
2. _____
3. _____

Realistic Choose a goal where there is a *real* chance you will be successful.
I think this goal is realistic for me because _____
_____

Timed How long do you estimate it will take to achieve your goal?
I think it will take me approximately _____

Your signature: _____ Teacher's signature: _____

© Helen McGrath and Toni Noble, 2003. This page from Bounce Back!® may be photocopied for classroom use.

WINNERS CARTOONS

BLM 10.7

Explain why each cartoon is funny and what comment it makes about how to be successful (or not!).

1.
- "I'M GOING TO MAKE A LIST SO I DON'T FORGET TO..."
- ".... UM...."
- "DAMN!"

2.
- "I'M GOING TO GET A PART TIME JOB AND SAVE MY MONEY TO BUY A BIKE."
- "MY PARENTS THINK IT'S A GREAT IDEA BUT I'M STILL GOING TO DO IT."

3.
- "AS SOON AS I GET ORGANISED I'M GOING TO TAKE A COURSE IN TIME MANAGEMENT."

4.
- "I HAVEN'T FINISHED MY ASSIGNMENT YET." "WHEN DID THE TEACHER GIVE IT TO YOU?"
- "8 WEEKS AGO!" "GEE, THAT'S SO SLACK THAT HE DIDN'T GIVE YOU MORE TIME."

5.
- MISTAKES & FAILURES TEACH YOU THINGS
- "GEE, I MUST BE GETTING A GOOD EDUCATION."

© Helen McGrath and Toni Noble, 2003. This page from Bounce Back!® may be photocopied for classroom use.

WINNERS PROBABILITY RACE

BLM 10.8

3 W	You put in the hard work required	4 W	You solved a problem along the way
5 W	You did what had to be done even though you wanted to watch TV instead	6 W	You made a good plan and followed it
7 W	You made an interesting mistake, but you learned from it	8 W	You took a bit of a risk
9 W	You planned your time-line well	10 W	You made your goal specific and realistic, not just wishful thinking
11 W	You found out what you needed to know first	Double O	You got distracted and took your eye off the goal
Double O	You didn't believe in yourself or focus on what you do well	Double O	You didn't make a good plan
Double O	You didn't put the work in		

© Helen McGrath and Toni Noble, 2003. This page from Bounce Back!® may be photocopied for classroom use.

CROSS-OFFS

BLM 10.9

keep	butterfly	happiness	finish	nine	swarm	eviction
concrete	your	lime	French horn	singer	eye	steel
Kilamanjaro	cheetah	crowd	excitement	hang-glider	on	ant
Everest	guitar	the	velvet	dictation	thirteen	flock
saxophone	conclude	polyester	leopard	wasp	Fuji	goal
three	jet	all	windscreen	trumpet	helicopter	the
time	pleasure	silk	bricks	lion	lemon	stop
fiction	gearbox	microphone	bonnet	seventeen	cease	and
aeroplane	keep	satin	wood	orange	fly	pride
hubcaps	panther	trombone	Kosciusko	herd	going	conviction

To find the message, cross off these words:
4 words that are brass instruments
4 words ending in -tion
4 words that are collective nouns
4 words that are mountains
4 words that are insects
4 words that are numbers
4 words that are building materials
4 words that are pleasant feelings
4 words that are big cats
4 words that are man-made flying machines or equipment
4 words that are materials
4 words that are parts of a car
4 words meaning 'to end'
3 words that are citrus fruits
3 words that are about a rock band performing

The secret message is _____

© Helen McGrath and Toni Noble, 2003. This page from Bounce Back!® may be photocopied for classroom use.